英汉语篇表征的批评隐喻研究

A Critical Metaphor Analysis of Representation in English and Chinese Discourse

张蕾 著

南开大学出版社

天 津

图书在版编目(CIP)数据

英汉语篇表征的批评隐喻研究 / 张蕾著. —天津：
南开大学出版社，2011.6
ISBN 978-7-310-03697-4

Ⅰ. ①英… Ⅱ. ①张… ②Ⅲ. ①英语—隐喻—对比研究
—汉语 Ⅳ. ①H315②H15

中国版本图书馆 CIP 数据核字(2011)第 069292 号

南开大学出版社出版发行

出版人:肖占鹏

地址:天津市南开区卫津路 94 号　　邮政编码:300071

营销部电话:(022)23508339　23500755

营销部传真:(022)23508542　　邮购部电话:(022)23502200

*

河北昌黎太阳红彩色印刷有限责任公司印刷

全国各地新华书店经销

*

2011 年 6 月第 1 版　　2011 年 6 月第 1 次印刷

880×1230 毫米　32 开本　8.75 印张　252 千字

定价:25.00 元

如遇图书印装质量问题,请与本社营销部联系调换,电话:(022)23507125

序

听到张蕾的《英汉语篇表征的批评隐喻研究》即将出版的消息，作为她的导师，我感到无比高兴。本书是在张蕾的博士论文基础上整理而成的，因此当她让我为本书作序时，便欣然答应下来。

曾经有一段时间，我对隐喻的语篇功能很感兴趣，阅读了一些相关文献，后来与廖美珍教授合作撰写了《隐喻的语篇功能研究》一文，发表在《外语学刊》2007 年第 6 期上。本文以隐喻概念的系统性和概念域之间的互动为出发点，把隐喻看作是一种重要的语篇策略，探讨了概念隐喻的语篇功能。我在阅读了更多的文献后发现，隐喻作为人类组织概念系统的重要基础，不仅是一种语篇组织策略，而且通过概念化、范畴化以及概念域之间的映射关系，在思想的表达和现实的表征过程中发挥着重要的作用。也就是说，隐喻具有重要的意识形态功能。在这一方面，有许多问题值得思考和研究：人们为什么用隐喻的方式来表达概念或表征现实？概念域之间的映射是如何实现的？为什么人们可以选择不同的隐喻概念来表征相同的现实？隐喻概念背后的动机是什么？诸如此类的一系列问题都可以在语篇分析，特别是批评语篇分析的理论框架内，通过具体的语篇分析找到答案。

当许多问题还悬而未决的时候，张蕾于 2007 年考入山东大学攻读博士学位，她逐渐对隐喻产生了兴趣，并开始关注隐喻的范畴化和概念化功能，将目光聚焦于隐喻在现实表征中的作用问题。张蕾不但勤奋好学，而且善于发现问题。在第 29 届奥林匹克运动会于 2008 年在北京举行之际，"奥运经济"一时成为国内外媒体报道和讨论的热点话题。张蕾从中发现，媒体在表征"奥运经济"时不仅大量使用隐喻，而且中西媒体在隐喻概念的选择上既有相似之处又有差别。那么这些相似或差异说明了什么？有什么样的理论价值？如何从纷繁复杂的隐喻现象中归纳出具有理论意义的模式？一个个的问题随即浮现出来，也正是带着这些问题，张蕾进行了系统的语料收集和分析工作。语料主要是主流媒体关于"奥运经济"的报道和评论。汉语语料来自《人民日报》和《中国经济周刊》，英语语料来自美国的《纽约时报》和《经济周刊》。语料收集只是研究的第一步，接下来的语料分析是极富挑战性的工作，因为隐喻的识别需要遵循严格的标准，否则就会影响研究的信度和效度。张蕾在前人研究的基础上确立了切实可行的隐喻识别标准，虽然这一点算不上是开创性的工作，但对语篇中的隐喻识别具有一定的启发和借鉴意义。有了隐喻识别的标准并非意味着接下来问题就能迎刃而解，因为从大量的语料中寻找隐喻的实例并逐一归类的确是一件苦差事。要出色地完成这项任务不但需要研究者的细心和耐心，更要有毅力。对范畴的分类是在语料分析的过程中逐步形成的，而且随着分析的深入要不断做出调整，每走一步都需要对分析的结果进行反复的检验，以保证分析数据的内部一致性。值得庆幸的是，张蕾克服了一个个困难，圆满地完成了研究任务。本研究一方面揭示了英汉大众经济语篇在表征"奥运经济"时所采取的隐喻化方式和策略及其异同，另一方面又从社会认知的角度阐释了隐喻表征背后的社会文化及认知动因。

从认知的角度看，概念隐喻是人们认识和感知事物的一种思维方式，是人类运用语言将世界概念化和范畴化的重要手段。从语篇组织的角度看，隐喻是人类将思想和意义组织为连贯的语篇的重要策略。因此，对隐喻现象的研究是语言学研究的一个弥久常新的课题，许多隐喻现象以及与隐喻相关的语言现象还值得我们做进一步的研究。希望张蕾在这一领域能够取得更具创新意义的研究成果。

在攻读博士学位期间，张蕾付出了很多，既要全力以赴地投身学业，又要照顾年长的父母和年幼的孩子。但她以坚强的毅力克服了一切困难，顺利完成了学业。这一方面得益于她的扎实功底，另一方面也得益于她勤奋好学和勇于探索的学品。我相信，张蕾在未来的学术研究的道路上一定会走得更远。

是为序。

苗兴伟

2011 年 1 月 22 日

前言

　　表征世界的语篇并不总是纯客观地反映所谓的"现实"。拥有权力的语篇生产者会控制被表征信息的大小和性质，从而左右接受者对有关事件的理解和看法。隐喻涉及不同概念域之间具有选择性的映射，它的使用和理解伴随着与其他认知元素的互动，同时它又是进行隐性评价的途径之一。隐喻的这些特性使它在语篇表征过程中发挥着重要的作用。

　　现有的隐喻表征研究将隐喻的语篇功能与对人类行为中最核心元素的阐释联系起来，包括语言与意识形态的关系，以及隐喻表征对社会现象的感知和看法的阐释功能。多数研究者都采用了批评话语分析的研究框架，主张对隐喻表征进行批评隐喻分析。不过在研究中完全依赖莱考芙和约翰的概念隐喻理论，忽略了传统隐喻之外的新奇隐喻的语篇功能，使研究结果绝对化。另外，语篇中认知过程和认知表征与社会群体之间的相互作用并没有得到清晰的阐释，无法驳斥隐喻表征分析中存在着过度解释的说法。实践方面也鲜有研究涉及发生在"第一世界"之外的社会现象，如处于高速发展中的中国经济。

　　本书尝试把认知语言学对隐喻的研究融入到 van Dijk 的社会认知模式中，对比分析英汉语篇中奥运经济的隐喻表征，揭示对同一经济现象的语篇表征是否存在着不同经济价值观的融合与冲突。书的主体部分由以下九章组成：第一章"导论"简要介绍了本研究的理论背景、研究目的、研究意义以及本书的结构；第二章"综述"介绍了认知语言学对隐喻的研究，并在隐喻实证研究转向的背景下对语篇表征研究，尤其是经济语篇中隐喻表征的意义建构功能进行了回顾和评析，旨在强调本研究的研究背景；第三章"理论框架"首先评析了批评话语分析的传统分析方法和最新兴起的批评隐喻分析方法。受到后者的启发，探讨如何把对隐喻的描述、阐释和说明与 van Dijk 的社会认知模式相融合，使隐喻作为思维方式，成为思维模式和支配思维模式的意识结构的中介面，作为语言现象，成为语篇与具体语篇中隐喻实现的中介面；第四章"方法论"介绍了语料的收集和分析过程，涉及对隐喻概念和分析单位的界定、语境在隐喻识别和分类过程中的作用以及隐喻研究中的主观性问题；第五章至第八章是本书的核心，主要运用前面构建的理论框架和介绍的研究方法对英汉语料中相同和独特的隐喻模式、同一模式中的不同概念场景以及各自概念合成和浮现意义的实现和功能进行了描述，并结合语篇和社会背景进行阐释和说明；第九章概述了本研究的结论和意义，并且对存在的不足及后续研究作了思考。

研究显示，两国媒体拥有共同的奥运经济思维模式，即发展模式和竞争模式，主要通过占支配地位的"生物体"、"旅途"、"战争"以及"体育游戏"隐喻模式来实现，其中概念源域均来自包括个体身体、心理和情感状态的人类内部现象，或源自各种社会经验的人际间现象。共同的思维模式反映了双方都把奥运经济看作不同经济主体间激烈、公开、透明的竞争，在竞争中注重策略、努力、忍耐与付出。另外，发展模式与竞争模式在隐喻表征过程的并存包容强调了奥运经济中的竞争对经济主体发展的重要性。这些共同点主要是由奥运经济作为体育商业事件的国际性所决定的。同时，以上反映自由市场观念的隐喻模式在中国媒体中大量存在，反映出迈向现代化的中国与世界逐渐融合的过程。然而，不同词汇在同一概念域内激活的各种场景，针对相同目标域采用的不同隐喻模式，以及相同隐喻模式或场景发挥的不同功能都折射出两国媒体思维模式上的差异以及它们对待相关事物不同的立场和观点。中方构建的竞争模式更加复杂，强调了奥运给当地经济带来的不仅是竞争，还有机遇。对中国经济的不同看法，以及北京奥运会对中国而言重大的政治和经济意义导致了双方发展模式上的差异。经济主体的隐喻表征差异还反映出不同的经济价值观和文化因素对隐喻使用的影响。总体上，美方在使用隐喻对奥运经济进行表征的过程中，对负面现象给予了更多的关注，例如对当地企业竞争力的质疑、大型建筑项目引发的争论，以及对中国经济的担忧。相反，中方构建了相对乐观的意象，把现实与企业未来的发展相联系，在报道中突出正面评价，对各种问题进行了弱化。

本研究的意义体现在以下三个方面：首先，研究结果显示了隐喻表征在揭示语篇隐含意义方面发挥的重要作用，充实了批评话语分析框架中的社会—认知分析模式。在把隐喻作为一种富含价值理念的认知语言现象进行分析的过程中，进一步弱化了传统隐喻与新奇隐喻的界限，强调了它们在表征现实中的相同作用。其次，研究在强调语言层面分析的同时，突显出历史文化元素、政治背景和经济价值观等社会结构对隐喻表征的隐含意义、评价意义和情感效应以及正负面态度意义的阐释作用。最后，研究中所采用的对比分析方法突显了不同国家由于意识形态和价值理念不同在使用隐喻中出现的差异，主张批评话语分析应该考虑社会的多样性。

本书的出版倾注了很多人的心血。首先，我要衷心地感谢我的导师苗兴伟教授。在我攻读博士期间，我始终得到他的细心指导和热情鼓励。导师严谨踏实的治学精神、深刻敏锐的学术眼光，还有他宽容待人的人文情怀，让我终身难忘。

其次，我要感谢在山东大学攻读博士研究生时的老师张德禄教授和刘振前教授。让我难以忘怀的还有我在南开大学攻读硕士研究生时的老师张迈曾教授、马秋武教授、苏立昌教授和李艺教授。是他们为我开启了语言学研究的大门，为我的研究奠定了语言学，尤其是功能语言学、语篇分析和认知语言学的理论基础。

感谢曾经主持我博士学位论文答辩的南京国际关系学院的张辉教授，南京大学的陈新仁教授，山东大学的刘世铸教授和马文教授。他们都为我的博士论文提出了宝贵的修改意见。

另外，天津外国语大学英语学院院长程幼强教授和许多同事在我求学期间提供了大力支持。为此，我向他们表示由衷的谢意。同时要感谢的还有我在山东大学的同学刘杨锦博士、崔凤娟博士和戴理敏博士等。

最后，我要特别感谢我的家人。没有他们的爱和支持，本书的出版是不可能的。

限于本人的研究水平，书中难免出现诸多纰漏和不妥之处，敬请各位前辈、学界同仁批评指正。

张蕾

2010 年 12 月于天津外国语大学

Abstract

Discourses are produced to represent the world. However, the representation is not always objective reflection of the "reality". The size and nature of the represented information are manipulated to reveal specific views of the producers in power and influence receivers' perception of the event concerned. Owing to its cross-domain conceptual and selective projection, interaction with other cognitive factors in its use and understanding, and its implicitly evaluative functions, metaphor is particularly involved in this function of representation.

A large amount of literature about metaphorical representation links the study of metaphor in discourse with understanding of something very central to human behavior, including the relationship between language and ideology in various political worlds, and the perception of specific domains within the socio-economic world. It is especially useful in exploration of the inner subjectivity of journalists of popular business discourse. Most of the existing studies in this field are carried out in the paradigm of Critical Discourse Analysis (CDA), which has contributed to the emergence of the fairly new approach of Critical Metaphor Analysis (CMA). However, its total reliance on Lakoff and Johnson's theory is so determinative and it ignores that discourse could guide us to both novel and conventional conceptual metaphors. In addition, the interface between cognitive processes as well as representations in discourse on the one hand and the social groups on the other hand is not constructed clearly enough to refute the criticism of over-interpretation. Practically, few studies concern economic events in fast developing countries, such as China, which is the region outside of the First World.

The present research establishes an integrated framework on the basis of metaphor studies in cognitive linguistics and CDA, especially the socio-cognitive approach developed by van Dijk. This proposed framework regards metaphor as both conceptual and linguistic phenomena that work as interface not only between the mental model and ideological structure dominating it, but also between discourse and its metaphoric realizations in text. The research is set in the case of a concrete business issue—Olympic Economy in the 2008 Beijing Olympic Games. As a fast-developing socialist country with a mixed economic system, China was put under the spotlight of the world thanks to the international sports event. This dissertation intends to test the hypothesis that Olympics-related economic activities will witness the integration of and clash between different economic ideologies by carrying out a comparative study of metaphorical representations of the 2008 Beijing Olympic Economy between Chinese and American media. For this purpose, two separate small size corpora were established on the basis of data collected from one authentic business magazine and one broadsheet newspaper in China and the United States respectively within the time range from September 1, 2001 to December 31, 2008. The relation between various aspects of the target domain and a set of source domains was established and special attention was given to realizations and functions of conceptual scenarios within each conceptual domain and some conceptual blending.

The results indicate that the two media share common mental model of Olympic Economy. Their developmental and competitive models of this international business event are realized by predominant metaphorical patterns—LIVING ORGANISM, JOURNEY, SPORT and GAME and WAR metaphors that are drawn from concepts concerning intra-phenomena of the human being, mainly the physical, mental and emotional states of individuals and the inter-phenomena of human beings, mainly their social experiences, including war, sport and game and journey. These similarities reveal their common thinking of Olympic Economy as a

2

fierce and open competition between opposite sides, requiring patience, strategies, hard work and sacrifice. The compatibility of these two models highlights the contribution of competition in Olympic Economy to the development of the entities concerned. This is largely decided by the nature of Olympic Economy as an international sports business with mature mechanism and to some extent shows the effect of China's integration with the international market in its process of modernization, which is marked by the frequent presence of those metaphors adhering to free-market ideology.

However, diverse conceptual scenarios activated by lexical choices within the same conceptual domain, different or even particular metaphorical patterns for the same entity or event and different functions of the same metaphorical pattern or scenario reveal differences in their mental models and their different views on participants and events. A more complicated competitive model is created by Chinese media to imply the juxtaposition of challenges and opportunities for local economy. Different views on China's economy as well as the political and economic significance of Beijing Olympics for China lead to different developmental models between the two media. In addition, different economic ideologies, plus cultural elements drive them to consider participants differently. All in all, American media give more space to critical voice in metaphorical representations of various aspects of Olympic Economy, indicating its negative evaluation of the competitiveness of Chinese companies, megaprojects and problems caused by the fast development of China's economy. Differently, Chinese media construct optimistic images in linking economic events with the political and social background in China. It also associates the current situation with companies' development in the future and attempts to tone down the current problems.

This research demonstrates the vital role linguistic analyses play in the revelation of metaphor functions, but we need to look further into

3

societal structure, including historical, cultural, as well as political factors and economic ideologies in order to give full explanation. Historical and cultural factors facilitate the understanding of implied meaning, embedded evaluation and emotional effect of a metaphor. The political factors justify the salience of the positive tone in Chinese media and its obscurity in the representation of troubles. Dominance of free-market ideology in American society and the mixture of free-market and socialist ideologies in China also give rise to their diverse thinking of Olympic Economy, which in turn reinforce their ideologies and influence the opinions of the readers and their perception of business activities relating to Beijing Olympics.

The findings support some basic ideas about metaphor, including its experiential motivation, conceptual and ideological nature and simultaneously demonstrate its function in exposing covert meanings in language use. Most importantly, this study enriches social-cognitive research under the paradigm of CDA. The study of metaphor as ideologically tainted language further blurs the boundary between conventional and novel metaphors, both of which can reveal the users' specific perspective to think of entities and events. Even one-shot metaphors with quite low frequency could perform the similar function and thus warn against the total dependence on statistics in the analysis of metaphorical representations. The comparative method adopted in the research clearly foregrounds underlying ideologies that nurture the diversity of metaphor use across different countries and thus advocates the idea that disparity across societies should be taken into account in the study of discourse in contemporary world. As a cognitively robust study in the paradigm of CDA, the present research enhances the belief that media discourse, including popular business discourse, is not always complete and neutral representation of the reality, but an effective channel to manipulate the public's understanding of significant events, such as Beijing Olympics and related business activities.

4

Contents

List of Tables

List of Figures

1

Chapter 1　Introduction

1.1 Background of the Present Research

No one can deny the overall power of the media in modern information societies. Together with other powerful elite groups and institutions, such as politicians, corporate managers, professionals and professors, media sometimes indirectly have the greatest influence on the lives of most people in society. It is said that media discourse is the main source of people's knowledge, attitudes and ideologies, both of other elites and of ordinary citizens. The media elites are ultimately responsible for the prevailing discourses of the media they control.

Traditional approaches to the role of the media in the reproduction of reality were largely based on content analysis: quantitative studies of stereotypical words or images representing certain social groups and events. These approaches treat media discourse as transparent messages whose contents may be analyzed in a superficial, quantitative way (van Dijk, 1991: 32-37).

The recent analytical approach examines the complex structures and strategies of media discourse and their relations to the social context with the aim to reveal the role of media in the reproduction of social reality. Its attention given to the dialectical relation between discourse and society can be traced back to the Marxist-influenced critical theory of the Frankfurt school, later followed by Habermas and Foucault. Their post-structuralist discourse analysis has provided important social theory for CDA (Fairclough, 1989, 1995; Wodak, 1996; Wodak & Meyer, 2001). Only with the inception of Critical Linguistics (Fowler et al., 1979; Fowler, 1991; Kress & Hodge, 1979), did linguistic theory come to be adopted by analyzing concrete discourse in the paradigm of CDA.

Originally, critical analysis of media discourse borrowed analytical tools from Chomsky's transformational grammar (Fowler et al., 1979; Hodge & Kress, 1988), but replaced it later with Halliday's systemic functional linguistics (Fowler, 1991). It is found that functionalist approaches are more useful than formalist ones, since the former like CDA is interested in the role of language in real use (Fairclough, 1989: 11; Wodak, 2001: 8). As a result, Hallidayan systemic functional grammar has become the main linguistic tool of CDA. It is only much more recently that the merits of cognitive linguistics in offering a theory of language for CDA have been discussed (Hart & Lukes, 2007: x). Researchers believe that CDA must account for the cognitive realities involved in discourse as language use, as expressed in the following extract:

We regard language as consisting of a related set of categories and processes. The fundamental categories are a set of "model" which describe the interrelation of objects and events. These models are basic schemata which derive in their turn from the visual perceptual processes of human beings. These schemata serve to classify events in the world, in simple but crucial ways (Hodge & Kress, 1993: 8).

In this connection, a number of theories that are subsumed by cognitive linguistics are applied in CDA, including conceptual metaphor theory, mental space theory, conceptual blending, conceptual framing, and framing in cognitive grammar. The present study attempts to demonstrate theoretical and practical contribution of cognitive linguistics to the research in the paradigm of CDA.

1.2 Rationales for the Present Research

Based on empirical evidence, this book takes an analytical and interdisciplinary approach to metaphor at cognitive as well as linguistic levels from a comparative perspective. The analysis is set in a broader social context with the aim to reveal the nature of media discourse as social practice used for representation and signification of certain social realities.

1.2.1 Theoretical Rationale

Discourse, including media discourse is language in action, through which producers and receivers interact with each other by way of mental representations of themselves and the groups they belong to (Chilto & Schäffner, 2002: 25; Fairclough, 2003: 49-53). These mental representations are stored in long-term memory as social knowledge about ideas, values and practices. They are arrived at both individually and collectively, and stimulated by produced text in communication.

In this connection, the representations in mind and in language-in-use are very crucial in the studying of the discourse meaning. We should intersect linguistic approach to media discourse with the cognitive approach. The standard cognitive ideas claim that metaphor is a part of human conceptualization and not simply a linguistic rhetoric that is prevalent in a variety of discourse (Chilton & Lakoff, 1995; Johnson, 1987; Kövecses, 2002; Lakoff, 1987, 1993; Lakoff & Johnson, 1980, 1999; Lakoff & Turner, 1989; Turner, 1991). This thought operates by mapping familiar source domains of experience onto more abstract domains. It transfers the logic of the source domain to the target domain. It also interacts with other cognitive factors and produces many entailments used for the reasoning of the target domain. The same abstract concept and

3

experience could be constructed and represented by different metaphors and the same metaphor can be realized in different linguistic expressions (Dirven, Frank & Pütz, 2003). Such selective nature of metaphor will enable us to present different ways of looking at our world (Lakoff & Johnson, 1980), so it can provide a conceptual structure for a systematized ideology. It can also arouse certain emotions (Goatly, 1997: 158) and articulate points of view. As a result, the choice of metaphor can invoke differences in evaluation besides those in ontological perspectives. In addition, metaphors with high frequency of occurrence are established as a mode of thought among members of a linguistic community, and are used to some extent in an automatic and effortless way (Lakoff & Turner, 1989: 55). These features enable metaphor to play an important role in the covert construction of reality, which is discussed in this book under the paradigm of CDA.

Incorporating metaphor study into CDA (Fairclough, 1989, 1992, 1995; Fowler, 1991; Kress & van Leevwen, 1996, 2001; van Dijk, 1977, 1988, 1997) that firmly sets linguistic analysis in social context could not only follow up one of the recent principal studies in cognitive linguistics that claim ideological stances are subsumed in metaphor, but also enhance the socio-cognitive research under the paradigm of CDA. In this way, the integration of metaphor study with CDA will give deep insight into the relationship between social structures, discourse and cognition.

1.2.2 Practical Rationale

Popular business discourses refer to journalistic texts that deal with current economic and business matters for an audience of experts and non-experts and seek to inform and entertain more generally (Deignan, 2006).

These journalistic texts, including articles from newspapers and magazines, basically deal with the description and evaluation of economic

4

performance of societies, the distribution of its fruits and the actions of public authorities (Reder, 1999: 9). They are one kind of media discourses that have been in the focus of many fields, because of their significant role in social life. They are the most accessible channel through which members in a community get to know some important business events and related people on the one hand and the people in power represent these entities on the other hand. The representations of these events and people invite readers to understand and interpret them in a certain way under the influence of shared situational, social and cultural factors. Because of these, such discourse can tell us a great deal about social meanings and stereotypes projected through language and thus, reflect and influence the formation and reconstruction of economic life (Bell, 1995: 23).

Owing to metaphors' cognitive characteristics, they are one of the available resources for journalists to impart abstract concepts to non-experts and help them to understand entities and events in the unfamiliar domain of economy in terms of domains with close relationship to their life. At the same time, metaphorical expressions could be used to dress up concepts, thus attract enough readerships with vividness. Most importantly, as an implicit element of evaluative resources, metaphor is in line with journalists' intention to interpret economic and business matters in a way that represents the views and actions of certain social groups subject to the social constraints and institutional relations, but at the same time avoid of being "biased" in their reports (Fowler, 1991). Consequently, metaphor contributes to a much more intangible form of ideologically tainted language in the popular business discourse. It is generally undetected and has the effect of conditioning and influencing the recipients' attitudes and opinions. So exposure of these covert meanings is quite important to the people involved. That is the very concern of this book through the examination of metaphorical representations of Olympic Economy in Chinese and English popular business discourse.

The concept of Olympic Economy was first put forward by Peter Ueberroth, who worked as president of the organizing committee for the 1984 Los Angeles Olympics. He created a financially successful competition that reversed a trend of heavy deficit spending by host cities and resulted in a surplus that financed youth sports in Los Angeles for many years. The concept refers to a variety of Olympics-related activities in the period preceding, during and succeeding the Olympics that result in certain economic values.

China won the right in 2001 to host the 29th Olympiad in the summer of 2008, and it was believed that this significant sports event would stimulate the economic development of the host city of Beijing and its economic effects would spread across the whole country through the regional and industrial interaction. Since Beijing's successful bid, it had been under the spotlight of the media at home and abroad. The launching of such Beijing Olympic Marketing Programs as sponsor authorization, sales progress, and licensing on September 1, 2003 had engaged over 600 Chinese and international business leaders. These local and international companies had spared no efforts to link their activities with the Olympics. Local and foreign media had traced closely the development in this movement, covering the bid, strategies and results of the marketing programs. In order to home this important sports event, China had invested a staggering amount of money for sports arena and at the same time facilitated the transformation of Beijing through demolishing many old buildings and building some modern ones. For these building projects, China invited famous foreign architects instead of domestic ones to design. Such huge investment had aroused most controversy. People worried that such huge investment would become a great financial pressure on the host city of Beijing for a long time after the Games. What's more, there was much discussion on the functions of these sports arenas after the Olympics.

Besides, the 29th Olympiad is different from other Olympics in the sense that it is the first Olympics that took place in one developing country that has a different economic system from other previous host countries. Most interestingly, China is experiencing economic transformation, which has a profound impact not only on itself but on the world. Its increasing integration with the international economy and its growing efforts to use market forces to govern the domestic allocation of goods have unleashed individual initiative and entrepreneurship and simultaneously encouraged foreign investment and foreign trade. Such a mixed economic system in a fast-developing socialist country has always been drawing close attention of the international world. The coming Olympics put it again under the spotlight of the world. We assume that Olympics-related economic activities will witness the integration of and clash between different economic ideologies. This book will help test this hypothesis by carrying out a comparative study of metaphorical representations of the 2008 Beijing Olympic Economy between Chinese and American media.

1.3 Objectives of the Present Research

The specific endeavor of this book is to discover and analyze how Olympic Economy is articulated on the basis of metaphor and how this plays a vital role in constructing an ideological view of economic reality. It will make explicit these socially constructed implicit meanings and test them for their ideological content.

The book focuses on the cognitive patterns of talking about Olympic Economy through description, explanation and interpretation of metaphorical representations in both Chinese and English popular business discourse for the purpose of manifesting the dialogic relation between cognition, ideology and discourse. This general objective will be further elaborated by the following few aspects:

Firstly, to explore whether a wide variety of metaphorical expressions

7

can be reduced to a fairly limited number of conceptual metaphors and thus indicate if there are similarities in the abstract reasoning in popular business discourse between these two countries and test the hypothesis that the western dominant economic value has an effect on Chinese economic ideology in its process of internationalization.

Secondly, to examine closely linguistic realizations of metaphors, including metaphorical linguistic expressions, their co-texts and various processes in them in order to demonstrate that certain semantic components of a source domain are highlighted and others are omitted to show the diversities between the two media in the metaphorical representation, which could reveal their different perspectives of looking at entities and events thus unearth their different views and opinions of Olympic Economy.

Thirdly, to examine the functions of metaphorical patterns and scenarios in the two media in an attempt to illustrate various aspects of Olympic Economy that have been highlighted in the representation, in order to reveal what is profiled and what is pushed to the background in their thinking about Olympic Economy.

Fourthly, to interpret and explain the above mentioned variations of metaphor use in context in order to explain why one type of metaphor is favored against another in one media and why specific scenario is given more priority in one media than the other with the aim to expose the implicit values and ideologies in these two economic communities by looking into historical, cultural and economic factors.

1.4 Outline of the Book

This book is divided into 9 chapters. Chapter 1 is the introduction. Chapter 2 outlines previous studies accomplished by domestic and foreign linguists under the guidance of paradigms in both cognitive and discourse

8

approaches to metaphor study with the aim to trace the development of metaphor studies and simultaneously locate the present research. It specially focuses on studies of metaphorical representations in business discourses with the aim to highlight the potential 'contribution of the present research.

The research is a study of metaphor use from the point of view of CDA, so an integrated theoretical framework will be established in Chapter 3 in an attempt to enrich cognitive aspects in the critical analysis of discourse. Before the elaboration of this framework, some theoretical background will be provided, with the intention to offer the rationale for the incorporation of different disciplines and at the same time illustrate what this framework could add to the current efforts by giving equal attention to cognitive, linguistic and socio-cultural aspects in the analysis of metaphor in discourse.

Chapter 4 is about methodology, which explains the procedures of data collection, addressing such issues as definition of metaphor, metaphorical units, subjectivity and the role of context in the identification and categorization of metaphors in the discourse analysis of metaphor. Besides that, it gives an overview of the procedures in data analysis, which is the focus of the next three chapters.

Chapter 5 to Chapter 7 form the section of data analysis, carrying out linguistic and cognitive analyses of frequent and less frequent common metaphors and particular metaphors respectively. Similarities in the metaphorical representations between these two media will be illustrated through frequent common metaphorical patterns. Diversities will be singled out in particular metaphors, preference for some metaphors revealed in quantitative disparity, and lexical choices for rich conceptual scenarios in the same metaphor.

Based on detailed data analyses, Chapter 8 will offer explanations from cognitive, social and cultural perspectives. Common dominant conceptual projections will reveal their similar understanding of entities and processes concerning Olympic Economy, which demonstrates to some extent the changing China's economic ideology under the influence of Western values or the integrations of different ideologies in this international sports economy. More attention is given to factors that give rise to diverse scenarios created in the same cross-domain mapping and particular conceptual correspondences with the aim to reveal different ideologies underlying the same economic phenomenon. All in all, the explanation attempts to shed light on the role of societal structure in the discourse of Olympic Economy.

Chapter 9 presents the conclusions in accordance with the description, interpretation and explanation in the preceding chapters and raises some challenging issues for the future research in relevant fields.

Chapter 2　Literature Review

2.1 Introduction

Metaphor has been studied for a very long time. The view of metaphor has shifted from a traditional view of a way of speaking in which one thing is expressed in terms of another to a recently-developed view of a cognitive phenomenon in which metaphor is considered to be a cognitive tool of vital importance in human cognition.

In the traditional approaches that subsume the comparison view and the substitution view, metaphor is a linguistic phenomenon without any involvement of cognitive activities. It is used for artistic and rhetorical purposes on the basis of resemblance between two entities (Kövecses, 2002: viii). The subsequent interaction view for the first time claims that metaphors sometimes function as "cognitive instruments." This view emphasizes that something new is created in the interaction between two terms, which is derived from the associative meaning of the two subjects concerned (Ortony, 1996). The creation of such similarity is a cognitive activity; however, the interaction view does not provide a detailed explanation of the characteristics of this cognitive process, which is fully explained by the mapping process in cognitive approaches to metaphor. The cognitive linguistic theory of metaphor, first developed by George Lakoff and Mark Johnson in their widely read book *Metaphors We Live By* (1980), focuses on the questions "what is metaphor?" and "how does it work in the mind?"

This chapter begins with an introduction to these studies with the purpose to trace the development of modern metaphor studies and simultaneously locate the current research. Then the review focuses on the studies of metaphorical representations in discourse approach. Special attention will be given to metaphorical representations in different types of business discourses in an attempt to highlight the potential contribution of this book.

2.2 Cognitive Approaches to Metaphor

For researchers who study metaphor from a cognitive perspective, the focus lies in the relation between language and thought: how metaphors construct our thought through conceptual mappings and how metaphorical expressions are processed.

2.2.1 Cognitive Nature of Metaphor

Pioneers of conceptual theories point out that metaphors primarily exist in thought instead of being a figure of language. They not only enrich the vocabulary for a speech community, but also help to construct the reasoning and conceptual system of human beings and to expand people's understanding through building up a relationship between two items. In this connection, metaphors provid people with new ways to understand and categorize experiences in one field by their experiences in another. In this way, people can use comparatively easy and familiar experiences to understand those difficult and strange ones (Gibbs, 1999: 145).

According to conceptualists, both language and understanding are metaphorical. Metaphor is part of everyday speech affecting the way people perceive, think and act, and is thus the way human beings live by. It claims that conceptual metaphors function at the level of thought, below language. They are used to describe the relationship that exists between two groups of ideas in people's mind. Such terms as source domain, target domain and mapping are conventionally used to express a conceptual metaphor. The source domain is usually a concrete domain employed for the representation of the target domain that is more abstract and requires more mental efforts in understanding. The structure and feature of the source domain is transferred by the metaphor to the target domain, and the process is called mapping from the source domain to the target domain. This process is composed of a series of psychological transformations by which an individual acquires, stores, recalls, and decodes information (Kail, 2001). A convenient way to express a metaphor in the conceptualist view is CONCEPTUAL DOMAIN (A) IS CONCEPTUAL DOMAIN (B), which is called a conceptual metaphor. The two conceptual domains in a metaphor are the coherent organization of experience (Kövecses, 2002), and domain (A) is understood in terms of domain (B).

Researchers generally identify conceptual metaphors through language. They search for patterns in the words and phrases that are generally called "linguistic metaphor", and use these as evidence for the existence of underlying conceptual metaphors (Steen, 1994). The relationship between metaphorical thinking and speaking is often described by saying that linguistic metaphors realize conceptual metaphors (Deignan, 2005). For example, the conceptual metaphor ARGUMETN IS WAR can be said to be realized by linguistic metaphors in such expression as "Your claims are indefensible" and "He attacked every weak point in my argument". A set of classical metaphorical mappings are hypothesized on the basis of recurrent linguistic expressions, such as ARGUMENT IS WAR and LIFE IS A JOURNEY, and other mappings that are related to human emotions (Lakoff & Kövecses, 1987).

2.2.2 Embodiment of Metaphor

Conceptualists believe that metaphors are based on embodied human

13

experiences (e.g. Lakoff & Johnson, 1980, 1999; Grady, 1997ab). "Embodiment" of meaning is essential to the cognitive view of metaphor, because a large portion of metaphorical meaning derives from people's experience of their body (Gibbs, Lima & Francozo, 2004). This phenomenon is discussed in motivation in cognitive linguistics. By "motivated" is meant "an account which appeals to something beyond the linguist's intuition that these senses are related, or that these two senses are more closely related than either is to a third sense" (Sweetser, 2002: 3).

In the study of metaphor, scholars have identified different types of motivations. For example, Kövecses (2002: 244) identifies two types of motivation, namely "correlations in experience and resemblance or similarity", which complement each other. Lakoff and Johnson (1999) have observed that metaphors have bodily motivation, and there are three ways in which simple or primary metaphors are embodied: the correlations are embodied in people's neuroanatomy; the source domains arise from the sensorimotor experiences of the human body; people repeatedly experience in the world situations in which source and target domains are connected. Among these, correlations in experiences are considered the basis for metaphor. For instance, we can conceptualize affection as warmth (Kövecses, 1986: 101) because of the correlation we experience in our childhood between the affective embrace of our parents and the comforting bodily warmth that accompanies it.

The embodied motivation of metaphor provides a natural, non-arbitrary reason for why people have the metaphorical mappings to better understand many abstract concepts (Gibbs, 2001). Metaphorical connections between different domains are perceived connections on the basis of objective similarities. People's access to them is through their experience, both physical and cultural. Therefore, the nature of a given metaphorical projection is partly determined by the nature of people's bodily experience. It is natural for human beings to borrow concepts and

14

vocabulary from the more accessible physical and social worlds to refer to the less accessible worlds of reasoning, emotion, and so on. This account for the phenomenon that the same metaphors are shared by unrelated languages. Although groups of people do not share language and culture, they do have one thing in common: inhabiting a human body, where the roots of the metaphorical connections probably lie in.

Research on EMOTION metaphors finds that they are motivated by bodily sensations that human beings experience when they have these emotions, including metaphorical ways of talking about ANGER (Gibbs, 1994) and LUST (Lakoff & Kövecses, 1987). Some cross-linguistic research supports the idea that metaphors for emotions are grounded in physical sensation (Emanatian, 1995; Yu, 1995).

2.2.3 Systematic and Partial Nature of Metaphor

A metaphorical concept is systematic and the language people use to talk about the concept is also systematic. That is to say, correspondences between the two domains are systematic. Aspects of the source domain are systematically correlated with aspects of the target domain. The correlation is a process of projection or mapping from the source domain to the target domain in a systematic way (Olson, 1998). Metaphorical expressions are determined by metaphorical concepts in a systematic way, and are also systematic, reflecting the systematic nature of metaphorical concepts and the nature of human activities. Systematicity allows people to understand one aspect of a concept in terms of another, and in this way hides other aspects of the concept. Different metaphors about one concept do not exclude each other, but form a complete and coherent system. Therefore, a concept can be understood in terms of a number of different metaphors (Kövecses, 2002).

Systematicity of metaphors is by no means absolute, and the mapping from the source domain to the target domain of a metaphor is partial. Only some features of the source domain are selected and projected onto the target domain to constitute a conceptual metaphor. The aspect emphasized in the target is called the highlighted part, which can be reflected in the lexicon of language. Because of the partial mapping of conceptual metaphors, researchers observe that the understanding of situations and events presented by any metaphor is therefore flawed. A metaphor will never give a completely accurate picture of its topic and every linguistic metaphor will inevitably highlight some aspects of the topic and hide others (Lakoff & Johnson, 1980: 10-14). For example, the term "seize" in the metaphor UNDERSTADING IS SEIZING just highlights the feeling we have when we quickly understand a new idea, but hides the lengthy pondering that often precedes understanding (Deignan, 2005: 23). Metaphors also distort because they present a simplified interpretation of situations. For instance, the metaphor LIFE IS A JOURNEY enables us to comprehend the abstract topic of life directly. However, human life is obviously far more complex than a literal journey. Aspects of human life are lost due to an artifically simple understanding of it that is suggested by the very metaphor.

Some researchers exploit both hiding and simplification of conceptual metaphors in order to show that metaphor is potentially ideological. They announce that metaphors in texts can be used to present a biased view of situation (Lakoff & Johnson, 1980; Lakoff, 1991). Since metaphors represent certain ways of thinking that are rooted in a common social practice, the biased pictures constructed by frequent metaphors of a community contribute to a collective bias of the members, reflecting the community's interpretation of the world. Such normative and reinforcing effect of conceptual metaphors requires us not accept them uncritically (Hawkes, 1972: 89; Mey, 1994: 62).

2.2.4 Complexity of Metaphor

Cognitive linguists have reached the consensus that conceptual metaphors are far from being simple one-to-one mappings, but are complex constructs. Kövecses's (1991, 2000) studies on metaphorical representations of emotion find that a particular abstract domain is understood in a variety of metaphors, each of which emphasizes different aspects of the topic. Such findings aroused the question concerning the generality and specificity of conceptual metaphors (Gibbs et al., 1997; Kövecses, 2002).

Grady (1997b) cleared the question by distinguishing primary and complex metaphors. Primary ones refer to simple, basic mappings that have a strong experiential basis and motivate metaphorical expressions within a variety of different areas of experience (Lakoff & Johnson, 1999: 49ff). They can combine to produce "complex metaphors", which correspond to the traditional conceptual metaphors of cognitive metaphor theory (Grady, 1997b). The "central mappings" put forward by Kövecses in his elaboration of "generalized metaphors" (2000) corresponds to Grady's "primary metaphors". They conceptually give rise to other constituent metaphors and entailments. From the center mapping COMPLEX SYSTEMS ARE BUILDINGS, many metaphors derive, including CAREERS ARE BUILDING, THEORIES ARE BUILDING, ECONOMIC SYSTEMS ARE BUILDINGS, A COMPANY IS A BUILDING and RELATIONSHIPS ARE BUILDINGS. These central mappings reflect major human concerns in cultural connection of the source domain and are most motivated experientially. Generally, a more hierarchically organized understanding of conceptual structure is shared by many cognitive theorists.

Apart from the phenomenon that a target may attach to several sources, a source domain may apply to several targets and a target may attach to several sources. For example, the BUILDING domain applies to

17

both THEORY and RELATIONSHIP, which are realized in such expressions as "Scientific knowledge is constructed by small numbers of specialized workers" and "The two have build a solid relationship". Kövecses names the range of target domains to which a given source concept applis the scope of metaphor (2002: 108-109).

Source domains often map ideas onto the target beyond the basic correspondences and produce rich entailments or inferences (Kövecses, 2005: 7). For example, if economy is conceptualized as a building and the process of building corresponds to construction of the economic system, then our knowledge about the building process can be used for the understanding of the creation of economic system, which is instantiated in such metaphorical language: "There is no painless way to get inflation down" and "We now have an excellent foundation on which to build".

2.2.5 Metaphor and Culture

Later, when the study extended to other languages than English, originally on emotion expressions, it was found that a particular abstract domain showed a particular cross-cultural disparity. Different conceptual mappings have been found for the abstract notions of Love (Yang, 2002), Anger (Kövecses, 2000; Taylor & Mbense, 1998). It was further indicated that some mapping enjoyed more central position than others in certain languages and cultures (Kövecses, 1995a, 1995b, 2002, 2005). For instance, the metaphor LIFE IS A SHOW is at the heart of American culture and can be found in every facet of American life and popular culture.

Such findings introduce cultural factors to studies on metaphor and have stimulated subsequent comparative studies across different languages and cultures under the framework of cognitive linguistics (Boers, 2003; Deignan, 2003; Kövecses, 2003, 2004; Maalej, 2004; Yu, 1998, 2004). These studies explore how speakers of different languages may use different metaphors to speak about common area of human experience. Such cultural motivation has attracted an increasing number of domestic scholars and produced a large amount of recent works. They have addressed similar and different conceptualizations of abstract concepts across cultures, including time and space (Chen, 2007a; Zhang & Ding, 2003; Zhou, 2000) and human emotions (Chen, 2007ab; Lin, 1998; Wen & Luo, 2004; Zhang, 2000). They have also compared similar and different conceptual functions performed by various elements of human basic physical and social experience between Chinese and English-speaking cultures, including the human body parts (Chen, 2007a; Wen & Wu, 2007), primary colors (Chen, 2003, 2007a), the natural phenomena of wind and water (Li & Feng, 2006; Xu & Zhou, 2006) and the eating activity (Yang, 2004).

These studies have to some degree extended the view of embodiment by taking culture into consideration. Metaphors are deeply grounded in culture and the most fundamental values in a culture are coherent with the metaphorical structure of the most fundamental concepts in the culture (Kövecses, 2003; Lakoff & Johnson, 1980; Sanday, 1994). This leads to one characteristic of conceptual metaphor that people are obliged to use them unconsciously at the very beginning (Shu, 2004). The conceptual domains concerned are metaphorically structured and stored in long-term memory as complex knowledge representations, containing organized information about related entities, actions and events. In this connection, pre-existing systems are activated when a linguistic metaphor is encountered (Cameron, 2001: 18).

These studies also point out the link between metaphor and culture is not always indirect, since many metaphors allude to knowledge that is shared as part of our cultural repository, but no longer directly experienced (Deignan, 2003: 270; MacArther, 2005). It needs to address the role of social structures, such as the authority of the source of transmission, to explain their survival in current usage. It would suggest that the meaning of some linguistic metaphors can be explained more fully with reference to former belief systems than through an analysis of possible physical origins alone.

Last but not least, these studies draw our attention to both linguistic and cognitive levels of metaphor research, because of the fact that two different languages could share the common conceptual metaphors but show similarities and differences in the linguistic expressions of these metaphors. Apart from these, these explorations are of particular interest to applied linguists in their attempts to make pedagogical use of metaphor research to facilitate learners' second language acquisition (Boers, 2000, 2001; Boers, Demecheleer & Eyckmans, 2004; Kövecses & Szabo, 1996; Lazar, 1996). The variation across different languages is also of great interest from the perspective that metaphor use may reveal a language-speaking community's world view or ideology. This point of view is taken by the present dissertation following some other research that will be reviewed in the discoursal approach to metaphor study.

2.2.6 Creativity of Metaphor

Lakoff and Turner (1989) initially address the creativity of metaphor in their book *More Than Cool Reason* when it is found that the poets share most of conventional metaphors with the normal people in the same culture, but their linguistic expressions strike us as novel and original. They achieve this figurative creativity by extension, elaboration, questioning and combining the conventional metaphors. All these creative cognitive processes result in novel metaphorical expressions.

Kövecses claims that these creative processes are not used only by poets, since many ordinary people endowed with the ability of creativity use metaphor creatively, which accounts for a great deal of variations in the use of metaphor (2005: 259). He further points out that the human cognitive potential goes beyond these processes and the Conceptual Metaphor Theory runs into difficulty in the explanation. For example, there is no natural correspondence between the source domain of BUTCHERY and the target domain of SURGEON, which expresses the main idea of the sentence "The surgeon is a butcher", namely, the surgeon is incompetent. The theory of conceptual integration or blending (BT) offers a solution.

Proposed by Fauconnier (1998) as well as Fauconnier and Turner (2002), this theory involves four domains in the analysis of metaphor: two input spaces, a generic space and a blended space also called blend (Fauconnier & Turner, 2002). The two input spaces correspond to the source domain and the target domain in CMT. Counterparts of the two input mental spaces are connected through a partial cross-space mapping. The generic space maps onto each of the input spaces, and contains what is common among them, that is, an element in the generic space maps onto paired counterparts in the two input spaces. The blended space is where material from the inputs combines and interacts. Conceptual blending is a great mental capacity and operates largely unconsciously.

In the blending process, structures from the two input mental spaces are projected to the new space called blend. It contains more specific structures that are related to the generic structure captured in generic space. They include structures that are not available in the inputs. The blend comes from the conceptual blending in the literal sense of blend of the two input spaces instead of from either of the two input spaces. The blend is not simply a copy of the source and the target, but it may include new elements that do not belong to the input spaces (Kövecses, 2002). Take the sentence "He was so mad, smoke was coming out of his ear" for example, in which we have an angry person as the target domain and smoke in a container as the source domain. There is no smoke in the target domain and no ear in the source domain, but the metaphor conceptually integrates

21

the two and creates a new conceptual blend: the angry person has a container that has ears from which smoke blows out.

Both CMT and BT regard metaphor as a cognitive phenomenon involving mapping between different conceptual domains, and both of them put limitations on the mapping process. However, there are differences between the two theories. CMT focuses on the explanation of conventional relationships based on unidirectional mappings from the source domain to the target domain. Differently, BT focuses on the conceptualization of novel metaphors and accounts for the interaction between the four mental spaces in the blending process. Mapping is multi-directional in BT, since elements in both input spaces are mapped onto the generic and blended spaces, and the result is an emergent structure which explicitly illustrates how new meanings come into being. This emergent structure is missing from CMT, which only consists of correlations and mappings from the source domain concept to the target domain concept.

In spite of differences between them, the two theories are complementary to each other. Metaphor in CMT is understood as entrenched and conventionalized relations between concepts. They are composed of stable knowledge structures that are stored in long-term memory. The conventionalized correlations and cross-domain mappings in CMT become inputs in BT and at the same time constrain the blending in BT. BT imitates dynamic mental activities of language users and is better at explaining novel metaphors. Blending can be both conventionalized and novel, and conventionalized mappings are often used in online mapping (Fauconnier & Turner, 1998; Huang, 2002). However, the multi-space network of BT is complex and the function of the generic space is not clearly stated (Luo, 2006). In order to give a satisfactory account for most metaphorical use of language and the understanding process, we need to combine CMT and BT. Conventional relationships between concepts can

22

be explained by CMT, and novel relationships, which are constructed online between concepts for local understanding, are explained through the network model proposed in BT. In a word, cross-domain mappings in CMT function as the basis of blending in BT, and BT provides new perspectives for cognitive studies of language.

2.2.7 Summary

In sum, findings in the cognitive approach to metaphor emphasize the role of metaphor to structure thinking and knowledge. They reveal its close relation with physical experience and indicate its linguistic instantiation, systematic as well as partial mapping and highlight its creativity, complexity and cultural implications. Because of these, research on metaphor from the cognitive perspective has become a starting point for a great number of studies in social science, including politics, philosophy, economics, cultural studies and education.

In spite of the breakthrough in the view of metaphor and its contribution to social studies, the cognitive approach is still criticized because of its methodology. Both intuitive and elicited data that are adopted in it derive from internalized language experience of individuals. Such data are different from naturally-occurring data. They tend to produce innovative rather than conventional metaphors that are the central concern of CMT. They can also be criticized because of their form A=B that is rare in naturally-occurring data. Those weak points have been complemented by research from the discourse approach.

2.3 Discourse Approaches to Metaphor

Because of linguistic, cognitive, and cultural features of metaphor, scholars have realized that for a full understanding of metaphor, we need to approach the phenomenon taking into account the real communicative contexts in which it occurs and which it helps to structure. This is fully voiced by Cameron in the following statements: "What I'm arguing for is the centrality of the contextual nature of language in use; the human and discourse context of language use is inherent in the joint construction of discourse goals and in the use of metaphor to achieve those goals. Processing metaphorical language takes place in context and draws on the discourse expectations of participants. It follows that the theoretical frameworks used to operationalize metaphor must do so too" (Cameron, 2001: 25).

In this connection, researchers from the discourse approach focus on the function of metaphor to create meaning by language users working under the conceptual metaphor paradigm. Their main interest is to reveal how people use language to creat meaning and metaphor is regarded as one of the tools in this process. These researchers distinguish themselves by making their analyses accountable to naturally-occuring data and are divided into two groups according to their different research questions and focuses, in spite of the fact that they all analyse a text as a product.

The first group adopting discourse approach look into the role metaphors play in the construction of meaning and how metaphors are interpreted in the interaction. They mainly concern spoken interaction and especially metaphor use for the expression of personal meaning. Their analyses are often limited to such specialized genres as health (Gwyn 1999; Levitt et al., 2000), education (Cameron & Deignan, 2003; Cortazzi & Jin, 1999) and reconciliation conversations (Cameron, 2007). The findings demonstrate the importance of metaphors in transmission of new concepts, helping people to understand, think and talk about their experience, and facilitating the participants to make extended efforts to explain themselves to and understand the other in the interaction concerning topics that are emotionally difficult to talk about.

All these studies take a dynamic and dialogic view of metaphor and analyze its usage in the face-to-face interaction and trace its function on a minute-by-minute timescale of utterance. They identify patterns of metaphor use in discourse as linguistic evidence of thinking and perspectives, while at the same time investigate how metaphors are negotiated and constructed across speaker. In one word, metaphor is seen as linguistic, cognitive, affective and social-cultural. There are some scholars who consider metaphors used in the spoken interaction in business activities, which will be introduced in the section for metaphor research on economic and business discourse.

The second group concerns the relationship between language and ideology and examines how metaphors work as filters when representing reality in line with Critical Discourse Analysis movement implicitly and explicitly. Since this perspective is taken by the present research, the next two sections will be set apart for a detailed review of relevant literature.

It is no doubt that a turn to discourse has outlined the recent tendency in metaphor studies. Scholars in China have more recently attached importance to the study of metaphor in the discourse, with such representative figures as Feng Xiaohu (2004), Liao Meizeng (1992, 2007), Lu Weizhong and Lu Yun (2006), Ren Shaozeng (2006a, 2006b), Wei Jidong (2005, 2006a, 2006b, 2006c), Wei Zaijing (2006), Zhang Wei and Zhang Delu (2007) and so on.

Inspired by the research carried out by Goatly (1997) and Koller (2003), these domestic scholars show great interest in the metafunctions of metaphors in discourse. They point out that conceptual metaphors play an active role in the conceptualization and explanation of our experience, facilitate the negotiation of discoursal meanings and the conveyance of the users' attitude, and work as an important foundation for the discourse processing and organization. These reflect the three metafunctions given by Halliday respectively—ideational, interpersonal and textual functions. Their research focuses on the textual function of metaphors in discourse, in which metaphor serves as the unifying factor ensuring the coherence of discourse. The systematic mapping of metaphorical concepts and the interaction between different conceptual domains activated by metaphors make metaphor a textual strategy. It not only forms systematic lexical cohesive networks, but also leads to mapping relations between chunks of discourse, which enables discourse to unfold with a specific mapping pattern.

In terms of ideational function of metaphor, several scholars have asserted the relationship between metaphor and ideological meanings, thanks to the partial and systematic mapping of conceptual metaphors (Hong & Zhang, 2002; Xin, 2007). Some scholars even take a step further by adovating the integration of CDA paradigm with cognitive linguistics in the discourse analysis of metaphor. However, they only discuss about the theoretical possibility and have not gone into empirical studies yet. In the next section, we will focus on the theoretical and empirical exploration of foreign researchers in this field. In other words, we will elaborate the studies of the second group of researchers we have mentioned in passing in this section.

2.4 Metaphorical Representation

Chilton (2004: 45-47) summarizes representation as one of three main strategic functions that linguistic expressions may perform in his study of political discourse. It has to do with controlling the amount and nature of information that others receive, and with evoking particular views of "reality". In this connection, representation is a way for discourse producers to manipulate the receiver's understanding of the reality by choice of giving information in terms of size and nature.

According to Chilton (2004: 51-52), metaphorical expressions are particularly involved in the function of representation, since their

26

interpretation involves the projection of material from source to target domains. The source domain provides a source for conceptualization. Intuitively, it is understood in a holistic way. If one part of it is accepted, so do other parts. For example, if you accept to use disease to represent immigrants, you will think of such people in terms of some other knowledge about disease, such as the idea that it should be removed from the body. These accompanying presuppositions will produce rich inferences about unstructured, vague and abstract phenomena. In addition, metaphors always interact with other conceptual factors in the production and perception of discourse, including structured culture knowledge stored in human mind. At the same time, metaphors are often used unconsciously. All these make metaphorical representations seem to be in line with common sense. Ideas and values underlying them become so subtle that it is hard for a normal reader to detect them.

Fairclough (2003: 131-132) also believes that metaphor is one available resource to produce distinct representations of the world. He points out that those different metaphors for competition between companies, including RACING and COMMUNITIES metaphors will produce different managerial discourses. His analyses emphasize that different combination of common metaphors usually produce different business discourses and such combination is deeply rooted in cultures.

Their ideas sum up many relevant studies and stimulate even more subsequent research on metaphorical representations in different genres, especially political and business discourses that link the study of metaphor in discourse with understanding of something very central to human behaviors.

The majority of studies on metaphorical representations in political discourse concern the relationship between language and ideology. Metaphor is regarded as a bearer of ideology which is "the structure of the values and interests that inform any representation of reality (Hawkins,

2001: 27). These studies examine how metaphors work as filters when representing reality in line with CDA movement implicitly and explicitly.

There has been a great interest in the interplay between the identity of special social groups and metaphor in political language. The studies concerned address a wide range of social problems, such as gender discrimination (Ahrens, 2010), immigrants (Charteris-Black, 2005; Santa Ana, 1999, 2002, 2003) and racism (Chilton, 2005a; Goatly, 2007; Hawkins, 2001; Musolff, 2007; Rash, 2005). These studies show that metaphor always constitutes the publicly shared world view. Such national ideology will drive certain policy decisions. Even more studies are concerned with the use of metaphor in public speeches, especially those produced by famous politicians and in special social settings (Akin, 1994; Charteris-Black, 2005; Cheng, 2006; Louis & Kathleen, 2008; Semino & Maschi, 1996). These rhetorical and critical analyses manifest the persuasiveness of appropriate metaphors in political speeches and demonstrate how they show the distance and solidarity between the speakers and the receivers. In this way, they provide particular insight into why the rhetoric of political leaders is successful and at the same time underline the importance of metaphor in the revelation of hidden ideologies. Other studies under the paradigm of CDA discuss metaphors used to talk about the 1991 Gulf War and the periods leading to it (Pancake, 1993; Rohrer 1995; Voss et al., 1992). More or less, these studies demonstrate the persuasive power of metaphor in political discourse. The very acceptance of these metaphors provides grounds for certain entailments that highlight some feature of reality and hide others (Lakoff & Johnson, 1980: 156-157).

In research on metaphorical representations in political discourse, scholars have gradually realized the importance of component features in the source domain. The conceptual scenarios they construct have been studied in international relationship (Wee, 2001), domestic policies

28

(Lakoff, 1996, 2002, 2004) and social debates (Musolff, 2003). Specific features of the source domain in a common metaphorical pattern are addressed in these comparative studies, which demonstrate that characteristic ideological contrasts can be revealed by internal meaning aspects of the metaphorical source domain that will be covered by surface similarities in common metaphorical patterns. For example, Musolff's study (2003) focuses on different conceptual scenarios constructed by the source domain BODY-HEALTH-ILLNESS in the German and British press coverage on European Union topics during the 1990s. Different cognitive models of the European Union are identified. The HEART DISEASE scenarios served in British debates mainly denounce the EU as rotten or sick at its centre, whilst the PREMATURE BIRTH concept was used in Germany to express a commitment to care for the euro.

In conclusion, ideology and its metaphorical manifestations in discourse have been a productive area of political discourse study in the research paradigm of CDA. All the above-mentioned findings reveal ideological power of conceptual metaphors. They are consistent with the view that conceptual metaphors construct our thinking and reasoning, and simultaneously enhance the theoretical status of metaphor studies in cognitive linguistics by giving critical reading of social and political worlds, ranging from gender and race to political wars. We will look at such exploration in the business world when we shift to the research on metaphorical representations in business discourse.

2.5 Metaphorical Representation in Economic and Business Discourse

Since metaphor is an important mechanism through which we conceptualize new ideas, comprehend abstract concepts, and give rational solutions to social issues, it plays a significant role in business discourse.

In the pioneering days of economic theory, a variety of metaphors were employed by economists in their works, including invisible hand for free market, trade barriers for tariffs, infant companies for beginning enterprises (Smith, 1776). A variety of metaphors can also be found in current economic discourse, such as cash-flow, equilibrium, collapse, burden, weak or strong currencies, up market or down-market, cycles, human capital, and elastic. Next, contributions made by both foreign and domestic scholars will be presented in the study of such metaphors.

Henderson (1982) was the first expert to broach this subject when he analyzed metaphors in scientific business discourse. In *Metaphor in Economics*, Henderson classified metaphors used in economic discourse into both conventional and more novel ones and pointed out the former kind had become conventional tools in economic description. He also indicated that there had been a shift in the categorization of the elements of production which were conventionally classified as capital and labor. His works were followed by McCloskey (1985), Bichieri (1988) and Mason (1990). McCloskey analyzed economic texts to show, for example, how rhetorical devices may be used to suppress uncertainty and give the impression that what is presented is the fact; Bichieri showed how relations among the production, circulation and distribution of goods could be expressed in terms of relations among body parts, which implied the conventional metaphor ECONOMY IS AN ORGANISM; Mason carried out a more detailed study of a sample of text from an economic textbook and noted various metaphorical constructs, such as the containment of ideas in chapters, branches of the tree of knowledge and the personification of various market abstractions.

For economists such an awareness of the rhetoric of economic models and description gives fresh insights into the subject itself. Applied linguists, such as Dudley-Evans and Henderson (1990), analyzed texts to give more profound insights into the rhetoric and discourse structure of "authentic" texts in the context of English for Specific Purposes (ESP), and examined the pedagogical significance of their analysis. Henderson (1986) proposed to raise students' awareness of the role of metaphors in theory construction and question formulation in economics as a social science. To him, introduction of metaphor to ESP would help economics students to recognize the metaphors behind commonly accepted economic models and encourage them to adopt alternative metaphorical perspectives with the aim to foster a questioning attitude.

In more recent years and at the moment, work on the metaphoric dimension of economics discourse is showing a dramatic increase. For organizational researchers, metaphorical language is found to be helpful in problem definition, strategy formulation, organizational reforms and the basic act of managing (Cornelissen, Kafouros & Lock, 2005). Metaphors are also handy in portraying company image (Oswick & Montgomery, 1999), effecting organizational change (Öztel & Hinz, 2001), and improving workplace performance (Phillips, 1998). Apart from these, many studies address the potential of metaphors in furthering sales in advertisement (Boozer, Wyld & Grant, 1992). Other studies focus on specific business activities and concepts. Smith's research (2005), for instance, addresses dominant metaphors used in negotiation and finds out that most of them are used unconsciously without being picked up by the respondents after looking at their contexts. His study suggests that early recognition of metaphors will bring full awareness of the intentions and implied suggestions of the other party, which will lead to opportunities for mutual advantage or compromise. White's study (2003) focuses on the metaphorical roots of the concept of growth, including ECONOMY IS A LIVING ORGANISM and ECONOMY IS A MECHANIC PROCESS, both of which can be subsumed under the conceptual framework of motion.

The above-mentioned studies have covered various domains of

economics, offering insights into theoretical formation, direction for business activities and implications for pedagogical designs in the field of ESP. They demonstrate social functions of metaphorical representations from the cognitive perspective. Except rich literature in scientific business discourse, there is a broad and intense interest among researchers in popular business discourse. Next is a more detailed review of what have been achieved by foreign scholars in this field in order to find out what the present dissertation could contribute.

Instead of analyzing metaphors in textbooks, organizational discourse and theoretical books on economics, many researchers have looked into metaphorical language in journalistic texts that deal with current economic and business matters for an audience of experts and non-experts.

Based on corpora of English, French and Flemish press texts and detailed frequency counts of the metaphors derived from such source domains as PATH, WARFARE and HEALTH, Boers and Demecheleer's study (1997) show that on the whole the same source domains are used, but with very different levels of frequency across the three languages. The most popular source domain in each language corresponds to national stereotypes which suggest that the speaker's culture influences their choice of metaphor. A later study (Boers, 1999) echoes such finding that speakers choose their source domains that are salient to them. It covers a number of linguistic metaphors drawn from the source domain of HEALTH in a corpus of *The Economist* and their frequency in editions written in each month of the year. The results indicate that HEALTH metaphors are more frequently used in articles written during the winter months. This research suggests that we use metaphors from source domains which are salient to us personally. Another research (Boers, 1997) gives attention to metaphors related to notions of HEALTH, FITNESS and RACING which are argued to reflect the free market ideology. Besides adopting tools offered by cognitive semantics, it reveals that the metaphoric description of an

32

economic scenario could indeed affect people's decision-making processes through a problem-solving experiment. Eubanks's study (2000) focuses on the conceptual metaphor TRADE IS WAR alone to develop a rhetorical model of metaphor, claiming that a single conceptual metaphor is employed in diverse ways, as determined by the speaker's personal discursive trajectory, as well as the discourse community's rhetorical etiquette. It demonstrates that metaphor is not just influenced by but actually is constituted by its concrete operation.

Rather than focusing on some predetermined metaphors, some scholars focus on certain economic phenomena. For example, White's study (1997) examines metaphors in a body of journalism dealing with 1992 currency crisis and provides extensive evidence of the widespread and systematic metaphors, such as MARKET TRANSACTION IS A METEOROLOGICAL PHENOMENON, MARKET IS A PLACE and MARKET IS A LIVING ORGANISM AS AN INTELLIGNET AGENT OR A SENTIMENTAL BEING and THE CURRENT CRISIS IS A WAR. These metaphors play an essential role in the textual cohesion and coherence, thus contribute to the communicative nature of press genre.

All these studies are important contributions to metaphor theory, directly or indirectly highlighting one of the basic ideas put forward in Lakoff and Johnson's theory that metaphor is grounded in physical experience. They also show the bidirectional relationship of metaphor research and popular business discourse. On the one hand, metaphor theory helps us recognize systematic patterns in the actual use of metaphoric utterances; on the other hand, the study of actual metaphor use in such discourse helps us reassess metaphor theory.

In the 2000s, there has been a growing call for the reconsideration of social aspects of metaphor use that was first underlined by Lakoff and Johnson in their original work when they state that INFLATION IS AN ADVERSARY not only gives us a very specific way of thinking about inflation but also a way of acting toward it. We think of inflation as an adversary that can attack us, hurt us, steal from us. Even destroy us. The INFLATION IS AN ADVERSARY metaphor therefore gives rise to and justifies political and economic actions on the part of our government: declaring war on inflation, setting targets, calling for sacrifices, installing a new chain of command, etc. (Lakoff & Johnson, 1980: 34) Animate and inanimate metaphors are distinguished (Charteris-Black, 2000, 2004: 135-169) in the examination of the way market movement and economic organizations are described in the corpus of *The Economist*, such as the use of animate metaphors to describe economy (e.g. growth, depression) and economic organizations (e.g. parent or sister company) and inanimate metaphors to describe market movement (e.g. rebound and slide). The choice made by experts depends on whether they are in or out of human controls and reflects the experts' way of looking at the market and relevant organizations. Koller's (2003) study combines quantitative and qualitative methodology in the exploration of metaphor clusters in economic discourse. It foregrounds the dominance of WAR metaphor which helps to masculinize discourse about marketing, sales, mergers and acquisitions. Enforced use of WAR metaphor helps to marginalize, if not eliminate, metaphoric femininity in the socio-economic sphere the metaphor is embedded in. Aside from WAR metaphors, the persistence of SPORT and EVOLUTIONARY STRUGGLE metaphors in business media discourse is also discussed in Koller's research (2004). It suggests the masculine bias evident in business reporting. In a word, her findings demonstrate that dominant metaphors in business discourse activate masculine patterns of behavior and thus subtly reinforce traditional gender bias in society.

In sum, Charteris-Black's study looks at the pragmatic aspect of metaphorical representations, demonstrating that different metaphors are chosen by users for different topics, which are determined by their rational thinking of entities and phenomena in business world. Koller's research, however, reflects how dominant metaphors in business discourse could illustrate social bias towards gender. Based on empirical studies, both of them enable us to be aware of the values and thinking in certain communities towards social phenomena through metaphor studies.

Other studies carry out comparative analyses of metaphor use concerning business reports on specific economic situations or debates about business issues. White and Herrera's research (2003) examines entailments of predominant metaphors, including BUSINESS IS A JUNGLE, COMPANIES ARE PEOPLE, MONOPOLIES ARE DINOSAURS in English and Spanish press about corporate consolidations in the world of telecommunications. Their findings enable us to unveil covert ideology that is actually tied up with and reinforces a long tradition within economic thought (Social Darwinism) or entrenched cultural values of gender roles. The study carried out by Caers (2006) investigates how *The Economist* metaphorically frames certain specific target domains (trade unions, government spending) differently from the *Guardian*, which is more socialist-oriented, as typified by their contrastive responses to particular situations and particular ideas during the Winter of Discontent, 1978-79, a turning point from Keynesian demand management to contentious monetarism. The findings reveal the underlying system of evaluation related to any specific target domains by looking at their highlighted aspects.

Such exploration of the inner subjectivity of journalists and their perception of specific domains within the socio-economic world has been complemented by the research on metaphor use in the Euro problem. Different source domains are identified in Italian and British press reporting in the represention of Euro (Semino, 2002). The conceptual domains of JOURNEY, SPORT, WAR and EXAMINATION are found to be consistent with an overall positive but apprehensive Italian view of the Euro and two metaphors LOCK and ONE SIZE FITS ALL reflect a

35

skeptical British view. Charteris-Black and Musolff's research (2003) looks at discussion of Euro in the *British Financial Times* and its German sister publication at a later point than Semino's when the Euro was weakening against other major currencies. Besides the shared metaphors that describe euro trading in terms of UP/DOWN MOVEMENT and HEALTH, English financial reporting employs many COMBAT metaphors in which the Euro is an active agent, while German reporting characterizes Euro as a passive beneficiary of the actions of such institutional bodies as banks and governments. This corpus-based study highlights the rhetorical importance of metaphor in media due to its ability to influence opinion and simultaneously reveals cognitive as well as pragmatic differences between different media. In conclusion, the cross-language analyses of metaphors about Euro foreground opposite stances taken by different European countries.

Different from the above studies that are based on comparison between different languages, the research of Vaghi and Venuti (2004) deals with the way the *Guardian* and the *Times* portrays the introduction of this new European currency by looking into their use of two structural metaphors (CONTAINER structural metaphors and MECHANICAL OBJECT structural metaphors). Both of them use THE EURO IS A CONTAINER metaphor to represent a possible future United Kingdoom membership of the European Monetary Union. But the *Guardian* has more positive mentions of such entry than the *Times*. As far as THE EURO IS A MECHANICAL OBJECT metaphor is concerned, they survey its subsumed processes with the two verbs join and launch. It shows that the *Guardian* uses join without assigning any specific metaphorical connotation and achieves significant positive connotation through the use of launch, which highlights the celebrative aspect of the event concerned. The *Times*, however, tends to attribute a negative connotation to the mechanical metaphors. Lauch is used relatively very rarely and is mainly found in uncertain contexts, and join too shows a dominant negative connotation. We can see that different connotations given to the same metaphors convey their positive and negative attitudes respectively towards a possible future adoption of the Euro in the United Kingdom.

All these socially-oriented studies of metaphor use emphasize the fact that metaphor plays a significant role in business discourse. It not only performs ideational function by conceptualizing the business world, illustrating how the same economic phenomenon is constructed by different communities, but more importantly offers ample evidence for interpersonal function by conveying evaluative stance and judgment due to the selective nature of conceptual mapping. The variation of metaphor use between different languages or different media in the same language reveals a language community's ideology and attitude towards special business issues. Such revelation is based on detailed analysis of salient source domains, including HEALTH, PATH, WARFARE, UP/DOWN MOVEMENT, ANIMAL, JOURNEY, MACHINE, BUILDING, CONTAINER, SPORT, GAME and MARRIAGE. Some of these studies single out only one of them, such as Eubank's examination of the WAR metaphor; some like Koller's research (2004) explore the function of the combination of different domains in conveying biased attitudes. Others start their analysis without any pre-defined metaphors but determine them after careful survey. Most of the researchers focused on conventional metaphors that show systematic and consistent mapping between source and target domains across texts except Semino (2002) who attached importance to "one-short" metaphors in her discussion of the economic aspects of the European Union.

A large majority of these studies base their conclusion on the corpus established by researchers themselves. This echoes a recent rise in the use of electronic corpora in metaphor research (e.g., Cameron & Deignan, 2003; Deignan, 2000, 2001; Peters & Wilks, 2003). Quantitative analysis of metaphor places the extrapolation of conceptual metaphors from linguistic evidence on a much firmer empirical footing than it was in the past. The adoption of a corpus methodology guides researchers to arrive at results that are more exhaustive and reliable than those obtained on the basis of introspection and/or the random collection of examples. However, quantitative methodology cannot replace qualitative analysis totally. In order to make up for the drawback of quantitative analysis, the lack of context, researchers combine quantitative and qualitative analyses and use concordance tools to show co-text of the key words in their research.

The comparative studies mentioned above, to some extent anticipate or respond to the call made by Deignan (2005) to develop the corpora to cover other languages than English. Charteric-Black and Ennis (2001) suggest the further line of enquiry into the economics of "non-western" cultures. Bratož's (2004) comparative analysis of linguistic and conceptual metaphors identified in Slovene and English economic and business articles focuses on the systematic organization in hierarchical structures of metaphor. The findings indicate that the metaphors identified in Slovene popular economic discourse are largely influenced by the Anglo-American traditions and values. A question arises here concerning whether the same influence has taken place in China. This dissertation attempts to find the answer to this question.

Kong Deming (2002) compared economic metaphors used in Chinese and German news reports through detailed analyses of seven kinds of conceptual metaphors. The application of these metaphorical concepts suggests the universality in cognition which is common among all nations. It also demonstrates subtle distinctions in the detailed application of metaphorical concepts due to national, social, and cultural differences. However, there is seldom research on different metaphor use between Chinese and English popular economic and business discourse that is based on naturally-occurring data and systematic analysis. The present

38

study will try to fill this gap and make a contribution to the current literature.

2.6 Summary

All in all, the cognitive approach to metaphor makes a breakthrough by emphasizing the role of metaphor in the construction of thinking and knowledge. It reveals the close relation between metaphor use and physical experience and indicates linguistic instantiations and cultural implications of metaphors. In this connection, research on metaphor from the cognitive perspective has laid a foundation for a great number of studies in social science, including politics, philosophy, economics, cultural studies and education. In spite of these, the cognitive approach is criticized for the intuitive and elicited data it adopts. These weak points of the cognitive approach based on internalized language experience of individuals have been complemented by research from the discourse approach.

The discourse approach to metaphor study enhances the basic view of cognitive linguistics that metaphor can be used to construct our understanding of the world. Detailed analyses of metaphorical representations in both political and economic discourses add weight to the argument that metaphor can give form to social and political ideas. They take linguistic, cognitive and socio-cultural aspects of metaphor into consideration in their analyses, thus link micro-level linguistic evidence with macro-level cognitive projections. In methodology, researchers have realized the limitation of intuitive and elicited data and chosen to base their conclusions on naturally-occurring discourse. They are not satisfied to limit their findings to a small size of materials and gradually apply techniques in corpus linguistics to improve the reliability of their research (Charteris-Black, 2004; Deignan, 2005).

Most research on metaphorical representations in political discourses is carried out in the paradigm of CDA. However, only a few studies in business discourses take this approach (Charteris-Black, 2004; Koller, 2003, 2004). In spite of the fact that some domestic scholars have given their attention to the interaction of CDA paradigm with conceptual metaphors in discourse analysis, representative work (Xin, 2007; Zhang & Jiang, 2008) still dwells on theoretical discussion about possible and potential integration of these two paradigms without systematic analysis of a large quantity of naturally-occuring data. Almost all the business phenomena that current studies have addressed are set in western cultures without expressing concern about international events involving some fast rising developing countries, such as China.

The present research will put forward an integrated framework based on CDA and cognitive studies of metaphor in an attempt to reveal hidden meanings in the representation of the 2008 Beijing Olympics.

Chapter 3   A Proposed Theoretical Framework

for the Present Research

3.1 Introduction

The present dissertation is a comparative study of metaphor use from the point of view of CDA, so in this part an integrated theoretical framework will be established with an attempt to enrich the cognitive dimension in the critical analysis of discourse. Before the elaboration of this framework, some theoretical background will be provided, with the intention to offer the rationale for the incorporation of different disciplines and at the same time illustrate what this framework could add to the current efforts by giving equal attention to cognitive, linguistic and socio-cultural aspects in the analysis of metaphor in discourse.

3.2 Theoretical Foundations for the Proposed Model

3.2.1 Traditional Approaches in CDA

CDA is a relatively new approach of discourse analysis that was consolidated as a cross-discipline between 1980s and 1990s. Different from discourse analysis and text linguistics with their descriptive goals, CDA regards discourse as a social practice and aims to reveal how "linguistic-discursive practices are connected to the wider socio-political structures of power and domination" (Kress, 1990: 85). This is echoed by

Fairclough in the following statements: CDA aims to systematically explore often opaque relationships of causality and determination between (a) discursive practices, events and texts, and (b) wider social and cultural structures, relations and processes; to investigate how such practices, events and texts arise out of and are ideologically shaped by relations of power and struggles over power and to explore how the opacity of these relationships between discourse and society is itself a factor securing power and hegemony (Fairclough, 1993: 135).

In a nutshell, CDA is concerned with making transparent the relationship between social practices and social structures that is opaque to common people. Along this research vein, the notion of ideology figures prominently and has been a central theme all along the critical analysis of discourse. Ideology is usually associated with political beliefs. However, it needs not necessarily be thought of in purely political terms. It can be seen as a set of beliefs which provide justification for what people do and say, as van Dijk defines it: The interface between the cognitive representation and processes underlying discourse and action, on the one hand, and the societal position and interests and social groups, on the other hand.... As systems of principles that organize social cognitions, ideologies are assumed to control, through the minds of the members, the social reproduction of the group. Ideologies mentally represent the basic characteristics of a group, such as their identity, tasks, goals, norms, values, position and resources (van Dijk, 1995: 18).

CDA's purpose, to some degree, is to unearth ideology, so as to reveal how it is expressed and constrains the social practices of discourse. Additionally, CDA explores the relationship between language and power. Foucault (1980) has emphasized that power is articulated through discourse. It is the mechanism through which language is the message or medium of authority. As a result, we need to get the deeper language structure in order to arrive at the underlying power in social practice. As

Fairclough (1992) articulates, CDA is interested in the link between language use and unequal relations of power. It investigates how relations of power exert control, operate through conformity to standards and are generally concealed from participants within a discourse.

Ideological power and powerful systems are encoded in the choices made within the language we are accustomed to use and acquires the appearance of objective commonsense and becomes so conventionalized that we are likely to accept them as natural (Fowler, 1991: 67). This is CDA that enables us to display to consciousness the patterns of belief and value that are encoded in the language.

According to Wodak (1999: 186), CDA is a research program with many facets and heterogeneous theoretical frameworks and methodologies, including Critical Linguists (Fowler, Kress, Hodge & Trew, 1979), Social Semiotics (Hodge & Kress, 1988), Fairclough's interest in social change (1992, 1995), van Dijk's socio-cognitive studies (1984, 1987, 1991, 1993, 1997), and the discourse-historical approach (Wodak, 1997, 1999).

Among these approaches, Fairclough's (1995: 59) three-dimensional model is one of the most comprehensive frameworks and has been central to CDA in the past twenty years or so. There are three focuses in this approach for the analysis of any communicative event: the text, which refers to the final product of the communication; the discourse practice, including the process of production and consumption and socio-cultural practice, which gives rise to the communicative event. These analytical focuses show that CDA has three dimensions: description of the text, interpretation of the interaction process, and its connection to the text, and the explanation of the relationship between the interaction and the social action.

In this connection, interpretation and explanation are two main stages of CDA and they are the very features that distinguish it from other traditional discourse studies. Interpretation is supposed to focus on the cognition of texts, whereas explanation deals with the link between texts and the socio-cultural context. However, most of the research tends to focus on the relation between linguistic analysis and the socio-cultural context. In other words, they focus on the explanation stage, while ignore the interpretation stage (O'Halloran, 2003: 2).

Even Fairclough himself highlights that his analyses deal with "the interrelationship of language and society, with the emphasis upon power and ideology" (Fairclough, 1989: 14). He introduces cognitive concepts that are stored in human mind, such as "Member's resources". They are representations stored in long-term memory, and then used by people in the production and interpretation of texts. In spite of this, Fairclough underlines "Member's resources" are socially determined and ideologically shaped, as "they are socially generated, and their nature is dependent on the social relations as well as being socially transmitted" (ibid: 24). Obviously, he gives priority to ideology and social factors at the cost of cognitive dimensions.

The lack of the cognitive dimension in CDA studies has drawn the attention of many scholars. Chilton (2005b) pointed out this important theoretical gap. He proposed to take cognition into account in order to overcome this missing link. Similarly, Wodak (2006: 179) stated that cognitive approaches "have been rejected and excluded from CDA by many of its practitioners out of unjustified reasons". In sympathy with them, van Dijk (2006ab) believed that critical discourse studies had shown little interest in the mental aspects of discourse and developed a more cognitively oriented framework that elaborates on the stage of interpretation in the sense of Fairclough' s framework (Fairclough, 1995: 59).

Van Dijk's socio-cognitive framework is an exception among the common trend of CDA. This approach emphasizes the significant roles played by both social and cognitive factors in the production and understanding of discourse.

"We shall see that adequate discourse analysis at the same time requires detailed cognitive and social analysis, and vice versa, and that it is only the integration of these accounts that may reach descriptive, explanatory and especially critical adequacy in the study of social problems." (van Dijk, 2001a: 98)

So there are three dimensions in his framework: society, cognition and discourse. Society involves both the local situation of spoken and written interaction, as well as more abstract properties of societies and cultures. Cognition is perceived in both personal and social senses, including beliefs and goals as well as evaluations and emotions and any other mental and memory representations and structures relevant to discourse. Discourse is regarded as a communicative event. It refers to not only the verbal products, but also the participants and specific contexts, including time, place and situation. This framework emphasizes the social meaning of the production and consumption of discourse. It is the product of social construction, characterized by local culture in certain time and space. The following figure shows the interrelationship of these three dimensions in CDA:

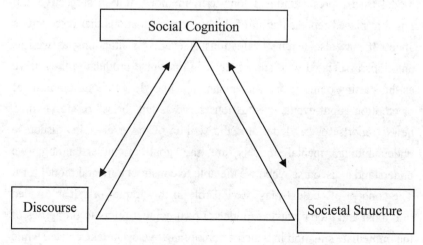

Figure 3.1   Discourse-cognition-society triangle

It shows that there is no direct relation between discourse structure and societal structure. They are mediated by the interface of cognition. In other words, what imposes controls on the production and comprehension of discourse, is not the social factors, such as power and economy, but "whether and how participants interpret, represent and make use of such external constraints, and especially how they do so in situated interaction" (van Dijk, 2006b: 163). The bidirectional arrows reveal the dialectical relation between the local structure of discourse and the global societal structure: societal structure shows up and is instantiated in discourse through the mediation of cognition; discourse in turn has social functions since it contributes to the formation or confirmation of social attitudes and ideologies.

Van Dijk (2001abc, 2006ab) uses the concept of "mental model" borrowed from contemporary cognitive psychology to account for "subjective constructs or definition of communicative situations". According to him, the production and understanding of discourse prominently involve the formation, activation or actualization of a mental model as a representation in long-term memory. It is a subjective and possible biased representation of the events or situations that discourse is about. It may also feature evaluations of events or situations, as well as emotions associated with such events. In discourse production they serve as the starting point of discourse, since our knowledge about, opinions of or emotion about events or situations serve as the "basis" of storytelling, news reports or a letter to the editor. Conversely, in discourse understanding, mental models are the goal of understanding: we understand a discourse when we are able to construct a mental model for it. The concept of context plays a vital role in this framework. It is divided into local and global context models. Local context refers to properties of the immediate situation in which a communicative event takes place, while global context is defined in terms of the social, political, cultural and historical structures. They are all mental representations constituting a part of long-term memory where people store their knowledge and opinions about events they have experienced or heard about.

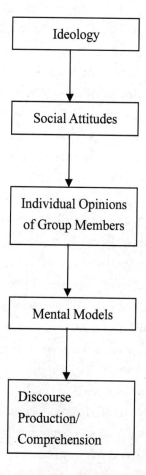

Figure 3.2   Mental models as an interface between discourse and society (Attia, 2007: 88)

Mental models represent not only personal beliefs but also social representations, which are knowledge, attitudes and ideologies. Van Dijk divides knowledge into three types: personal, group and cultural. Among them, cultural knowledge is shared by all component members of a society and is the common ground of all social practices, such as discourses. He further asserts that metaphors, as properties of discourse, should be understood in terms of socially shared cultural knowledge (van Dijk, 2001d, 2002). Besides knowledge, the mental representation contains the opinions and evaluative beliefs about events and participants. These opinions and beliefs may be personal, but they are generally derived from the socially shared attitudes, which may be controlled by ideologies (van Dijk, 2001c, 2002). In this way, both knowledge and opinions can be representative of the ideology of the community the very person is identified with. Thus, these mental models constitute the input of discourse production and comprehension, as is illustrated in Figure 3.2.

In brief, van Dijk's framework spells out the interface between the social and the personal through the relations between personal representations in the mental models on the one hand, and the socially shared representations of groups, on the other hand. This, to some extent, solves the puzzle of some scholars who hesitate to consider cognitive factors in their studies since they think there is no access to states of individual minds. It could also solve similar problems faced by metaphor studies in discourse production and comprehension.

3.2.2 Critical Metaphor Analysis

So far, scholars have reached the consensus that CDA could benefit a lot from borrowing ideas from cognitive studies (Attia, 2007: 83). Only discourse analysis gives concern to what goes on in people's mind, would it introduce new development in language studies (Chilton, 2005b: 23). Dirven et al (2005) similarly stated that "cognitive linguistics provides analytical tools for a critical assessment of ideologies, not 'ideal ways' of conceptualizing". From the part of literature view, we can see that some scholars have applied metaphor as an analytical tool in their studies due to critical properties of metaphor. Maalej (2007: 134-138) justified the incorporation of metaphor into CDA by pointing to the following nature of metaphor: it is so pervasive in language, thought and discourse; it can be used both intentionally and unintentionally; and it has psychological reality.

Wodak (2006) took a step further by calling for a framework that is capable of incorporating sociological, cognitive and linguistic categories. CMA developed by Charteris-Black (2004) is such an attempt. According to this framework, metaphor plays an important role in the construction of the covert meaning in discourse. It is an integrated approach that brings together perspectives from CDA, corpus analysis, pragmatics and cognitive linguistics to describe, interpret and explain metaphor use in a particular type of discourse. It is claimed that both individual and social aspects will affect the choice of metaphor, and complements a cognitive semantic view of metaphor with pragmatic factors.

Metaphor is defined by incorporating linguistic, cognitive and pragmatic orientations: It is a formal statement with semantic tension, showing a shift in the conceptual system and has the underlying purpose of influencing opinions and judgments of the recipients (Charteris-Black, 2004: 19-22). To analyze such metaphors, a three-stage method is adopted, which is in line with Fairclough's description, interpretation and explanation. In each stage, corpus plays a significant role: in the identification stage, a sample of texts is analyzed to identify candidate metaphors, which are then examined in relation to the three orientations. Words that are commonly used with a metaphoric sense are then classified as metaphorical keywords and the presence of these keywords is measured quantitatively in the corpus. Then, corpus contexts are examined to determine whether each use of a keyword is metaphoric or literal. Interpretation considers establishing a relationship between metaphors and the cognitive and pragmatic factors that determine them. This involves the identification of conceptual metaphors, and where feasible, conceptual keys. Explanation of metaphors involves identifying the social agency that is involved in their production and their social role in persuasion. The formation of conceptual metaphors and conceptual keys and illustration of the typical evaluation of metaphors will assist in explaining why they can be persuasive. Evidence for the ideological and rhetorical motives can be aided by comparing the findings for a particular mini-corpus with those for the same metaphors in a much larger corpus or comparing different sections of the same corpus (ibid: 34).

It can be seen that CMA adopts a hierarchical cognitive model of metaphor, organized into conceptual keys, conceptual metaphors and surface metaphorical linguistic expressions. Such a model supports Lakoff's notion of inheritance hierarchy and achieves economy of description as well. Most importantly, the identification of the conceptual key at the abstract level offers us an access into the thoughts of the encoders that underlie language use and reveals that metaphor choice is motivated by ideology. Besides the conscious choice of the encoder on the one hand, CMA attempts to consider unconscious acceptance of decoders on the other hand by focusing the analysis on the function of metaphors to arouse particular emotions in specific genres, including political, religious and media discourses. In this way, based on a broader range of naturally-occurring data, CMA refers to both individual and social consideration and takes into account both sides in communication, thus to some extent enrich research in the paradigm of CDA.

CMA has been employed to analyze a variety of discourses. However, there are still some problems in this paradigm. Firstly, the line between conscious and unconscious use of metaphors is not as clear-cut as Charteris-Black claims in his analyses, attributed to encoders and decoders respectively. The encoders are often likely to use metaphors unconsciously (Goatly, 1997), especially conventional ones, since they belong to a stock of established beliefs and conceptualizations that are generally shared by members of a community. The underlying conceptual mappings evoked by linguistic expressions can be taken as the common sense that is echoed by van Dijk's "common ground" or "mental model" in his social-cognition approach.

Secondly, the total reliance on Lakoff and Johnson's theory is too determinative, since discourse could guide us to both novel and conventional conceptual metaphors. The conventional metaphors do not need much cognitive processing, and arise with unconscious nature. On the contrary, linguistic metaphors that do not activate conventional conceptual metaphors are more linguistically creative and require us to make more cognitive efforts (Maalej, 2007: 137). The new conceptual metaphor underlying them not only reflects the change of the user's conceptual system, but also influences the perception and actions of the receivers. So we need to complement conceptual metaphor theory with conceptual blending theory in the analysis of metaphor use.

Thirdly, CMA faces the same criticism as CDA does. It is claimed that casual receivers are only concerned with the central idea of discourse at the cost of little cognitive work. They will not go through the detailed analysis analysts are engaged in, so CMA is criticized for its over-interpretation (O'Halloran, 2007: 169). Common readers are supposed not to compositionally process the metaphors to infer a macro-concept as analysts do. Such criticism, however, ignores the double functions of metaphor—its social and cognitive nature. It is the interface between cognitive processes and representations in the discourse on the one hand, and the social groups on the other hand. This interface should work as the starting point to illustrate the motivations and functions of metaphors in discourse.

A proposed theoretical framework will be set up in the following section in an attempt to fill up the deficiencies of current metaphor studies in the paradigm of CDA.

3.3 The Proposed Theoretical Framework

The theoretical framework for the present research is firmly rooted in critical approaches to discourse as social practice. It is concerned with the ideological and mystificatory structures of discourse.

In a more general sense, discourse is regarded as an element of social life that is in dialectical relation with other elements (Fairclough, 2003: 214). It is a particular type of language use that is constitutive of knowledge that tells us how things are, together with the evaluations and legitimating of, and purpose for these things. Such knowledge is activated in the specific context. This implies that people may, at different times and in different texts, choose different discourses to represent the same practice (Caldas-Coulthard & van Leeuwen, 2003: 158). So discourse is the point where ideology and language meet. It is the instrument of the social construction of reality (Kress, 1996: 193). From such collective discourse arise particular instances of talk or text situated in time and place. The collective discourse decides the nature of the concrete ones.

As far as the topic in the present research is concerned, metaphors appear in concrete discourse. In this sense, they are metaphorical expressions realized by specific words, word groups, clauses or sentences about Olympic Economy in journalistic texts. The constant mapping across certain conceptual domains and derived conceptual blending reflected by these linguistic metaphors will denote underlying metaphor users' knowledge of, understanding of and evaluations of Olympic Economy, the content in the abstract sense of discourse. At the same time, metaphors in concrete discourse will reinforce the conceptual metaphors and conceptual blending in abstract discourse, which reveal how social groups represented by metaphor users conceptualize Olympic Economy in the way that is most appropriate for their political, economic and legal systems. In this way, the analysis of metaphorical representations of Olympic Economy will look into metaphor in both abstract and concrete discourse. The concrete realizations of metaphor, namely metaphorical expressions become the starting point in this process. As a result, we need to consider linguistic factors and cognitive configuration, as well as social and situational contexts in the proposed framework.

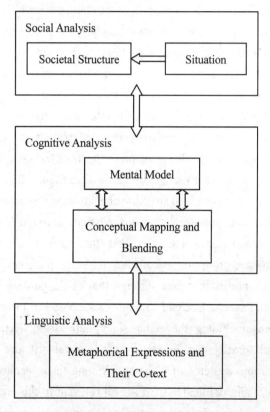

Figure 3.3   A proposed theoretical framework of the present research

Drawing primarily from two important strands of critical social research—CDA, especially van Dijk's socio-cognitive framework and

CMA (Charteris-Black, 2004), an integrated framework (Figure 3.3) has been constructed with the aim to apply metaphorical structures to CDA in an explicit way. It adopts a three-stage analytical framework: linguistic analysis, cognitive analysis, and social analysis, which are represented respectively by the three big boxes from the bottom to the top. Linguistic analysis is primarily text based, covering syntax, lexicon, local semantics, topics, schematic structures, global coherence in the studies under the paradigm of CDA. In this research, it is concerned with metaphorical expressions, the surface realizations of underlying conceptual metaphors and their co-text. Social analysis refers to the general context and situational context in which the concrete discourses with embedded metaphorical expressions are produced and understood. They are mediated by cognitive analysis, which will look into how Olympic Economy is conceptualized in the two media by making explicit the cross-domain mappings and conceptual integration on the basis of text description.

The social analysis presented by the two paralleling boxes on the top in the figure examines societal structure and situation respectively. Societal structure refers to enduring relationships between individuals or groups of individuals, emphasizing the idea that the society is grouped into structurally related groups or sets of roles. It also refers to embedded social institution and norms in social systems that could guide and shape the action of social agents. Societal structure is supposed to inform important social systems including the economic system, legal system, political system and cultural system. In other words, societal structure is the parent system of various systems of a society. Among them, economic system, cultural model and political system are all relevant to the present studies. There is a very close relationship between economic and political systems. The political system determines the economic pattern of a country. Economic systems decide the government's role in the operation of economy, the relationship between different participants in economic activities, the ways to deal with capital and human resources. Cultural models are presupposed, taken-for-granted models of the world that are popularly shared by the members of a society and play an enormous role in their understanding of that world and explain their behavior in it (Quinn, 1991: 84).

Another element in social analysis is the situational context. In the present research, it includes the mega sports event of Beijing Olympics, together with political and economic events in the run-up to it. These social factors will possibly activate relevant scenarios in mental models. These models feature a large amount of personal and socio-cultural knowledge and are much more detailed than the discourse based on it. The activated scenarios will guide social members in both Chinese and American societies in the production and comprehension of metaphors representing Olympic Economy. They are what cognitive analysis deals with.

The framework adopts a hierarchical cognitive model of metaphor, organized into mental model, conceptual metaphor and integration, and surface metaphorical linguistic expressions. The term of "mental model" is borrowed from van Djik's socio-cognitive framework. In this research, it is the subjective contructs or definition of Olympic Economy, reducing this hard-to-grasp complicated business phenomenon to its essential characteristics and making it comprehensible to readers. The mental model is a dynamic cognitive structure that is based on socially or culturally shared knowledge and the situational contexts.

The mental model will decide encoders' ways to perceive the target domain, such as business activities in terms of other domains whose features and properties they believe will project the counterparts of the reported event. Through such choice of conceptual metaphors as well as subsequent inferences and entailments, certain properties of business event, concerning related participants, resources and backgrounds can be foregrounded. The corollary of this is to add bias to the media discourse,

55

favoring special perspectives on reported events and participants. Since metaphor influence perception, the choice of metaphors will help to consolidate accepted mental models that are usually in the interest of a dominant group represented by the encoder.

In this connection, the mental model is manifested in and perpetuated by conceptual metaphors. In other words, metaphors are semantic manifestations of mental models. As Pielenz (1999: 170f) says, conceptual metaphors mirror the basic social norms, socio-cultural experiences and collective beliefs of a speech community. They may include conventionalized metaphorical ways of speaking, as well as the skills to construct fresh or deliberate metaphors.

Metaphor not only works as an interface between the cognitive structure underlying a discourse and ideological structure dominating it, but also links discourse and its metaphoric realizations in text. It is believed that metaphorical expressions in surface text derive from dominant metaphors. These expressions may help to enhance cognitive models governing discourse and become a starting point to study cognitive and ideological factors of discourse.

Close examination of metaphorical expressions will reveal that lexical choices for the source and target domain will reveal reporters' positive or negative opinions towards related event and people (Dirven, Frank & Pütz, 2003: 8). Besides, they can stimulate certain emotions among recipients (Charteris-Black, 2004: 11-12). Some tuning devices including modal verbs, adjective and adverbs, and attitudinal epithets will modify linguistic metaphors in the co-text (Cameron & Deignan, 2003; Goatly, 1997: 171-197), tone down their potential strength or oppositely mark them for even greater emphasis and sometimes activate conceptual blendings. In addition, various processes embedded in metaphorical expressions concern different participants in the represented action. There is an ideological dimension within the reporter's decision to which participant a particular

56

role is assigned or to whom a particular metaphor is assigned (Wolf & Polzenhagen, 2003).

All these linguistic resources will reify the prevailing metaphor and in turn become vital clues to dig out the underlying ideological structures. They may also manipulate ideal readers who live in the same community dominated by similar ideological structures. They will be steered by the metaphors permeating the discourse to the very interpretation that fits with the reporters.

In a word, this framework incorporate both cognitive linguistics and Critical Discourse Analysis to consider linguistic, cognitive and social perspectives of metaphors with the purpose to compare popular business discourses produced in different countries with claimed disparate ideologies. Its cognitive interface between ideology, discourse and text analysis precludes the weakness of CDA paradigm to some degree and the linguistic analyses provide evidence to counter the criticism of subjective interpretation in CDA.

3.4 Summary

With the consensus that CDA could benefit a lot from borrowing ideas from cognitive studies, ideas about metaphor have been incorporated into discourse analysis that is interested in unearthing the convert meaning, which not only reflects but also reproduces the existing societal structure and power relation. CMA is one of such attempts to address cognitive dimensions CDA aims to enhance in its efforts to highlight some social problems and social structures in terms of discursive structures. As an integrated approach, it describes, interprets and explains metaphor use in discourse, considering both individual and social aspects in the choice of metaphor, and complementing the cognitive semantic view of metaphor with pragmatic factors.

However, the total reliance of CMA on Lakoff and Johnson's theory is so determinative that it ignores that discourse could guide us to both conventional and novel conceptual metaphors. In addition, the interface between cognitive processes as well as representations in discourse and the social groups is not constructed clearly enough to refute the criticism of over-interpretation.

A proposed theoretical framework for the present research is set up to overcome the current difficulties in this direction on the basis of metaphor studies in cognitive linguistics and the socio-cognitive approach of CDA. The framework is composed of three stages: linguistic analysis, cognitive analysis, and social analysis. Among them, cognitive analysis, which is organized hierachically into the mental model, conceptual metaphor and integration, and surface metaphorical linguistic expressions work as the interface not only between the mental model and ideological structure dominating it, but also discourse and its metaphoric realizations in text.

Chapter 4   Methodology

4.1 Introduction

The present research sets out to examine how metaphor operates in the case of a concrete business event—Olympic Economy in the 2008 Beijing Olympics. It takes a critical perspective with the aim to reveal covert meanings in media discourse. Relevant popular business discourse is considered in both formal terms (its lexical and grammatical characteristics) and semantic terms—as a cluster of types of meaning that are systematic reflexes of a specific way of making sense of the world. In this study, it concerns metaphorical expressions in each concrete discourse, with special attention to implications of metaphorical expressions and grounding of each metaphor, and at the same time, infers the underlying cognitive patterns that indicate the special way of classifying and constructing this specific economic event.

The critical perspective also regards popular business discourse as social practice and analyzes it against its wider social context. In this connection, the use of metaphor in it is assumed to be the product of a complex interaction between social, cultural, cognitive and linguistic factors impinging on the producer of a text at a particular time in a particular situation.

In an attempt to reveal how the use of metaphor gives rise to specialized ways of talking about Olympic Economy, it makes no difference whether metaphor producers intentionally seek ways of speaking about Olympic Economy that will tend to create favorable or unfavorable attitudes or their thinking leads them naturally to some kind of metaphors. Since metaphor mediates between cognition and emotion to influence our intellectual and emotional responses, both directly through describing and analyzing things and indirectly through drawing unconsciously emotional associations of words, the value of which are rooted in cultural knowledge. As a result this dissertation considers both conventional and novel metaphors against integrated contexts including social, cultural and situational factors.

It is hypothesized that conceptual metaphors realized by linguistic expressions and their inferences and entailments will reflect different ways the two media look at the same economic matter. The present critical approach not only describes differences in the harness of metaphors, enabling us to understand what Olympic Economy is in a society, but explains how it can be and ought to be, revealing what are obscured by the linguistic expressions.

In a word, the present study aims to reveal the importance of metaphorical representations in the construction of an ideological view of economic reality through description, explanation and interpretation of metaphorical expressions concerning Olympic Economy in both Chinese and American popular business discourse. In order to achieve this, specific data were collected and analyzed according to predetermined procedures.

4.2 Data Collection

Two electronic text corpora were compiled for the research, one Chinese and the other English. The articles were retrieved from the websites of the following periodicals and newspapers: *Business Week* (BW), *China Economics Weekly* (CEW), *The New York Times* (NYT) and

People's Daily (PD).

Business Week was established in 1929 and has a worldwide circulation of 1,155,785 copies. As the biggest business magazine, it enjoys 5,300,000 readers across the world. In terms of education and profession, 86 percent of them hold a university degree and have top management position in the line of finance, banking, telecommunication and manufacturing industries. It is supposed to provide not only the latest business information, but authentic comments and analyses of economic events. Its counterpart *China Economics Weekly*, the only business weekly in China, is under the management and auspices of People's Daily Agency. It was first published in 2002 as a comprehensive political-and-economic magazine and enjoys similar readership with *Business Week*. Up to now, *China Economics Weekly* has reached the circulation of 186,000 copies and become the most authentic resource of economy. *The New York Times* is the largest metropolitan newspaper in the United States. Founded in 1851, it is distributed internationally. *People's Daily* is the official newspaper of Chinese central government. Established in 1948, it is regarded as the bridge between the government and the people and the window through which the outside world comes to know about China.

The articles to be included in the corpus were selected from the above newspapers and magazines using two main criteria: the date of publication and the relevance to the topic. All selected articles are machine-readable texts published between September 1, 2001 and December 31, 2008. We decided to fix the time span to the time when Beijing succeeded in the bid for holding the Games and nearly half a year after the Games since this time range provides us with the opportunity to investigate the very beginning of preparations for the Games and different attitudes of the media towards them and to check their predictions on Olympic Economy.

61

As for the relevance to the topic, I decided to select those articles containing the phrase ào yùn jīng jì [奥运经济] in Chinese and its English equivalent "Olympic Economy" as well as the word "Beijing" in American media. All these elicited articles were arranged chronologically and unrelated ones were deleted after reading the title and the leading paragraph. In addition, attention was given to a number of considerations in the corpus building. Firstly, since the project does not aim to carry out genre analysis, the data collection ignores genre issues and results in articles from different pages of the same newspaper. Similarly, because the present study attempts to reveal the underlying ideology entrenched in a society, the data collection did not take into account the individual factors of the reporters, such as gender and social status.

As a result, a total of 170 articles (see Table 4.1 and Table 4.2) were collected from these four sources. The Chinese corpus contain 170,711 characters, which was divided by 1.6 to make the Chinese characters comparable to words citation （Xu, 2007）. This produced 121, 936 words. With 81,124 words of the English data, the total size of the corpora amounts to 203,060 words in all.

Table 4.1   Data from Chinese media

Publication	Number of Article/ % of Corpora	Number of Character	Average of Article Length
CEW	26/29.5	77.881	2995
PD	62/70.5	92,830	1497
Total	88	170,711	

Table 4.2 Data from American media

Publication	Number of Article/ % of Corpora	Number of Word	Average of Article Length
BW	42/51.2	42,637	1015
NYT	40/48.8	38,488	962
Total	82	81,124	

4.3 Identification of Metaphorical Expressions

The analysis starts from the linguistic level. Recently an increasing number of researchers have realized the value of corpus analysis and adopted it in their cross-linguistic studies of metaphor use, such as Charteris-Black (2003), Deignan and Potter (2004), Kövecses (2005) and Semino (2006). However, there is not, as yet, a well-established and reliable automatic method for identifying metaphorical expressions in a large database. Similarly, there are at the moment no widely available corpora that have been annotated for metaphor. In the current adoption of corpus analysis, almost all the searching terms are predetermined, including vocabulary relating to specific source (Koller, 2004, 2006) or target domain (Stefanowitsch & Gries, 2006) with the help of dictionaries and thesauri and "key words" which occur unusually frequently in a particular dataset as compared with a larger reference corpus (Charteris-Black, 2004). In some cases, the researchers exploit a smaller corpus with manual analysis alongside a larger corpus (Cameron & Deignan, 2003; Charteris-Black, 2004; Musolff, 2004; Semino, 2002). All these methods in corpus analysis have facilitated the investigation in the pattern of metaphor use, but could not predict important patterns of variation at the level of individual examples. Because of this, the present study opts for a manual survey with the aim to find all extracts containing metaphorical linguistic expressions.

Expressions were identified as metaphorical when they illustrated any domain incongruity in reference or attribution. Incongruity was taken as involving the understanding of and/or reference to an economic entity, agent, or process in terms belonging to an experiential domain different from business, irrespective of the degree of innovation of the metaphorical expression.

In this respect, metaphorical expressions in this study concerns business terms included in economics dictionary that are in line with the above definition, such as expansion and strategy. Derived from the battlefield, they conventionally describe the business activity to enlarge the market share and general planning of a participant in the business world. They could reveal experts' shared thinking of the business event, which have been accepted by common people in a society.

The criterion of incongruity also appears to be applicable to similes. They are one way of talking about one thing in terms of another through the use of such expressions as "like", "as", "as if" and so on. This is a form of incongruity that has been acknowledged by the user, who utilizes a construction of juxtaposition between the two domains. The research also considers personification, the animate metaphors in which the metaphorical unit involves animate collocate in its primary semantic sense but the topic term is not animate, like the noun growth in the expression market growth.

Besides, the present study covers metonymically-motivated expressions, including both metaphors from metonymy and metonymy-based metaphors. They are both grounded in physical experience, but different in the aspect whether there is ambiguity between the literal and figurative interpretation (Deignan, 2005: 63-67). There is a semantic gap between literal and figurative meanings of metonymy-based metaphors. For example, hot with a literal sense describing something having a high degree could denote strong feelings in its figurative sense, exemplifying the primary metaphor TEMPERATURES STAND FOR EMOTIONS. However, the short of co-text sometimes will make it difficult to tell apart the literal sense from the figurative one of such metaphor from metonymy as back away. Because of this, the manual method is a helpful way to consider the co-text and even wider context that is necessary in the distinction between metaphorical sense and literal one.

Image metaphors and those with cultural heritage are also taken into account in the study. The former involves the mapping of visual images, such as the description of buildings' shape as some geometric figures. The latter is rather culturally grounded (Zinken, 2003; Zinken et al., in press), including stereotypes, stock characters in art work and school knowledge. They are motivated by the reporters' adaptation to a certain cultural structure or substructure, which leads to specific imaginative resources.

So the present research not only considers conventional metaphors, but also examines novel metaphors or new uses of conventional metaphors as well. It is proved that novel metaphors are often used in politics to steer strategies and set agendas (Billig & Macmillan, 2005; Van der Valk, 2003) and Semino (2002) used to signify their importance in business discourse in her term "one-shot" metaphor.

Moreover, given that the identification of such domain incongruities is subjective, this process was assisted by referring to *Collins Cobuild English Language Dictionary* and *Macmillan English Dictionary—US Edition* for English corpus and *Modern Chinese Dictionary* for Chinese corpus respectively. *Chinese Idiom Dictionary* was also used to pick out metaphoric Chinese idioms. Steen points out the advantage of relying on a dictionary rather than one's intuitions: [...] convenient to adopt a dictionary as a concrete norm of reference, so that you have an independent reflection of what counts as the meanings of words for a particular group of users of English (Steen, 2007: 97).

The chosen dictionaries are based on a large corpus of contemporary English and Chinese from a wide range of sources. So they became a reliable tool to support our intuitions in the identification. They were used mainly to identify the basic sense of those candidate expressions, in order to determine whether the original conceptual domain is different from the topic concerned.

The whole process to identify metaphorical expressions was carried out through two separate stages, which are set apart by three months. The different results will be singled out for further discussion with one expert in metaphor study. In this way, some ambiguous cases have been settled.

The resulting metaphorical lexical units contain single words that are single headwords listed in dictionaries and multiword units, including generally phrasal verbs, compounds, poly-words and proper names. These units discussed in each section of this dissertation appear in bold type within quoted examples and in the main text, whereas the metaphorical schemas underlying them appear in capital letters according to mainstream cognitive notation. The number of instances, Chinese characters and English translation for Chinese metaphors are put in parentheses and square brackets respectively after the metaphorical units when it is necessary.

4.4 Categorization of Metaphorical Expressions

Altogether 1,993 metaphorical expressions are identified in the collected data, with 1,133 in Chinese and 860 in American media. They were classified into different groups according to the source domains they adopt by identifying their basic meanings. In this way, all the individual metaphors were categorized and were arranged numerically according to the frequency of the different source domains that surfaced.

In this phase, the neighboring text plays a decisive role for some lexical units whose basic sense could be used in more than one conceptual domain. Take the Chinese word zhàn shèng [战胜] [to beat] for example. It could refer to the triumph in either war or contest. Whether to categorize it into the WAR or the SPORT and GAME metaphor is dependent on the scenario its co-text has created. In the following discourse, the conventional term **bào lěng mén** [爆冷门] [to have unexpected result] used in sports event helps us to categorize zhàn shèng as one type of SPORT and GAME metaphor.

(1) 伊利**战胜**了可口可乐等名牌，一举夺得 2007-2008 年度"最佳营销奖"，**爆**出了一个不大不小的**冷门**。

[The company of Yili beat such famous international brand as Coca-Cola to acquire the award of "2007-2008 Annual Best Marketing" and has become a modest black horse.]

(CEW, August 11, 2008)

4.5 Analytical Procedures of the Research

The identified metaphorical expressions establish associations between various aspects of the target domain (i.e. Olympic Economy) and a set of source domains. The source domain will immediately trigger a number of key features that are routinely related to concepts in the source domain. They have been stored in the producer and reader's memory as a kind of socially-shared knowledge. As a result, the choice of one source domain over another can result in positive and negative attitudes toward the entity in question, depending on the attitudes toward the items of the source domain. In this connection, frequent source domains in the representation of Olympic Economy are analyzed. Particular source domains to each media and those with obvious disparity in frequency between these two media are also considered in spite of their low instantiations in order to reveal comparatively preferable ways of representing the same topic. The presence of metaphorical expressions relating to the same source and target domains across a number of texts within the corpus is termed metaphorical pattern in the research.

However, simply the identification of the source conceptual domain can hardly reveal comprehensively how the ideologies underpinning the newspapers influence their representations. It is necessary to examine how the source domain is signified and which aspects of the source domain have been given extra attention by analyzing the semantic-orientation of the signifying expressions. In this connection, the concept of scenario (Grady, 1997ab; Musolff, 2004, 2006; Semino, 2008) is referred to frequently in the present study. It is smaller but richer mental representation than the source domain, including particular situations and settings, entities, goals and actions that are related to the source domain. The emphasis of conceptual scenario aims to determine which aspects of a metaphorical mapping can dominate the discourse for Olympic Economy. The results will steer us to specific features of the source domain journalists intend to emphasize, which will be transferred to the topic in question.

In order to have comprehensive description, interpretation and explanation of metaphorical representation, the quantitative method was adopted throughout the dissertation. Meanwhile the data was quantified with statistical measurements to show the frequency of certain metaphorical pattern and conceptual scenario, which verifies the relevant results. For the purpose of quantification, I counted as separate instances of metaphorical language all metaphorically used words relating to the same source domain that occur within the same clause.

The above procedure was followed separately for the two separate corpora. The respective results were compared for the similarities and differences in the metaphorical choice and use in these two media. Inferences about the motivations of these similarities and differences were further made with the purpose to unearth the underlying ideology of Olympic Economy. The next three chapters will present detailed analysis of metaphorical patterns, conceptual blends, scenarios and use of these metaphorical constructions. First, I will go to the most frequent metaphorical patterns shared by these two media.

Chapter 5   Analysis of Frequent Common Metaphorical Patterns

5.1 The Overview of Metaphorical Patterns

1,133 Chinese and 860 English metaphorical expressions are identified respectively in the collected data. The more instances of metaphors in the Chinese corpus may be explained by its larger size. It has a little lower metaphorical density than the English counterpart, with 9.29 and 10.6 metaphorical expressions identified in every 1000 Chinese and English words.

Table 5.1   Source domains in metaphorical representations

Source Domain	Chinese Data			English Data		
	Occurrence of Token	Frequency per 1,000 words	Percentage of Chinese Token (%)	Occurrence of Token	Frequency per 1,000 words	Percentage of Chinese Token (%)
LIVING ORGANISM	207	1.7	18.3	209	2.58	24.3
JOURNEY	204	1.67	18	152	1.87	17.7
SPORT & GAME	170	1.39	15	173	2.13	20.1
WAR	169	1.31	14.9	166	2.05	19.3
MACHINE	94	0.77	8.3	26	0.32	3.02

continued:

Source Domain	Chinese Data			English Data		
	Occurrence of Token	Frequency per 1,000 words	Percentage of Chinese Token (%)	Occurrence of Token	Frequency per 1,000 words	Percentage of Chinese Token (%)
PHYSICAL ENVIRONMENTAL PHENOMENON	69	0.57	6.1	35	0.43	4.07
PERFORMANCE	53	0.42	4.5	19	0.23	2.2
BUILDING	50	0.41	4.4	29	0.36	3.37
NATURAL RESOURCES	40	0.33	3.5	8	0.098	0.93
FOOD	36	0.3	3.2			
TEXTILE	/	/	/	22	0.27	2.6
CONNECTION	/	/	/	17	0.21	1.98
EXAMINATION	12	0.1	1.06	/	/	/
ART	12	0.1	1.06	/	/	/
FORTUNE	9	0.073	0.8	/	/	/
Others	10	0.08	0.88	4	0.049	0.47
Total	1,133	9.22		860	10.29	

5.2 Representation of Olympic Economy as a Living Organism

5.2.1 Introduction

The general metaphor ECONOMY IS A LIVING ORGANISM is regarded as an initial framework to handle the understanding of economics (Henderson, 1982: 149; White, 2003). But the productivity of this general metaphor is more obvious at the three basic levels of the plant, animal or human. These sub-categorizations give us three mappings: OLYMPIC ECONOMY IS A PLANT, OLYMPIC ECONOMY IS AN ANIMAL or OLYMPIC ECONOMY IS A HUMAN. All the three sub-domains share overlapping features so that some metaphorical expressions could be assigned to two or even three of them. Some attributes are more proper to one of them. For example, the propensity for growth is the salient feature of a plant (Charteris-Black, 2004: 77).[1]

Table 5. 2   Distribution of LIVING ORGANISM metaphors

Sub-conceptual Element	Chinese Media		American Media	
	Token	Percentage (%)	Token	Percentage (%)
HUMAN LIFE	197	95.2	147	64.5
ANIMAL LIFE	9	4.3	8	3.5
PLANT LIFE	1	0.5	73	32
Total Token	207		228	

Metaphors from the domain of organism are an important group comprising more than 18% and 24% of all metaphors representing Olympic Economy in the collected Chinese and English data. Such metaphor enjoys the greatest density in both media, reaching 1.7 and 2.58 per 1,000 words respectively. It is a little more prevalent in American media than in Chinese media. All the three underlying conceptual mappings have instantiations in the data (see Table 5.2) in spite of disparity in figures. OLYMPIC ECONOMY IS HUMAN LIFE is the only predominant type of LIVING ORGANISM metaphor in Chinese media. Whilst, the large majority of English LIVING ORGANISM metaphors are divided by two conceptual elements, HUMAN LIFE and PLANT LIFE. Next, a close examination of each sub-domain will be presented.

5.2.2 Representation of Olympic Economy as Human Life

Kövecses (2002: 16) points out that the human body is one of the most popular source domains in the English language. In the discourse of Olympic Economy, we have found that concepts concerning human relationship, human behaviors, human psychology as well as human body parts are used to talk about business events and entities. These personifications transfer inanimate and insensible objects into animate and subjective roles, and thus highlight the development, psychological state and social aspects of the target domains. Linguistic devices derived from the concept of human life are comprehensively exploited in the discourse concerned, constructing the scenarios of PHYSICAL and INTELLIGENT AGENT, as well as SENTIMENTAL and SOCIAL BEING.

5.2.2.1 Representation of Olympic Economy as a Physical Agent

In representing Olympic Economy as a physical being, various aspects of the target domain are depicted in terms of physical characteristics of human beings, including body part and appearance, life span, health and strength. Table 5.3 and Table 5.4 show the conceptual elements that are sorted by basic mappings. They are listed in the order of discussion. For subordinate conceptual categories, the number of tokens is listed in the last column as sub-token, which is the sum of figures for individual functions of metaphorical expressions.

Twenty-one Chinese metaphors constructing Olympic Economy as physical being are used to talk about the image of companies in terms that originally describe a person's appearances, including much more lexicalized metaphor **xíng xiàng** [形象] in such structure as **shùlì qǐyè xíngxiàng** [树立企业形象] [to set up the image of an enterprise] and more novel metaphor **fēng fàn** [风范] in the title **zhǎnshì qǐyè fēngfàn** [展示企业风范] [to Show the Demeanor of the Company].

In American media, the noun giant with the literal sense describing a person in big size conventionally refers to any large and successful business organization. In the discourse (1) concerning competition between domestic and international sneaker brands, world-famous companies Nike and Adidas are like giants, who make the domestic Li-Ning appear weak. Here the linguistic metaphor of giant is compatible with the SPORT metaphor activated by the phrasal verb lag behind that constructs the disadvantageous situation faced by the less powerful company in the market in terms of a rival coming behind in a race.

(1) Today Li-Ning lags behind giants Nike and Adidas even at home.

(BW, May 1, 2008)

Another metaphor makeover describes the host city as a person trying beauty treatment to improve her appearance. This refers to China's various measures to change Beijing's image for the coming Olympics.

Table 5.3   Chinese metaphorical representations of Olympic Economy as a physical agent

Sub-conceptual Element	Expression	Pinyin	English Translation	Individual Token	Sub-token
APPEARANCE	形象	xíng xiàng	image	19	21
	风范	fēng fàn	demeanor	2	
LIFE SPAN	成熟	chéng shú	mature	9	30
	生存	shēng cún	to survive	6	
	成长	chéng zhǎng	to grow up	5	
	孕育	yùn yù	to conceive offspring	4	
	诞生	dàn shēng	birth	4	
	出生	chū shēng	birth	2	

continued:

Sub-conceptual Element	Expression	Pinyin	English Translation	Individual Token	Sub-token
STRENGTH	强大	qiáng dà	powerful	10	15
	活力	huó lì	vitality	5	
HEALTH	调控	tiáo kòng	to regulate	18	32
	健康	jiàn kāng	healthy	8	
	瘦身	shòu shēn	slimming	4	
	痼疾	gù jí	chronic disease	2	

Compared with Chinese media, American media prefer to borrow some concepts from the human body instead of appearance to describe structures and features of Olympic constructions. For example, the surface of buildings is described as the **skin** of human body, and the materials that surround buildings are conceived of as the clothing humans wear, realized by the adjective **clad** after the copula "be". They have become jargons in the field of construction. The description of buildings as human body recurs when the section that link other parts of the city with the National Theatre is termed as a giant **umbilical cord**, which refers originally to the long flexible cordlike structure that connects a fetus to the placenta. Our knowledge about close relationship between fetus and placenta enables us to infer the integration of this new building with the layout and style of the whole city.

The specific way of American media to look at buildings as biological organism is also reflected in its convergence of evolution of living organism with progress in these projects. This is realized by the noun **gestation** that describes the process of constructing a building as conceiving a new baby. The other metaphor **born** with similar basic sense depicts the development of Chinese technology.

Table 5.4 **English metaphorical representations of Olympic Economy as a physical agent**

Sub-conceptual Element	Expression	Individual Token	Sub-token
BODY PART	skin	8	11
	clad	2	
	umbilical cord	1	
APPEARANCE	giant	4	6
	makeover	2	
LIFE SPAN	survive	3	10
	immaturity	3	
	gestation	2	
	born	1	
	come of age	1	
STRENGTH	strong	11	34
	powerful	9	
	strength	8	
	power	6	
HEALTH	healthy	4	7
	pain	2	
	painful	1	

There are more metaphorical expressions concerning human birth in the Chinese corpus, including the nouns **chū shēng** [出生] and **dàn shēng** [诞生] sharing the basic sense of a baby's birth and the verb **yùn yù** [孕育] meaning conceiving offspring. They are used for different aspects of the target domain. As a conventional metaphorical expression, **dàn shēng** [诞生] acts together with **chū shēng** [出生] to construct the appearance of

Olympics-related products in the market, such as the unveiling of the mascot for the 2008 Beijing Olympics in (2).

(2) 作为奥运会的核心识别元素，奥运会吉祥物从**诞生**之日就受到世人的普遍欢迎。

[As a basic element of Olympics, its mascot was warmly welcomed by the world since its birth.]

(PD, November 11, 2005)

Chinese media also highlight metaphorically the appearance of a new marketing strategy, such as the recessive marketing program adopted by non-official sponsors. The word **yùn yù** [孕育] is adopted in the discourse about opportunities produced by Olympic construction projects for companies and the introduction of new management into these projects.

Besides human birth, more expressions conveying different periods of human life span are adopted in metaphorical representation. The verb **shēng cún** [生存] and its English equivalent **survive** have become lexicalized metaphors for the survival of companies in the economic domain, concerning their most basic and vital requirement as a living organism. The Chinese verb **chéng zhǎng** [成长] and adjective **chéng shú** [成熟] conventionally metaphorize the full development of an organism. In the discourse concerned, they describe the development and maturity of the following phenomena: the sponsorship campaign, the marketing strategy and plan, the brand development and the introduction of new products. For example, the following extract (3) concerns Olympic books whose development is said to reach maturity.

(3) 对奥运书籍的开发，营销手段更加**成熟**了。

[As far as the development of Olympic books is concerned, the marketing strategy had become more mature.]

(PD, August 20, 2004)

The maturity of marketing programs is instantiated only once in English discourse "Olympic sponsorships **came of age** when Peter

Ueberroth exploited them to subsidize the Los Angeles Games in 1984".
However, the word **immaturity** with the opposite sense from **came of age**
has three instances pointing to the underdeveloped Chinese market, as in
the following title:

(4) Chinese Market **Immaturity** Was a Draw

(BW, July 31, 2008)

Chinese metaphors that are drawn from the sub-domain of physical
development, ranging from birth to maturity, are also used to highlight
the development of relevant companies, the main entities in Olympic
Economy, as well as the development of China's economy, and the
affected entities in Olympic Economy. For example, in the following
discourse (5), the adjective **chéng shú** [成熟] highlights the facilitating
forces of Olympic business opportunities in the development of Chinese
enterprises.

(5) 这个机遇将大大提高中国企业的竞争力，使中国企业变得更
加**成熟**起来。

[This opportunity will improve greatly the competitiveness of
Chinese enterprises and make them become more mature.]

(PD, October 29, 2001)

Besides body part and life span, the physical state of a person is used
to enhance the vigor and liveliness of participants in the business activity.
Such a metaphorical pattern is quite significant in American media, with
34 instances of expressions realized in nouns as well as verbs. Words
related to physical strength, such as **strength** and its adjective **strong**
describe a robust person with physical power, who is not easily injured.
The word **power** and its adjective **powerful** refer to the ability to act
efficiently. They all point to the economic power of the companies
concerned and their great influence in the business community, as
expressed in the following extracts:

(6) Beijing's thinking has been that if China has a locally produced alternative, it could reduce the amount of royalties it would have to pay to foreigners while helping Chinese tech companies become more **powerful** globally.

(BW, November 23, 2004)

(7) InBev's China Business in southeastern China will be enhanced by Anheuser-Busch's **strength** in northeastern China.

(BW, July 14, 2008)

In Chinese media, we find such terms with similar senses as **qiáng dà** [强大] and **huó lì** [活力]. Besides representing the power and influence of companies, they highlight brisk market, prosperous China's economy and profound influence of Olympic Economy as in this example:

(8) 奥运无疑都会为文化体育、会展旅游等第三产业的发展增添**活力**。

[The Olympic Games will undoubtedly add vitality to such tertiary industries as culture, sports and convention-exhibition tourism.]

(PD, September 5, 2008)

There are only three HEALTH metaphors in English discourse. Besides the most conventional one **healthy**, the metaphoric noun **pain** in the structure "the **pain** of fewer tourists" highlights the negative effect of China's restrictive security measures on the tourism industry. Its adverbial form in the title "**painfully** understaffed" signifies the underdevelopment of environmental protection, showing doubt on China's ability to hold up the claim for a "Green Olympics".

In contrast, HEALTH metaphors are quite prominent in Chinese media, realized by **tiáo kòng** [调控], **jiàn kāng** [健康], **shòu shēn** [瘦身], and **gù jí** [痼疾]. **Tiáo kòng** [调控] originally refers to how stress response systems regulate the internal and external conditions of an organism to keep balance between them. Thinking of Olympic Economy as a living organism, the term **tiáo kòng** [调控] concerns its macro-control, as is expressed in the following example:

(9) 在奥运经济日益升温之时，我们是否也应当想一下：对奥运进行调控？

[When Olympic Economy heats up day by day, should we think of regulating it?]

(CEW, August 23, 2004)

As the Chinese equivalent of **healthy**, **jiàn kāng** [健康] in Chinese media represents the same phenomenon in Olympic Economy—wholesome operation of marketing programs and the development of China's economy. In contrast, there are much fewer metaphors concerning human illness. Only one metaphor **gù jí** [痼疾] is used with low frequency to underline the huge investment into Olympic construction projects, as in (7), in which the problems produced by these projects are compared to a chronic disease that is hard to get rid of according to our common sense.

(10) 抑制了"超投资、超规模、超标准"的**痼疾**。

[Inhibit the chronic illness of extra investment, super-scale and super standard.]

(PD, September 23, 2005)

These problems had spurred wide debates in China. For the consequence of the debate, the Chinese media use **shòu shēn** [瘦身], as in (11) to refer to the government's final decision to impose tight control on these projects in order to save money and become more efficient. The physical fitness of an individual converges with the more abstract concept of fitness in the sense of being highly competitive in business. In modern society, the increasing value given to physical fitness has made it a cultural aspiration in the West. This ideal has been applied metaphorically by corporate culture to conceptualize corporate performance. Here Chinese media use it to construct the measures taken by Chinese central government to deal with the thorny problems that bring trouble to every host country. The cultural value subsumed by this metaphor implies the positive evaluation of domestic press on Chinese government's role in the control of Olympic preparation.

(11) 北京奥运场馆**瘦身**计划的启迪。

[Inspirations of Beijing Olympic arena's slimming plan.]

(PD, August 28, 2004)

The above analyses demonstrate that both media conflate various physical aspects of human beings with entities and events in Olympic Economy. Common conceptual scenarios are constructed in them with corresponding metaphorical patterns, such as the mapping between the survival of being and companies, the convergence between the birth of beings and appearance of economic phenomena, as well as the conflation between strength of human beings and power of companies. These mappings are even realized by equivalent expressions.

In spite of these similarities, differences arise when we look at tokens and functions. Quantitatively, American media give priority to the STRENGTH scenario, while Chinese media to LIFE SPAN and HEALTH scenarios. Correspondingly, the function of companies' powerful influence and development are significantly dramatized in American and Chinese media respectively. Besides, there are distinct aspects of the target domain these two media highlight through metaphors of physical beings, judging from metaphorical functions, such as the macro-control of Olympic Economy in Chinese media and various aspects of the preparation for Beijing Olympics in American media. Generally, American media construct more comprehensive scenarios than Chinese media, since it represents both positive and negative aspects of Olympic Economy, including mature Olympic Economy itself and problems in the preparation, such as technology and environmental protection, whilst Chinese media only emphasize the positive effect of Olympic Economy on China's economy and great opportunities for companies.

5.2.2.2 Representation of Olympic Economy as an Intelligent Agent

The most salient feature of a person that distinguishes it from animal and plant is his or her intellectual dimension. Journalists are found to recur to this aspect when they describe companies and talk about complex marketing programs. Companies will be described as intelligent agents, who are able to carry out rational functions, such as perception, interpretation, evaluation, judgment and decision making. The function of such metaphor can be seen from the following examples taken from the English corpus:

(12) Super 8 Hotels is **getting ready for** the 2008 Olympics in Beijing.

(NYT, October 22, 2006)

(13) The company also **tailors** its marketing.

(BW, October 8, 2007)

(14) The 18-year-old company once **ruled** China's sneaker business.

(BW, May 1, 2008)

Table 5.5   English metaphorical representations of companies as rational agents

Function of Metaphor	Expression	Individual Token	Sub-token
Preparation for OE	get ready for	6	7
	prep	1	
Active Participation in OE	tailor	5	15
	embrace	3	
	lure	3	
	grab	1	
	woo	1	
	grip	1	
	steal	1	
Domination in OE	rule	1	1

These metaphors originally describe human behaviors with clear purposes. The phrasal verb **get ready for** with 6 instances not only represents the preparation of individual companies and the host city, but also the technological maturity for the Olympics. The verb **tailor** with the basic sense of cutting or styling material or clothes to satisfy certain requirements activates the conceptual domain of clothing and fashion, in which the tailor is the very agent to alter garments. Blended with the business domain that are signified by the neighbouring words "company" and "marketing", this metaphoric verb represents the reality that companies adapt their marketing strategies to the Olympic market, in which companies correspond to tailors, and their marketing strategies correspond to clothes. The word **rule** represents the fact that Li-Ning Company used to be an authority in sneaker business, implying its power and influence among domestic companies. Representatively, these examples illustrate the three main functions metaphors perform when they construct the company as an intelligent being. These functions are listed in both Table 5.5 and Table 5.6 in the order of discussion with individual linguistic metaphors in both media. **Prep** (1 instance) shares the similar sense and function with **get ready for**. The two verbs **lure** and **woo**, with the similar basic meaning of attracting others with the promise of some reward, construct the efforts made by companies to attract more consumers taking advantage of the Olympics. **Steal**, with the basic sense of taking others' objects without their permission, conveys strategies in the marketing competition by companies, signaled by the collocate "share". There are richer and more varied instantiations in the Chinese corpus for the same functions.

Table 5.6 Chinese metaphorical representations of companies as rational agents

Function of Metaphor	Expression	Pinyin	English Translation	Individual Token	Sub-token
Preparation for OE	筹划	chóu huà	to plan and prepare	2	4
	未雨绸缪	wèi yǔ chóu móu	while is fine weather, mend your sail	1	
	厚积后发	hòu jī hòu fā	successive success after profound accumulations	1	
Active Participation in OE	抓住	zhuā zhù	to grab	6	23
	接触	jiē chù	to contact	3	
	牵手	qiān shǒu	to hold the hand	3	
	担负	dān fù	to take up	2	
	肩负	jiān fù	to take on	2	
	担任	dān rèn	to take the office of	2	
	创作	chuàng zuò	to create	1	
	揩油	kāi yóu	to get advantages at expense of others	1	
	抢客	qiǎng kè	to seize the clients	1	
	投身	tóu shēn	to throw oneself to	1	
	大展身手	dà zhǎn shēn shǒu	to give full play to one's skills	1	
Domination in OE	迎来	yíng lái	to come to a specific stage	1	3
	拿回	ná huí	to take back	1	
	站稳脚跟	zhàn wěn jiǎo gēn	to gain steady footing	1	

Metaphorical representations of the preparation for Olympic Economy are realized by Chinese idioms **wèi yǔ chóu móu** [未雨绸缪], which reflects that companies make beforehand plans for any predicted situation in the competition. There is also variation of conventional expressions. For example, the idiom **hòu jī bó fā** [厚积薄发] with the basic meaning "profound accumulations and gradual emergence" is transformed to **hòu jī hòu fā** [厚积厚发], to depict successive success of a company in the market after many years of accumulation in various aspects. Apart from idioms, the verb **chóu huà** [筹划] signifies the meticulous planning of companies in the preparation stage.

Participation in marketing competition is constructed metaphorically by a series of verbal groups. Both **qiān shǒu** [牵手] and **jiē chù** [接触] concern close cooperation between companies in the field of construction and marketing. Another word **chuàng zuò** [创作] signifies company's innovative ability in brand development. The word **kāi yóu** [揩油] expresses the same metaphorical meaning as the English word **steal** and **qiǎng kè** [抢客] concerns competition between companies in the marketing programs[2].

In the representation of companies as rational agents, the verb **zhuā zhù** [抓住] with 7 instances figures significantly in the Chinese corpus. As a two-argument verb grammatically, it originally describes holding some physical objects by animate agents. In the following discourse, it is employed to depict how companies take advantage of business opportunities provided by the Olympic Games. In the same discourse, any company that achieves unexpected success in this process is described as a competitor in a race or contest about whom little is known. This scenario is constructed by the noun **hēi mǎ** [黑马], which is the literal translation of the English nominal group **dark horse** derived originally from the domain of horse racing. The mixture of different metaphors enables the media to set companies' action in the competitive situations.

(15) 中国广大中小企业只要**抓住**机会，成为"**黑马**"的几率并不低。

[It is greatly possible for many middle-and-small-sized companies in China to become dark horses if they could seize this opportunity.]

(PD, December 30, 2005)

Five other instances of **zhuā zhù** [抓住] metaphor are identified. They all point to the fact that no companies involved want to miss this great opportunity and all of them plan to have full participation. This is further constructed by **tóu shēn** [投身] and **dà zhǎn shēn shǒu** [大展身手]. They shed light on efforts and passions of these rational agents. The same function is realized in English discourse by similar metaphors, including such verbs as **embrace, grab** and the noun **grip** in the following examples:

(16) In the U.S., Haier's portable wine coolers have **grabbed** 30% of the market.

(BW, October 8, 2007)

(17) To be sure, Nike firmly dominates the athletic footwear business and is unlikely to **lose its grip** anytime soon.

(NYT, January 28, 2006)

(18) He attributes the company's brand popularity to its strong local roots as well as its willingness to **embrace** international business practices.

(BW, August 28, **2006**)

In addition, three Chinese verbs **dān fù** [担负], **dān rèn** [担任] and **jiān fù** [肩负] share the similar basic sense of undertaking certain responsibilities by some intelligent agents. In the discourse of Olympic Economy, they represent how sponsors, builders and technical suppliers service for the Olympic Games, as expressed in this example:

(19) 各家国内外赞助企业，**肩负**起为奥运会提供优质服务、保障奥运会成功举办的责任。

[Domestic and international sponsors have taken up the responsibility to offer high-quality service to see that the Olympics will be held successfully.]

(PD, April 30, 2007)

They attach importance to the role of famous sponsors at home and abroad in the Olympics and draw our attention to the social responsibility of business communities and thus foreground the close relation between economy and sport.

In Chinese media, the power of companies is indirectly illustrated by their achievements that are signaled by a set of verbal groups, such as **yíng lái** [迎来], **ná huí** [拿回] and **zhàn wěn jiǎo gēn** [站稳脚跟] in the following extracts. Respectively, they indicate Chinese companies' progress in brand development, opportunity they gained in construction projects and their great influence in the new markets. All these demonstrate their increasing power.

(20) 中国企业**迎来**了品牌建设的最佳时期。

[Chinese enterprises have come to the flush of brand development.]

(CEW, June 4, 2007)

(21) 公司**拿回**近百万平方米的施工任务。

[The company has taken back the construction work that amounts to nearly million square meters.]

(CEW, March 1, 2007)

(22) 公司牢牢地在外埠市场上**站稳了脚跟**。

[The company has gained an extremely firm footing in the "out-of-town" market]

(CEW, August 11, 2008)

Apart from these above common functions of metaphors depicting companies as rational agents in a variety of processes, some other metaphors, such as **jǔ shǒu tóu zú** [举手投足] [every act and every move] (1 instance) and **wén jī qǐ wǔ** [闻鸡起舞] [to rise upon hearing the crow

87

of a rooster and practise the sword] (1 instance) respectively depicts the ease of a successful company as a person in the construction line and constructs the company as a diligent warrior who rises to exercise on hearing the cock crows in the morning and gets ready for the battle. The latter is compatible with the neighboring WAR and SPORT metaphors activated respectively by zhēng tiān xià [争天下] and jìng zhēng [竞争] in the following discourse:

(23) 大多国内企业要与外国企业**争天下**的实力还不够，还需**闻鸡起舞**，加倍努力，才能增强未来与外国企业**竞争**的实力。

[The majority of domestic enterprises are not strong enough to strive with foreign companies. They need to rise upon hearing the crow of a rooster and practise the sword and redouble their efforts. Otherwise, they would not grow strong enough to compete with foreign rivals in the future.]

(PD, October 29, 2001)

We can see that in the representation of companies as rational people in the preparation for, participation and domination in Olympic Economy, both media highlight active participation of companies in Olympic Economy, especially marketing strategies they take. The rich entailments produced by its metaphorical representations extend beyond human behaviors and reflect the psychological state of the agents in some cases. Apart from having more realizations of such metaphors, Chinese media stress social aspect of companies' economic activities in the construction of their responsibility in the Olympics. In addition, we notice a mixture of LIVING ORGANISM metaphors with SPORT and WAR metaphors. Compatibly, they highlight the behavior of companies in the competitive background of Olympic Economy.

Behaviors of rational human beings are also referred to in the representation of abstract and complicated economic phenomena. The following table lists the scenario of human actions for this target domain, including actions conveyed by metaphorical expressions and the corresponding agents and patients.

Table 5.7　Metaphorical representations of business phenomena as rational agents

Expression	Pinyin	English Translation	Metaphorical Meaning	Token	Agent	Patient
带来	dài lái	to bring	to produce, to result in, to lead to	5	various marketing programs	profits, sales increase, and brand values
				2	related industries	profits for host city
抬头	tái tóu	to raise the head	to be active in the market	1	fake mascots	/
为他人做嫁衣	wèi tā rén zuò jià yī	to make clothes for others' wedding ceremony	to create opportunity	1	holding Olympics in China	foreign companies
接踵而至	jiē zhǒng ér zhì	to come one after another	to take place successively	1	marketing campaigns	/
量身定做	liáng shēn ding zuò	to measure and customize	to dedicate...to	1	Olympics-related projects	investors from Hong Kong
担负	dān fù	to take up	to shoulder (responsibility)	1	commercial emblem	historical responsibility to spread Olympic spirit
jump	/	/	to rise suddenly	4	profits	/
				2	fees for marketing	/
				1	number of hotel	/
climb	/	/	to increase	1	sales	/

89

Among the six types of Chinese metaphorical expressions that transfer human rational and physical behaviors to the general and complex concept of marketing programs, 83.3% of them (10 out of 12 instances) are neutral and positive constructions. Benefits of Olympic Economy are demonstrated through the metaphor **dài lái** [带来] and the social function of Olympic products is highlighted by the metaphor **dān fù** [担负]. The two metaphoric idioms **jiē zhǒng ér zhì** [接踵而至] and **liáng shēn ding zuò** [量身定做] represent enormous business opportunities in the Olympic market. The negative metaphors include the verb **tái tóu** [抬头] and Chinese proverb **wèi tā rén zuò jià yī** [为他人做嫁衣]. The former describes the return of fake mascots to the market. The latter originally refers to poor girls making wedding clothes for a living but having no money to marry. It has developed into a conventional metaphor describing a person working hard for others. Blended with the conceptual domain of marketing opportunity and competition in the Chinese market due to the holding of Olympics, the proverb dramatizes the possibility that only foreign companies instead of domestic ones garner benefits of the Olympics although the whole country is busy preparing for the coming Olympics.

In this way, we could come to the conclusion that Chinese media construct a more comprehensive picture of Olympic Marketing Programs in terms of human action and behavior. In most cases, the media shed light on advantages of taking part in Olympic Economy, in terms of great benefits and endless business opportunities. Simultaneously, however, it leaves space to abnormal competition and failure of some companies in the competition for partnership.

In English corpus, the intransitive verbs **jump** and **climb**[3], originally describing human physical upward move, indicate the sudden rise of agents concerned. The increasing profits and sales enhance the positive effects of Olympic Marketing on successful sponsors, while the increasing fees for marketing highlight some price participants have to pay if they want to take advantage of such business opportunity. Statistically, Chinese corpus adopts more metaphors of human behavior than American one. Another difference arises when we look at agents and patients in the listed processes. The two metaphoric verbs used by American media are intransitive and only highlight the relevant agents. As a result, the constructed processes take place as self-initiated actions of the personalized phenomena without any interference of external forces. In contrast, 85.7% processes represented in Chinese media include both agents and patients, highlighting the effects behaviors of agents bring to patients.

5.2.2.3 Representation of Olympic Economy as a Sentimental Being

There is also a sentimental dimension to a person and this aspect, highlighted by both media, also provides a further highly structured sub-domain, giving us the metaphor COMPANIES ARE SENTIMENTAL BEINGS. In such case where the feelings and emotions of the person predominate, the aspect of companies that is put forward is their psychological states. The following extracts contain metaphors that reflect such psychological states as surprise in (24), hope and expectation in (25) and (26), confidence in (27), and willingness in (28) taken from the English corpus, and aspiration in (29) as well as aloofness in both (30) and (31) from the Chinese counterpart.

(24) There are some very large, well-known companies that were **caught completely off guard** on this restriction on pollution.

(BW, July 3, 2008)

(25) G E **hopes** to put Olympic-specific ads at local airports and on highway billboards.

(NYT, October 9, 2007)

(26) VisionChina Media (VISN) is **expecting** a bonanza this summer.

(BW, May 28, 2008)

(27) China Mobile has shown its **confidence** in the domestic

91

technology by putting the business under its unlisted parent company.

(BW, April 9, 2008)

(28) He attributes the company's brand popularity to its strong local roots as well as its **willingness** to embrace international business practices.

(BW, April 9, 2008)

(29) 而对于很多本土企业来说，对这个梦想的 "**渴望**" 尤为强烈。

[While for many local companies, the aspiration for this dream is much more intense and strong.]

(CEW, August 11, 2008)

(30) 与北京2008奥运会食用油独家供应商——金龙鱼四处可见的 "奥运概念" 营销相比，鲁花显得格外 "非奥运"，甚至有些过于**安静**。

[Different from Golden-dragon, the exclusive supplier of edible oil for the 2008 Beijing Olympics, which carries out widespread promotions, related to "Olympic Concept", Luhua looks extremely "non-Olympic", and even somehow too calm.]

(CEW, August 4, 2008)

(31) 与其他 "非奥运赞助企业" 挖空心思做奥运营销相比，鲁花显得有些 "**超脱**"。

[Compared with other non-sponsors who spare no efforts to carry out Olympic marketing, Luhua appears to be somehow detached and behaves above the event.]

(CEW, August 4, 2008)

Altogether, there are 11 instances of such metaphor in the English corpus against 4 realizations in Chinese. Nearly half of such metaphors in English are concerned with the psychological state of expectation, which is realized in Chinese through such expressions as the noun **kě wàng** [渴望] [aspiration] (1 instance) and the compound verb **mèng mèi yǐ qiú** [梦

寐以求] [to dream of] (1 instance) with more strength and intensity. Apart from the emotion of surprise, in which the company is described as a passive agent in (24), all the other metaphors in English describe positive and active emotional responses from companies that could explain their eagerness and full participation in Olympics-related business activities. Differently, the Chinese corpus mentions negative and inactive response of some non-sponsors, which gives light to mixed attitudes among Chinese companies towards Olympic Economy, as expressed in (30) and (31).

5.2.2.4 Representation of Olympic Economy as a Social Being

A rational, healthy person is at the same time a social organism, with certain social relationship and social status. In the construction of a company as a human being, both media do not ignore this social aspect, with 37 English and 51 Chinese instances of metaphorical expressions.

Table 5.8   Chinese metaphorical representations of Olympic Economy as a social being

Sub-conceptual Element	Express-ion	Pinyin	English Translation	Individual Token	Sub-token	Function
SOCIAL STATUS	老大	lǎo dà	head of any group	2	10	company's position in competition
	龙头	lóng tóu	head of any group	2		
	风头	fēng tou	publicity	2		
	资历	zī lì	qualifications	1		
	新秀	xīn xiù	an up-and-coming youngster	1		
	鼻祖	bí zǔ	an originator	1		
	巨擘	jù bò	giant	1		

continued:

Sub-conceptual Element	Expression	Pinyin	English Translation	Individual Token	Sub-token	Function
SOCIAL RELATION	合作伙伴	hé zuò huǒ bàn	partner	33	41	connection of company & industry with OE
	家庭	jiā tíng	family	3		
	联姻	lián yīn	to marry	3		
	热恋	rè liàn	to fall in deep love	1		
	攀附	pān fù	to seek connections in high places	1		

Both media describe companies as a specific kind of people with certain social status (see Table 5.8 and Table 5.9). In Chinese, we have **lǎo dà** [老大], **lóng tóu** [龙头], **bí zǔ** [鼻祖], as well as the lexicalized metaphor **jù bò** [巨擘]. They stand for founders in a line or leading companies in an industry, like GE in illuminating industry and Tsingtao Beer that take active part in Olympic Economy. Another noun **xīn xiù** [新秀] referring to an up-and-coming youngster in a field, is used to talk about newly emerging companies with good performance in the Olympics. The structure **zī lì lǎo** [资历老] describing people with long credentials of certain service is employed for companies with a long history. Moreover, the compound noun **fēng tou** [风头] with the basic sense of publicity one receives enables the media to talk about the situation that companies are faced in terms of social status of a person. This is well expressed in discourse (32), in which the real sponsor lost its advantage in Olympic Marketing to the non-sponsor of Nike. Altogether, these metaphors point to the situation these related companies are located in business competition.

(32) 耐克的**风头**盖过了真正的赞助商"锐步"。

[Nike received more publicity than Reebok, who is the real sponsor of the Olympics instead of Nike.]

(CEW, August 11, 2008)

Table 5.9 **English metaphorical representations of Olympic Economy as a social being**

Sub-conceptual Element	Expression	Individual Token	Sub-token	Function
SOCIAL STATUS	high-profiled	5	12	company's position in competition
	ambassador	4		
	upstart	3		
SOCIAL RELATION	parent	2	5	relation between companies
	sister	2		
	sibling	1		
	partner	17	20	connection of company & industry with OE
	love affair	2		
	marry	1		

In English discourse, **upstart** shares the same function as **xīn xiù** [新秀], referring to the fast developing Chinese companies. However, **upstart** arouses different emotional response due to its primary sense standing for people who have risen quickly to wealth or power but seem to lack dignity or ability. The inherent derogative sense implies the negative evaluation of American media on these companies. **Ambassador** primarily refers to a diplomatic minister of the highest rank as permanent representative to another country or sovereign. In the discourse of Olympic Economy, it stands for the Chinese brand that is acknowledged in the world as the representative of Chinese quality products. **High-profile** has the basic sense referring to a position attracting much attention. It modifies famous international enterprises, such as in the expression "**High-profile** Beijing Olympics sponsors Kodak and Lenovo", which emphasizes the well-publicized stance of these enterprises. Besides, it describes Olympic megaprojects that had drawn much public attention in the structure "a number of **high-profile** projects".

In the English corpus, some conventional metaphors are identified to talk about close relationship between different companies in terms of family network, such as **parent**, **sister** and **sibling** as modifiers of the word "company", with 5 instances in all. The metaphoric verb **marry** highlights the incorporation of Olympic spirits with products of such company as Lenovo in their marketing strategies. The FAMILY metaphor is realized in Chinese media by the noun **jiā tíng** [家庭] and the verb **lián yīn** [联姻]. They do not refer to the interrelation between companies, but shed light on the cohesive power of Olympic Economy that attracts so many companies, as expressed in one of typical examples (33), in which the Beijing Olympic Games is like a family and any companies that have connection with it are family members.

(33) 这三家企业先后**联姻**到奥运这个大**家庭**中。

[These three enterprises connected themselves one by one to the powerful family of Olympics.]

(PD, March 17, 2006)

Such close relation between company and Olympic Economy is enhanced by metaphors with the basic sense concerning social relationship between human beings. The most outstanding expressions are **hé zuò huǒ bàn** [合作伙伴] and the English counterpart **partner** due to their most pervasive occurrence. Both of them are conventional metaphorical expressions standing for cooperating participants in economic activities. In the topic of this dissertation, they refer to any companies that have contributed to Olympic Economy. Different from balanced relationship and mutual benefits conveyed by the conventional verb **lián yīn** [联姻],

96

the use of **pān fù** [攀附] and **rè liàn** [热恋] indicate imbalanced relationship between the agent and patient in the following extracts.

(34) 央视网成了各家视频网站争相"**攀附**"的对象。

[CCTV net has become the object many video websites are scrambling to seek connection with.]

(CEW, August 11, 2008)

(35) "会展经济"**热恋**北京奥运

["Exhibition Economy" falls in deep love with Beijing Olympics.]

(PD, June 24, 2004）

Conventionally, the patient of lexicalized metaphor **pān fù** [攀附] stands for powerful authorities that can bring fame and fortune to anyone who can seek connection with them. Here, it becomes the web of CCTV, with which a great number of video web sites are eager to obtain cooperation in the coverage of Olympic sports events. **Rè liàn** [热恋] implies the brisk feature of exhibition economy relating to Olympic Marketing. Both of them highlight great attraction of Olympic Economy to different companies in spite of low tokens. The scenario of human relationship is also realized in the English corpus by other metaphors than the conventional one **partner**. The expression **love affair** dramatizes the close attention and great support China's economy gives to professional sport. This indirectly implies the effect of Olympics on China.

The above evidence demonstrates that metaphorical constructions in terms of the HUMAN RELATIONSHIP scenario in both media highlight the allure of Olympic Economy by virtue of almost similar metaphorical expressions.

In all, by representing Olympic Economy as a social being, both media draw our attention to the power of this international sports business and the status of companies in it. They are highlighted by similar metaphors concerning social status and social relation. Apart from quantitative disparity, Chinese media shed more light on the allure of

Olympic Economy due to its richer metaphorical expressions. Another difference arises in the function of FAMILY metaphors. They are used in American media for relationship between companies besides the close relations with Olympic Economy companies try to establish.

5.2.3 Representation of Olympic Economy as Animal Life

By far, we have seen diverse aspects of the conceptualization of Olympic Economy as human beings. We can now move a step down the Great Chain of Being to the animal level. When the animal level is used as the source domain, we have the metaphors FINISHED BUILIDNG PROJECTS ARE ANIMALS and COMPANIES ARE ANIMALS.

The first metaphor is absent in the Chinese corpus, but has 6 instances in the English corpus.

(36) The CCTV center seems to flatten out from some vantage points and **bear down on** you from others.

(NYT, July 13, 2008)

(37) This sprawling **web** has completely reshaped Beijing since the city was awarded the Olympic Games seven years ago.

(NYT, July 13, 2008)

(38) All these projects have been **tracked** for years, creating little oohs and aahs of delight as they emerge physically similar to the computer-generated imagery that preceded them.

(BW, April 27, 2007)

The verb phrase **bear down on** in the example (36) enables the press to transform the aggressive nature of a predator to the building and arouses an unpleasant feeling among the receivers. When coming to the network of roads, trains, subways, canals and parks extending through Beijing in (37), the media compare it with a spider web, which is a vicious trap designed to capture and control innocent victims. Through such a metaphor, the media depict the aspect of city transformation as behaving in a way that should not, with the implication that such behavior of the devouring of the weaker is to be considered merciless. The verb **track** in (38) originally describing the action of following the trail of an animal implies these projects involved are not quite new in the design, since they had drawn our attention for a long time. Besides these expressions that entail negative evaluation of buildings and trigger negative emotional response to buildings and Beijing transformation, animal life is drawn upon in the expressions that activate image metaphors for the description of building's structures, such as **dragon** and **dragon-shaped**. The idiom **white elephant**, a conventional way in American society to describe large and unwieldy things that are either nuisance or expensive to keep up, is used to refer to the financial pressure Olympic building projects imposed on the host city.

The second metaphor COMPANIES ARE ANIMALS is activated by six types of linguistic metaphors, one in the English corpus and five in the Chinese corpus. Dominant companies are depicted as dogs (2 instances) in the English corpus. In the Chinese corpus, companies involved in the competition are described as tigers and bees and companies making a hit overnight in the Olympics are referred to in terms of soaring horses. Besides that, the company breaking the current balance in a line is compared to a catfish. These ontological correspondences are realized by such expressions as **top dog**, the Chinese idioms **hǔ shì dān dān** [虎视眈眈] [to look at fiercely as a tiger does], **fēng yōng ér shàng** [蜂拥而上] [to swarm onto like groups of bees], and **fēi huáng téng dá** [飞黄腾达] [to take off rapidly like the legendary horse] with 1 instance respectively, the Chinese verb **téng fēi** [腾飞] [to blast off] and the Chinese noun **nián yú** [鲇鱼] [catfish] with 3 instances respectively.

The idiom **hǔ shì dān dān** [虎视眈眈] and **fēng yōng ér shàng** [蜂拥而上] are conventional metaphors conveying negative attitudes of the users. The scenario of predators preying on something delicious corresponds to the situation in the market where competitors are ready to chase and scab any chance that could bring them interests. The produced blending highlights the fierce competition in the market. The scenario created by the metaphor **fēng yōng ér shàng** [蜂拥而上] brings a picture before our eyes, in which a large group of bees swarm onto the same thing for exclusive possession. In the discourse of Olympic Economy, it draws our attention to the intensity of competition. Both **fēi huáng téng dá** [飞黄腾达] and **téng fēi** [腾飞] use the scenario of a flying horse to depict the fast developing companies. The word **nián yú** [鲇鱼] in (39) reminds us of the jargon "catfish effect" used in the human source management. It derives from a European legend about fishing, in which some catfish are put into a container full of sardine and begin to swim feverishly in this unknown environment. In this way, delicate sardine can be kept alive and would be sold later at a much higher price. In the human source management, a catfish refers to a new competitor that could stimulate the whole group. Here, Leishi, as an unknown company before becoming an Olympic partner, is the new competitor in the lighting industry. To other companies, the latest arrival of this competitive rival arouses sense of danger and thus urges them to better their work. In the same discourse, the ANIMAL metaphor **nián yú** [鲇鱼] is mixed together with the WAR metaphor that is activated by the word **lǐng jūn** [领军]. Such a mixture depicts the very leading company in the lighting industry as head of an army. This compatible mixture embeds the influence of a new powerful company in the competitive market.

(39) 作为**领军**企业，雷士有望成为中国照明行业的"那条**鲇鱼**"。

[As a leading enterprise, Leishi is expected to become "that catfish" in Chinese lighting industry.]

(CEW, August 11, 2008)

The analysis demonstrates that ANINMAL metaphors are adopted by the two media to highlight different aspects of Olympic Economy. Chinese media use these metaphors to foreground the fierce competition in Olympic Economy and its positive effects on the industry involved. American media employ the ANIMAL metaphor to imply its negative attitudes towards the megaprojects for Beijing Olympics.

5.2.4 Representation of Olympic Economy as Plant Life

PLANT LIFE metaphors only enjoy sporadic realizations in Chinese discourse, such as the novel expression **yī zhī dú xiù** [一枝独秀] with one instance, which originally refers to one particularly thriving branch of a tree. In the discourse concerned, it represents one successful company in a line.

However, PLANT LIFE metaphors are an important group comprising 32% of all LIVING ORGANISM metaphors in American media. It refers to the plant life when it talks about the expansion of Olympic construction projects through the noun **growth** (2 instances) with the basic sense denoting the increase in size of a living organism. All the rest of its PLANT LIFE metaphors are adopted to represent China's economy in the context of Olympic Economy with 71 instances in all.

Many of these are realized by a conventional metaphor for the growth of a plant. It is activated by the noun **growth**, its adjective form **growing** and the corresponding verb **grow**. Altogether, they account for nearly 70 % of the total PLANT LIFE metaphors with 51 tokens out of the total 73. Generally, the expansion and development of economic activities are represented as a natural process of biological growth of a plant, which is the central scenario constructed in English LIVING ORGANISM metaphors. Another metaphor activated by the word **boom** plus its adjective form of **booming** describes the flourishing economy. Basically, a scenario of growth would show a cyclic situation within which certain factors would contribute to and foster effective growth while others would impede or diminish it. Next, we will unearth these factors by looking into the varieties of the GROWTH metaphor.

101

The **growing** metaphor (11 instances) is used to modify the city of Beijing, specific industries in China, and the Chinese market respectively. Among them, the target referent of the Chinese domestic market with variant expressions takes up nearly half of these metaphors. The GROWTH scenario constructed by the verb **grow** typically highlights the notion of increase by quantifying the extent of the increase in question. In these metaphors, the term **grow** appears with such core quantity modification collocates as percentage, factor or other numeric values, as seen in the following examples:

(40) China's economy has been **growing** by double-digits annually.

(NYT, March 30, 2008)

(41) The industry has **grown** from virtually nothing in 1979, when the communist government lifted a ban on ads, to as much as $16 billion last year.

(BW, June 25, 2005)

The social entities depicted like a growing plant in these examples are China's economy and specific industries, which are involved in a natural process rather than through the agency of companies and government. Such a natural process is codified into compound nouns that show the grammatical modification of the word growth, including **economic growth, double-digit growth, traffic growth** and **tourism growth** with 5 instances in all. There are other 8 grammatical modifications which provide a further way in which the scenario of growth is extended. They are divided by the binary opposition of positive and negative connotations of the modifiers (Table 5.10).

Table 5.10   Grammatical modification of Growth

Positive		Negative	
high continued exceptional breathtaking	GROWTH	explosive unrestrained torrid blistering	GROWTH

The positive modifiers draw our attention to the magnitude and vitality of China's economic growth and its profound influence. The modifier "unrestrained" describes the economic growth as something that is hard to control, implying that the economic growth with great magnitude and force is easy to run out of our human control. The two-word expression "explosive growth" names the features of two different conceptual inputs, one is the danger of an explosive, and the other is the natural development of a plant. These features are integrated into the target scenario concerning the development of China's economy, producing the blended meaning, which dramatizes the danger of the fast development. Similarly, in the expressions "torrid growth" and "blistering growth", the adjectives "torrid" and "blistering" with the similar basic sense referring to extremely hot and dry weather arouse our unpleasant feelings. Blended with the scenario of plant growth, these two expressions imply unpleasant results of the fast developing economy in China. The juxtaposition of positive and negative evaluation of China's economic growth enables the readers to notice the developing economy at high speed in China and the problems it has produced.

The same binary opposition of positive and negative evaluation proceeds in GROWTH metaphors, in which **growth** is used in the semantic role of affected participant and the syntactic role of object (Table 5.11). "X" is fleshed out in the contexts of the representation of China's economy (look at examples 42-44) as some circumstance, for example, pollution due to the fast development, government activities, the recession in the U.S. and inflation in China. They highlight a variety of factors at home and broad that will hinder the development of China's economic growth.

(42) China's soaring energy use and resulting pollution are a serious threat to the country's continued prosperity and **growth**, not to mention the well-being of its citizens.

(BW, August 22, 2005)

103

Table 5.11   Growth as affected participant

"X"...............GROWTH	"Y"...............GROWTH
a threat to	contribute to
interrupt	sustain
cut	drive
pressure on	

(43) "If the U.S. is falling into recession, and we think it is, it will mean downside pressure on exports from China and on economic **growth**," said Huang Yiping, chief Asia economist at Citigroup.

(NYT, October 9, 2007)

(44) While the Chinese economy is still **sizzling** and investment continues to **pour into** the country, analysts are beginning to worry that if rising inflation does not cut Chinese **growth**, then weakening demand in the United States for Chinese-made goods will[4].

(NYT, March 19, 2008)

On the other hand, the Olympics as the referent of Y emphasizes the opportunities this sports event provides for China's economy, as expressed in one typical case (45), in which "that" refers to the tourism growth in Beijing due to the holding of the Olympics. It facilitates the development of the lodging industry in Beijing. The scenario of GROWTH is strengthened in the same discourse by the metaphoric verb **seed** and metaphoric noun **boom**. The metaphor **boom** is as conventional as that of **growth**, signifying the fast development of China's economy. The verb **seed** is the extension of the highly conventionalized use of **growth** and **boom** to refer to the economic expansion. It represents a conceptual identity in the precondition for the growth of a healthy plant and a healthy economy. It is based on an isomorphoric correspondence between the sequence of events that lead to a successful outcome in the natural world and in the world of business. Apart from the recurrence and extension of the LIVING ORGANISM metaphor, the verb **drive** activates the MACHINE metaphor. The juxtaposition of animate and inanimate metaphors also appears in the scenario of GROWTH as an agent, which will be examined in the following section.

(45) While that **drives growth** for the thousands of four- and five-star hotels filling China's cities, it has **seeded** a much larger **boom** in economy.

(BW, April 3, 2008)

In a word, in the scenario of GROWTH as a patient, American media highlight the positive effect of the Olympics on China's economy, but simultaneously draw our attention to the concomitant problems of the fast-developing economy with magnitude.

In several cases, the word **growth** fulfills the classical role of semantic agent, which refers to the participant carrying out the action in the situation concerned. In some instances, it performs as the syntactic subject, as in (46); however, in the other cases, it is positioned after the preposition in both active and passive voice, like the structures in (47) and (48). They all stress consequences of the economic development in China, including effects on companies and changes in people's lifestyle.

A significant phenomenon in the scenario of GROWTH as an agent is that growth is captured as a mechanical activity. The verbal expression **ratchet up** in (43) transports us to the world of force dynamics and mechanics.

(46) The mainland's blistering **growth** has **ratcheted up** demand for corporate loans, and rising incomes mean affected participants are salting away more money in bank deposits.

(BW, August 28, 2006)

(47) Some major hotel companies stand to profit from this potential **growth**.

(BW, March 27, 2007)

(48) **Propelled**[5] by double-digit gross domestic product **growth** and

105

rising urban incomes—up more than 12% last year—increasingly well-off Chinese are opting to travel within China for fun and relaxation.

(BW, April 3, 2008)

The juxtaposition of the natural and mechanical worlds may seem to be an incompatible alliance of radically distinct and mutually exclusive source domains for the same target domain. However, at a more abstract semantic level, both domains configure the identical scenario, in which a dynamic process is acted upon by the element that drives the speed, intensity or scope of that process (White, 2003). As a natural phenomenon, the growth of a plant is clearly a dynamism that can increase or decrease and can be acted upon in various ways as to bring about these effects or impede their happening. The metaphors derived from the mechanical world similarly evidence the core purpose of acting on dynamic processes. The fast-growing economy in China is described as an engine that gives impetus and vitality to business activities. The power of China's economy is given more priority by MACHINE metaphors in Chinese corpus, which will be analyzed in detail in the part for MACHINE metaphors.

We can see that in the representation of Olympic Economy as a living and animate organism, both media create common conceptual scenarios in the corresponding metaphorical patterns, especially in the construction of this sports business in terms of the most basic human experience— physical aspects of human body. Besides, both identify the active participation of companies in Olympic Economy with human rational behaviors, and conflate the power of this international sports business and the status of companies in it with social status and interrelationship of human beings. These mappings are even realized by equivalent expressions in these two media.

In spite of these similarities, differences arise when we look at the frequency and functions of different metaphoric patterns and scenarios. OLYMPIC ECONOMY IS HUMAN LIFE is the only dominant type of

LIVING ORGANISM metaphors in Chinese media. Whilst, the large majority of English LIVING ORGANISM metaphors are divided by two conceptual elements, HUMAN LIFE and PLANT LIFE. This suggests that American media emphasize rational reasoning and psychological factors in Olympic Economy on the one hand, and natural development without human interference on the other hand. This difference is also reflected by different metaphoric verbs when they construct business events in terms of human actions.

In addition, American media give priority to the STRENGTH scenario, while Chinese to LIFE SPAN and HEALTH scenarios. Correspondingly, the function of companies' power and development are significantly dramatized in American and Chinese media respectively. Besides that, Chinese media shed more light on the allure of Olympic Economy by virtue of the metaphor of human social relationship, which is realized in metaphorical expressions with higher frequency than those in American media.

Differences also lie in the different functions the same metaphor, such as COMPANIES ARE ANIMALS performs in the two media. Such differences lead to diverse aspects of the target domain these two media highlight, such as the macro-control in the management of Olympic Economy in Chinese media and various aspects of the preparation for Beijing Olympics in American media in the representations of Olympic Economy as a physical being. Sometimes, the lexical choice will underline different aspects of related entities and events in Olympic Economy. For instance, metaphorical expressions originally denoting rational human behaviors in the representation of companies reveal the social responsibility Chinese media emphasize that companies should take up in Olympic Economy.

Although Chinese media address abnormal competition and failure of some companies in the competition for partnership by virtue of HUMAN

BEHAVIOR metaphors, they shed more light on the positive side of Olympic Economy, especially opportunities granted to companies and China's economy. Comparatively, American media dramatize negative aspects of Olympic Economy, especially the problems faced by the host country in the preparation for Beijing Olympics, which echoes the wide debates inside China and doubts outside China. The media also foreground problems produced by China's fast-developing economy.

5.3 Representation of Olympic Economy as a Journey

5.3.1 Introduction

JOURNEY metaphors can be traced back to the PATH image schema, which is based on our physical experience of motion in space. Its constituents include a starting point, a destination, a path connecting the two, and the direction of the movement. This image schema provides a way of metaphorically constructing goals as destinations, ways of reaching goals as forward movement, problems as obstacles to movement, and success or failure as reaching, or failing to reach a destination. This schema can be seen as providing the basic structure of the more complex JOURNEY domain, which contains richer and more culture-specific knowledge about travelers, modes of travels, impediments to travel and so on (Semino, 2008: 92). The JOURNEY metaphor has been used to frame many abstract and complex concepts, such as love (Lakoff & Johnson, 1980: 44) and life (Lakoff & Turner, 1989). In these cross-domain mappings, a journey is taken as a prototype purposeful activity involving the movement in physical space from a starting point to an end point or destination. Lakoff (1993) used to reformulate the JOURNEY metaphor as PURPOSEFUL ACTIVITY IS TRAVELLING ALONG A PATH TOWARDS A DESTINATION. Later, Charteris-Black (2004: 74)

108

incorporated this into a political conceptual metaphor: PURPOSEFUL
SOCIAL ACTIVITY IS TRAVELLING ALONG A PATH TOWARDS A
DESTINATION. As far as the present topic is concerned, I will transform
the metaphor into: OLYMPIC ECONOMY IS TRAVELLING ALONG A
PATH TOWARDS A DESTINATION.

The JOURNEY metaphor amounts to 356 instances in the collected
data, with 204 in the Chinese corpus and 152 in the English corpus. It is
the second most productive metaphor in the Chinese corpus, occupying
18% of its total metaphorical expressions. Although the JOURNEY
metaphor ranks after LIVING ORGANISM and WAR metaphors in the
English corpus, it still produces 17.7% of its metaphorical realizations.
Rich expressions construct comprehensive scenarios of a journey in these
two media, including PATH and DIRECTION scenarios, FORWARD and
BACKWARD MOVEMENT scenarios, FACILITATING as well as
DEFACILITATING FORCE scenarios, and the one concerning different
modes of travelling. Among them, the four conceptual scenarios presented
in Table 5.12 figure significantly in both media. Altogether, their instances
reach 191 and 144 in Chinese and American media, taking up more than
93% and 94% of JOURNEY metaphors in them respectively.

Table 5.12   Quantity of main conceptual scenarios in JOURNEY metaphors

Main Conceptual Scenario	Chinese Media		American Media	
	Token	Percentage	Token	Percentage
PATH	25	13.1%	17	11.8%
FORWARD MOVEMENT	95	49.7%	66	45.8%
FACILITATING FORCE	60	31.4%	30	20.8%
DEFACILITATING FORCE	11	5.8%	31	21.5%

Table 5.12 tells us the FORWARD MOVEMENT scenario is the most dominant scenario JOURNEY metaphors construct in the two media, taking up almost half of the total realizations. Although there is no marked quantitative disparity in the PATH scenario, Chinese media produce twice FACILITATING FORCE scenario as many as American media and have more instances of the FORWARD MOVEMENT scenario. In contrast, the DEFACILITATING FORCE scenario enjoys much more realizations in American media than in Chinese media. In the following section, I will investigate each of these scenarios with the regard to reveal ideological trends in the representation of Olympic Economy that lead to these quantitative similarities and differences, as well as to unearth more differences that are hidden behind these statistics.

5.3.2 The PATH Scenario

The PATH scenario generally represents the whole process of business activities, such as various marketing programs and construction projects for Beijing Olympics. It includes the starting point, the middle stage and the destination, constructing metaphorically what economic entities had experienced while they prepared for the bid of these activities and carried out their plan after the success of grabbing these opportunities, and whether they achieved their goals at last or not.

Table 5.13   Chinese metaphors for the PATH scenario

Expression	Pinyin	English Translation	Token	Metaphorical Use
起步	qǐ bù	to start	2	奥运营销刚刚**起步** [The Olympic marketing just starts.] (PD, April, 22, 2005)
起点	qǐ diǎn	starting point	1	北京承诺为企业分享奥运商机提供一个公平的**起点**。 [Beijng promises a starting point with equality for enterprises to share Olympic business opportunity.] (PD, April, 26, 2004)

110

continued:

Express-ion	Pinyin	English Trans-lation	Token	Metaphorical Use
路	lù	road	11	联想的奥运之**路**已经逐渐进入**冲刺**阶段。 [Lenovo's path to Olympics has gradually entered sprint phase.] (CEW, October 9, 2005)
旅	lǚ	trip	2	在奥运会开幕之际，大部分企业的奥运之**旅**已至**收官**阶段。 [On the occasion of opening the Olympics, many companies' Olympic trip has come to the end.] (CEW, August 11, 2008)
途径	tú jìng	way	2	奥运有无限商机，参与其中也有很多种**途径**和方式。 [Olympics has boundless opportunities and there are many ways to take part in them.] (PD, September 12, 2007)
历程	lì chéng	course	2	这种"少投入、高产出"的活动，成为 2008 年中国企业奥运营销**历程**中，较为成功的一次事件营销。 [Characterized by "less input and much output", this activity has become one successful case in the course of Olympic marketing experiended by Chinese companies in 2008.] (CEW, August 11, 2008)
捷径	jié jìng	shortcut	2	与北京奥运会的赞助商合作，将成为中小企业**搭乘"奥运快车"**的**捷径**。 [Cooperating with Beijing Olympic sponsors will become a shortcut for medium-and-small-sized companies to take "Olympic Express".] (PD, June 17, 2005)
弯路	wān lù	tortuous path	2	这些企业成功进入北京奥运会，肯定会在整个行业中形成示范作用，可以让更多的中国企业少走一些**弯路**。 [The successful entry of these companies into Beijing Olympics makes them play an exemplary role in the whole line and help even more Chinese businesses achieve more with less cost.] (PD, April 4, 2008)

continued:

Express-ion	Pinyin	English Trans-lation	Token	Metaphorical Use
到达终点	dào dá zhōng diǎn	to reach the destination	1	宏观调控与具体实施这样 "政企分开" 的管理模式，会促使北京奥运工程建设朝着良好的方向**迈进**，就**像疾速飞奔的地铁列车**一样平稳、有序、安全正点地**到达终点**。 [Macro control and the management pattern of separating government and enterprise ensure the progress and quality of projects and urge the building projects of Beijing Olympics to stride towards a good direction and reach the destination on time in a smooth and orderly manner like a fast subway train in a dash.] (PD, September 23, 2005)

There are a variety of Chinese and English metaphorical expressions representing this process, which are listed in Table 5.13 and Table 5.14. The starting point is represented by the Chinese verb **qǐ bù** [起步], the Chinese noun **qǐ diǎn** [起点] and the English phrase **get under way**. They construct the initial stage of the marketing program or the initial operation of marketing plans by specific companies.

Table 5.14 English metaphors for the PATH scenario

Expression	Token	Metaphorical Use
get under way	1	As the JWT work for Lenovo and Yili **gets under way**, Mr. Doctoroff said, the challenge the agency faces creatively is "to marry the product characteristics with the spirit of the Olympics." (NYT, November 14, 2007)
way	2	Even when that began to change, the primary **way** Chinese companies competed was on price. (NYT, April 12, 2008)
path	2	China's most ambitious brands hope to follow the **path** originally trod by Japanese and Korean giants. (BW, October 8, 2007)

112

continued:

Expression	Token	Metaphorical Use
course	2	If the nationalism gambit proves effective, sponsors may stay the **course** and try to build on their relationship with Chinese consumers. (BW, May 28, 2008)
goal	7	The **goal** of both government officials in Beijing and China's top companies for the past few years has been to move toward higher-value production. (BW, October 8, 2007)
reach	3	The real point of sponsorship is to use the Olympics to **reach** potential customers. (NYT, June 1, 2008)

There are richer expressions for the middle phase of this journey. In Chinese media, **dào lù** [道路], **tú jìng** [途径], **jié jìng** [捷径], **wān lù** [弯路] are four lexicalized metaphors for the PATH scenario. **Dào lù** [道路] and **tú jìng** [途径] refer generally to the channel through which companies participate in Olympic Economy. **Jié jìng** [捷径] conventionally connotes a quick way for some purpose. In the quoted discourse, it represents metaphorically how small companies, which could not establish the direct connection with the Olympics, managed to obtain business opportunity through contracting with sponsors. **Wān lù** [弯路] constructs how companies will waste time and money if they do not take right measures in the marketing, as travelers choose a tortuous path that takes them away from the destination. Like the word **lì chéng** [历程], the two characters **lù** [路] and **lǚ [旅]** generally represent companies' experiences in the Olympic marketing. Mixed with SPORT and GAME metaphors activated by **chōng cì** [冲刺] and **shōu gōng** [收官], they highlight the competition these participants are engaged in the course of their development.

In addition, the PATH scenario is used together with other JOURNEY metaphors that create minor scenarios, such as that concerning the mode of travelling activated by the the nominal groups **kuài chē** [快车] and **liè chē** [列车]. Such juxtaposition highlights the concrete measures comapies choose to take part in Olympic Economy.

Compared with 21 tokens in Chinese media, only 6 tokens of metaphorical expressions in the American media represent the middle stage experienced by companies in Olympic marketing programs that ranged from September 1, 2003 to the end of Beijing Olympics. However, American media give more space to the DESTINATION scenario through the term **goal**[6], which is used to signify what companies inspire to achieve in Olympic Economy, as expressed in (49), in which the aim of Chinese companies is to internationalize their brands.

(49) The explicit **goal** was to **elevate** the brand from a Chinese one to a worldwide one.

(NYT, June 20, 2008)

The media also adopt expressions indicating the arrival at the destination, such as **reach**, the English equivalent of the Chinese expression **dào dá zhōng diǎn** [到达终点] to conceptualize companies' successful operation of their marketing plans.

Judging from linguistic realizations of the PATH scenario in the two media, it seems that Chinese media represent a more process-oriented PATH scenario, while American media represent a more goal-oriented one.

5.3.3 The FORWARD MOVEMENT Scenario

Traditionally, we evaluate positively the forward movement towards the destination. **Step** or **pace**, as both noun and verb are conventional ways of talking about the progress towards a goal. Their corresponding Chinese characters **bù** [步], **mài** [迈] and **zǒu** [走] with similar basic meanings are the most prevalent realizations of the JOURNRY metaphor in Chinese media, altogether accounting for about 29.6% of the total tokens of the JOURNEY metaphor with different collocations functioning grammatically as nouns or adverbs (see Table 5.15 and Table 5.16). Here, they create the similar scenario, signifying gradual forward movement of

114

the agent towards the destination. The agents include companies as well as China's economy plus its specific sectors. Simultaneously, the FORWARD MOVEMENT scenario shows the concern about the current status and future development of China's economy by virtue of the prepositions **jìn** [进] or **rù** [入] and **xiàng** [向] respectively.

The compound nouns **bù fá** [步伐], **jiǎo bù** [脚步] and **yī bù** [一步] establish the mapping between a phase of the journey towards a specific destination and the progress made by companies and the host country in Olympic Economy, such as in the following sentence:

(50) 奥运 TOP 是联想国际化**道路**上的重要**一步**。

[To become Olympic TOP is a very import step for Lenovo on the road of internationalization.]

(CEW, August 23, 2004)

Table 5.15 Chinese metaphors with the character bù as a noun

Expression	Pinyin	English Translation	Token	Metaphorical Meaning
逐步	zhú bù	gradually	7	the prolonged process of marketing
进一步	jìn yī bù	further	5	other measures after one progress
第一步	dì yī bù	the first step	4	the initial trial in the marketing
步伐	bù fá	a pace	4	speed of development
脚步	jiǎo bù	a step	3	development
一步	yī bù	a step	3	development
下一步	xià yī bù	the next step	3	other measures after one progress
大步	dà bù	stride or at good speed	2	fast development in marketing
初步	chū bù	initially	2	the initial trial in the marketing

115

The adverb **zhú bù** [逐步] implies that the Olympic Marketing Program is a prolonged process, requiring patience and plans; the other two adverbs **jìn yī bù** [进一步] and **xià yī bù** [下一步] signal other measures companies or China will take after making certain process in the Olympic market. The last adverb **chū bù** [初步] shares the same basic meaning as the noun **dì yī bù** [第一步] to mark where companies begin with the marketing. The compound word **dà bù** [大步] is used as a noun meaning a stride or an adverb with the sense of walking with big steps to signify the quick development achieved by companies.

In 30 out of 33 tokens of Chinese metaphors with the character **bù** [步], Chinese companies are the very agents that are responsible for the progress conveyed in these metaphors. In this way, Chinese media mainly concern the progress and advance achieved by Chinese companies in Olympic Economy, which is ranging from sponsorship, sales, ticketing, brand building and promotion activities that are in line with careful planning.

The phrasal verbs with Chinese characters **bù** [步], **mài** [迈] and **zǒu** [走] reaching 39 tokens in all mark clearly the direction of forward movement due to the prepositions **chū** [出] [out of], **jìn** [进] or **rù** [入] [into] and **xiàng** [向] [towards] (see Table 5.16). The first three prepositions activate the CONTAINER metaphor, which indicates the place where the agent gets out of and gets into respectively and implies changes the agent experiences in this movement. In the discourse of Olympic Economy, used together with **bù** [步], **mài** [迈] and **zǒu** [走], these prepositions represent what the participation in the business competition could bring to the companies, as expressed in the following examples (51) as well as (52), and its influence on China's economy, as expressed in (53) as well as (54). The nouns following the preposition **xiàng** [向], including wài bù shì chǎng [外埠市场], guó jì huà [国际化], hǎi wài [海外], quán qiú shì chǎng [全球市场] and shì jiè [世界] indicate very clearly the destination in the scenario of forward movement, which implies the goal Chinese companies inspire to achieve. In all its 5 instances, **mài jìn** [迈进] appears after the prepositional phrase beginning with the preposition **xiàng** [向], as in (50), showing the direction of forward movement. Therefore the vast majority of the listed expressions focus on the future development of the agent concerned. They focus on what companies and China's economy intends to achieve by taking advantage of Olympic Economy.

Table 5.16 Metaphoric phrasal verbs with Chinese characters mài, zǒu and bù

Expression	Pinyin	English Translation	Token
走向	zǒu xiàng	walk towards	16
走出	zǒu chū	walk out of	13
迈进	mài jìn	march into	5
迈出	mài chū	march out of	2
步入	bù rù	step into	2
迈向	mài xiàng	march towards	1

(51) 作为中国企业**走出去**的成功代表，7 年的奥运进程也是联想的国际化之**旅**。

[As a representative of Chinese enterprises who have successfully gone global, the 7-year course of the Olympics is a journey of internationalization for Lenovo.]

(PD, September 9, 2009)

（52） 只有中国市场的**阵地**更加稳固，国际化的**脚步**才能踏实地**迈出去**。奥运会就是雷士照明**迈向**国际化进程的最佳契机。

[Only with a firm position in Chinese market, could the step towards internationalization be steadily and surely strided. The Olympics are such a chance for Leishi to stride towards internationalization.]

（CEW, August 11, 2008）

（53）在外企争先恐后地**进驻**、国内企业巨头积极参与下，中国照明行业将快速向集团化、规模化、品牌化方向**迈进**，一大批中小照明品牌将被**淘汰出局**。

[With the panic rush of foreign enterprises and active participation of prestigious local companies, Chinese lighting industry will speed up its grouping, scalization and branding and an army of medium-and-small-sized brands will be put out of business.]

（CEW, August 11, 2008）

(54) 随着奥运会的结束，大陆经济是否进而**步入**衰退，成为两岸热议的焦点话题。

〔Whether the mainland economy could head for a recession or not had become a subject of feverish speculation between the Cross-straits as the Olympic Games finished.〕

(PD, September 1, 2008)

An interesting point in these examples is that apart from being used together with other JOURNEY metaphors, such as **lǚ** [旅] in (51) and **jiǎo bù** [脚步] in (52), the FORWARD MOVEMENT scenario activated by **zǒu chū** [走出], **mài chū** [迈出], **mài xiàng** [迈向] and **mài jìn** [迈进] is embedded in other metaphors, including the WAR metaphors signaled by **zhèn dì** [阵地] [battle field] in (52) and **jìn zhù** [进驻] [to advance into] in (53), and the SPORT metaphor activated by **táo tài chū jú** [淘汰出局] [be eliminated out of a competition] in (53). Such mixture of metaphors indicates the co-existence of the development and competition in Olympic Economy, implying the direction these Chinese companies choose in the face of fierce competition.

Apart from the above lexicalized metaphors, more creative metaphorical expressions (23 tokens in all) conveying mobility have been identified (see Table 5.17) to dramatize the progress in Olympic Economy.

All of them have basic senses that convey the forward movement and progress without reference to any hindering forces and difficulties. Let's look at their metaphorical creation in detail.

The word **kāi pì** [开辟] implies a new way in a variety of business activities, such as a new channel for sponsorship or a fresh way to get financial support for Olympic construction projects. Its synonymy **kāi tuò** [开拓] conceptualizes the expansion of companies into new markets, entailing opportunities for their future development. **Chāo yuè** [超越] interprets metaphorically the reality that some companies have won the competitive advantage over their rivals in the competition due to their success in Olympic Economy, like Lenovo in the listed example. The metaphoric noun **fēi yuè** [飞跃] conceptualizes the fast development of some brands. The development of Olympic business and associated brands are also constructed by another compound verb **qián xíng** [前行] conveying forward movement in space. In addition, the verb phrase **shàng tái jiē** [上台阶] illustrates that China's economy as well as individual companies have developed to a new stage in a variety of aspects through participating in Olympic Economy. This metaphor contains the basic image schema of GOOD IS UP (Lakoff & Johnson, 1980: 16).

Table 5.17   Other Chinese metaphors conveying mobility

Expression	Pinyin	English Translation	Token	Example of Metaphor Use
开辟	kāi pì	to open up	6	**开辟**国内企业赞助中国体育代表团和中国奥委会的先河 [To open up a new way for domestic companies to sponsor Chinese sports delegation and Olympic Committee] (PD, May 8, 2008)
超越	chāo yuè	to surpass	5	联想**超越**麦当劳 [Lenovo has exceeded McDonald's] (PD, August 29, 2008)
飞跃	fēi yuè	leap	4	品牌的**飞跃** [The Leap of Brands] (CEW, August 11, 2008)

continued:

Express-ion	Pinyin	English Translation	Token	Example of Metaphor Use
开拓	kāi tuò	to open up	4	**开拓**外埠市场 [to develop market in other cities] (CEW, March 19, 2007)
前行	qián xíng	to move forward	2	品牌**前行** [advance of brands] (CEW, August 11, 2008)
上台阶	shàng tái jiē	to walk up a step	2	服务水平**上**了一个新**台阶** [The service has reached a new level] (CEW, August 11, 2008）

All the above metaphorical constructions work together to stress the progress achieved by Olympic industries and associated sponsors, appliers and partners. They contain positive evaluation of business activities and any elements contributing to relevant achievements, which will be further highlighted in the FACILITATING FORCE scenario.

In English data, the mobility is signaled by metaphoric verbs, nouns and adverbs. They are listed in Table 5.18 in the order of token numbers with one instance of metaporical use for each of them.

Table 5.18　English metaphors conveying mobility

Expression	Token	Metaphorical Use
move (v.)	10	The best Chinese companies will find **ways** to **move** ahead in both emerging and developed markets against big branded multinationals.　(BW, August 28, 2006)
step (n.)	8	In Beijing this summer, Lenovo will take the next **step**. (BW, April 25, 2008)
ahead	8	Many of the projects would have gone **ahead**. (BW, June 18, 2008)
move (n.)	6	Many of the **moves** are to protect sponsors. (NYT, July 11, 2008)

continued:

Expression	Token	Metaphorical Use
lead to	6	Hosting the Olympics could **lead to** long-term improvement in the city government's credit worthiness, rather than to a huge financial **burden**. (BW, June 18, 2008)
go forward	4	The sooner infocomm vendors realize this and act, the better their prospects will be **going forward**. (BW, June 14, 2007)
stride	4	The country is **making strides** to protect intellectual property rights.　　　(BW, December 4, 2006)
rush (v.)	4	The N.B.A. is **rushing** to **expand** its presence in China as quickly as possible before the Beijing Olympics. (NYT, September 19, 2007)
rush (n.)	3	The **rush** to get the city ready for the Olympic Games is creating not just stadiums and new housing. (NYT, June 26, 2005)
hustle	2	To do that, Lenovo **hustled** to win the right to design the Olympic torch a first for a company. (BW, October 8, 2007)
leapfrog	2	But Beijing chose to **leapfrog** those technologies and develop its own system using taxi GPS data. (BW, July 23, 2008)
further	2	Lenovo is using its status as a top sponsor of the Beijing Olympic Games to **further** boost its exposure. (BW, October 8, 2007)
make the leap	2	Chinese companies aim to **make the leap** from low cost and low quality to become world brands of real repute. (BW, October 8, 2007)
forge	1	However, that has not deterred China from **forging** ahead with its floating-car program. (BW, July 23, 2008)

continued:

Expression	Token	Metaphorical Use
pace	1	Beijing is already planning to build a second airport by 2015 to keep up with the torrid **pace** of air traffic growth. (BW, February 29, 2008)
mileage	1	The BUCG has gotten the most **mileage** from the Games. (BW, April 24, 2008)
milestone	1	For Internet television, the Beijing Games represent a **milestone**. (NYT, August 18, 2008)
far	1	The theater's construction was too **far** along for major design changes. (NYT, September 19, 2004)

Move, used as verb as well as noun, is the most prevalent way in the collected English data to conceptualize economic progress in terms of spatial movement. It represents not only companies' participation in business activities, but also the Chinese government's measures for the macro-control, copyright protection and anti-pollution in the preparation for the Olympic Games. Such collocated adverbs as "ahead" and "forward" indicate mobility towards the destination. Another lexicalized metaphor **step** used as a noun stands for one actual stage of a business activity or a concrete measure taken by the Chinese government to control pollution. The word **ahead** is used as an adverb in the phrasal verb **go ahead** or as a preposition in the expression **be ahead of**. With the literal sense of occupying the leading position on a path, it implies in the discourse of Olympic Economoy, the smooth development of building projects or advantages of successful companies in the market. Another adverb **forward** performs the similar function in the structure **go forward**. The phrasal verb **lead to** originally implies a certain goal of a journey. In the quoted example, it stands for those benefits the Olympics could bring to the host country. As the equivalent of Chinese expression **dà bù** [大步],

the metaphoric noun **stride** highlights the great progress both domestic and foreign companies have made in the Olympic market and great efforts made by the Chinese government in the preparation. Like **move**, the metaphor **rush** also appears as verb and noun. With the basic sense denoting sudden and violent movement, it depicts the quick reaction taken by companies and gives light to the emergence of a large number of building projects in a short period of time in the preparation for the 2008 Beijing Olympics, as is expressed in the quoted example. The verb **hustle** expresses the similar metaphorical meaning. The verb **leapfrog** primarily connotes fast advance on the path. In the discourse in question, it dramatizes the great progress China has made in technology. The adverb **further** shares the same metaphorical sense and function as the Chinese metaphoric adverb **jìn yī bù** [进一步]. So does the idiom **make the leap** as the Chinese nominal group **fēi yuè** [飞跃], representing considerable progress that companies have made in marketing programs. The verb **forge** describes China like a person who moves with a sudden increase of speed and power, implying China has intensified the development of its car industry. The noun **pace** denoting the speed of forward movement represents the development of China's tourism industry. The covered distance away from the departure point, expressed by the adverb **far** and the nouns **mileage** and **milestone**, construct altogether the achievement in Olympic Economy and the development of related industries.

With 95 and 66 instances in Chinese and American media respectively, we can see the FORWARD MOVEMENT scenario is the most pervasive concept in the JOURNEY metaphors of these two media. They represent the progress achieved by companies in Olympic Economy and effective measures taken by the government in the operation of Olympic Economy. The two media even share equivalent terms in the metaphorical construction. However, Chinese media highlight the direction in the forward movement, which implies the intended inspiration of Chinese businesses.

5.3.4 The FACILITATING FORCE Scenario

The forward mobility is facilitated by external forces in the scenario of a journey constructed by collected English and Chinese data. In English, it is realized by the three verbs **push** (26 instances), **accelerate** (3 instances) and **propel** (1 instance), with the similar basic meaning of making physical things move forward more quickly. They emphasize the efforts to intensify various marketing programs, as expressed in (55), or to facilitate the construction of Olympic infrastructure, as depicted in (56).

(55) NBC has accelerated its Olympic commitment.

(NYT, June 7, 2003)

(56) In anticipation of the Summer Olympics this August, China's capital is pushing to complete construction projects to welcome millions of tourists.

(BW, April 8, 2008)

Such physical movement entails psychological determination of the agents involved, which are sometimes referred to through metonymy, such as "China's capital" in (56) instead of the direct reference in (55).

The word **push**, used as verb or noun, is quite outstanding in American media with the highest frequency of 26 tokens in all the expressions for the JOURNEY metaphor. As a verb, with the basic sense of applying steady force to move some object or spurring somebody to achieve better results, it constructs self-compelling process in most cases (9 out of the total 17 instances), in which companies devote themselves to various marketing programs as the typical examples (57) and (58) illustrate. In other cases, it represents the material processes in which an agent spurs the patient to advance. In six such processes, the Chinese governments at both municipal and national levels exert external incentive to various patients, including companies in (59), Olympic construction projects in (56), and the high-technology needed for the Olympics in (60). In another two instances, the Olympics and its accompanying phenomena become the facilitating force.

(57) Even as the likes of Lenovo, ZTE, Huawei, and Haier push their brands overseas.

(BW, October 8, 2007)

(58) G.E. is still clearly pushing a big chunk of money at the Olympics.

(NYT, October 9, 2007)

(59) The Chinese government is pushing its companies to amplify their ad messages to compete with foreign brands.

(NYT, July 20, 2008)

(60) Smaller cities push high-speed Internet use as Beijing and Shanghai continue their momentum on the coattails of the Olympics and World Expo.

(BW, June 14, 2007)

Used as a noun, as in the typical example (61), **push** metaphorically describes the determined efforts made by companies to enter new markets or new lines. There are other 5 instances of **push** metaphors performing the same function. Modified by the adjectives "new", "renewed", "global", "big", and "strong", it expresses consistency, intensity and great scope of marketing measures. Besides, the other three instances of **push** metaphors highlight China's efforts in the preparation for the Olympics, including measures in catering and technology.

(61) Coca-Cola is also making its own big push into China.

(NYT, July 20, 2008)

We can conclude that in most cases, **push** involving physical entities and events creates a JOURNEY scenario, in which companies are described as rational people whose initiative and determination to participate in the marketing program urge them to make efforts. In addition, it highlights the governments' role in Olympic Economy.

The FACILITATING FORCE scenario is created in Chinese media

by the following four phrasal verbs **tuī dòng** [推动] (26 instances), **cù jìn** [促进] (16 instances), **jiā kuài** [加快] (10 instances), and **tuī jìn** [推进]（8 instances）with the basic sense of pushing, propelling, quickening and accelerating. More than 75% of such FACILITATING FORCE metaphors are constructed in the discourse about China's economy in the context of Beijing Olympics.

In the conceptualization of China's economy as a journey, there is an assumption that it has a predetermined goal to achieve, which is described as the destination of the journey. Facilitating forces could help to reach this destination more quickly and more easily.

The above-mensioned metaphorical expressions conveying facilitating forces represent China's economy through material processes, in which an agent passes on forces to make the patient move on, as instantiated in the following examples:

(62) 自奥运申办成功以来，奥运经济就一直有力地推动着中国尤其是北京地区的经济增长。

[Since the successful bid for holding the Olympic Games, Olympic Economy has propelled the growth of economy in China, especially that of Beijing district.]

(PD, August 1, 2008)

(63) 中国奥委会的市场开发促进中国体育营销上升到一个新的高度。

[The market development carried out by Chinese Olympic Committee (COC) has facilitated the elevation of Chinese sports marketing to a new level.]

(PD, May 9, 2008)

(64) 北京奥运会成功举办后，如何利用奥运加快经济转型，是人们关注的话题。

[After Beijing Olympics, people are concerned with the issue how to take advantage of the Olympics to facilitate the economic transformation.]

The agents, the source of impetus, are marked explicitly in these examples. They are Beijing Olympics or its concomitant features and activities. Besides the general concept of "Olympic Economy", the agents allude to more concrete concepts of the international model, economic measures as well as the market development of COC. These abstract and complex economic phenomena have been personified as animate agents in the FACILITATING FORCE scenario.

The affected patients in those processes include national and local economy, as expressed in (62). However, in most cases, they represent more concrete industries, such as the sports marketing in (63), and any concepts that highlight changes in economy, for instance the notion of industry transformation in (64).

The analyses of conceptual elements in these material processes draw our attention to the positive effects of the Olympics on the economic development in both national and local regions. This justifies the economic development that is depicted more clearly in the FORWARD MOVEMENT scenario, in which China's economy is described as a traveler moving forward and approaching its predetermined destination.

One interesting point is that this force schema is often used together with other scenarios in JOURNEY metaphors. Look at one typical example of such double metaphor (Charteris-Black & Musolff, 2003: 167):

（65）以奥运促进首都经济社会的发展，加快首都发展步伐。

[The Olympic Games will give impetus to the economic and social development of the capital and speed up its forward step.]

(PD, August28, 2004)

In this discourse, economy in Beijing is described as a traveler whose forward movement that is presented by the metaphoric noun **bù fá** [步伐] has been accelerated, which is activated by the verb **jiā kuài** [加快] with the basic sense of increasing the speed and the verb **cù jìn** [促进] as the equivalent of the English word propel. Their juxtaposition strengthens the important role played by the Olympics in the development of its host city. In some discourses like (63), the FACILITATING FORCE scenario is used together with the ORIENTAL metaphor GOOD IS UP, which is realized by the verb **shàng shēng** [上升] and the noun **gāo dù** [高度]. This mixture highlights the positive functions of these facilitating forces and thus implies business opportunities produced by Olympic Economy.

Apart from China's economy, the FACILITATING FORCE scenario is instantiated in the representation of concrete marketing programs, construction of building projects as well as the development of relevant companies. In the discourse (63) about Beijing construction, JOURNEY scenarios recur, which are activated repeatedly by the noun **liè chē** [列车], phrasal verbs **mài jìn** [迈进] and **cù jìn** [促进], and verb phrase **dào dá zhōng diǎn** [到达终点]. Here **mài jìn** [迈进], a quite popular Chinese JOURNEY metaphor, is used in the co-text **cháozhe liánghǎo de fāngxiàng** [朝着良好的方向] [towards good direction], implying an optimistic prospect for the project. The neighbouring simile triggers our knowledge about the subway train, including the high speed and fixed routine, which is transferred to the domain of building projects, highlighting its fast and smooth advance in accordance with the predetermined schedule. The metaphor of subway train is extended by its reaching the destination, indicating the project will be finished on time. All these positive metaphors point to the benefits the agent of this discourse could bring to the Olympic building project concerned. That is the function of the macro control and management mode in the building project, which in turn will benefit the development of the host city.

(66) 宏观调控和政企分开的管理模式，保证了工程的进度与质量，促进北京工程建设朝着良好的方向迈进，就像急速飞奔的地铁列车，平稳、有序、安全、正点地到达终点。

[The macro control and the management pattern of separating governments and enterprises ensure the progress and quality of projects and urge the building projects of Beijing Olympics to stride towards a good direction and reach the destination on time in a smooth and orderly manner like a fast subway train in a dash.]

(PD, September 23, 2005)

In sum, 29.7% and 19.7% of Chinese and English JOURNEY metaphors construct the FACILITATING FORCE scenario, which is more favored by Chinese media. Apart from the quantitative disparity, there are differences in its function between these two media, which lead to different aspects of Olympic Economy they intend to foreground. Chinese media highlight positive effects of the Olympics on the economic advance of the host country, while English media dramatize the great efforts made by companies in the Olympic market.

5.3.5 The DEFACILITATING FORCE Scenario

In contrast with the FACILITATING FORCE scenario, there are resisting forces preventing the advance towards the destination, which is realized by the nouns burden, curb, bottleneck, roadblock, obstacle, setback, and hurdle in the English data. Through them, physical barrier and obstruction on the path converge with the abstract and intangible difficulties in the business world.

Our knowledge of what may block or obstruct movement towards a predetermined destination is employed here for a negative evaluation of the cause of the constraint entailed by the FACILITATING FORCE scenario. Among the four instances of burden metaphor, three of them are modified by the adjective "financial", meaning that the large amount of money needed to pour into Olympic construction projects has created a big problem to the government and thus constrained the further development. This is another way to address the financial problem caused by these megaprojects besides the metaphor white elephant in the conflating of Olympic Economy with a living organism.

We can see that the metaphor burden expresses deep concern about the problems of megaprojects in the preparation for Beijing Olympics that had produced wide debates in China. There are even richer metaphors in the representation of other business problems. Curb is used as both metaphoric noun and verb. In spite of different grammatical functions, they convey the same metaphorical meaning, standing for the constraints Chinese central government imposes on traffic and some industries in the coming days to Beijing Olympics. The noun bottleneck with the primary sense of traffic jam in a narrow road describes difficulties that poor infrastructure imposes on the capacity of Beijing Airport, which brings negative influence to the tourism industry during the Olympic Games. The fourth noun setback, meaning an unfortunate happening that hinders or impedes advance in its original sense, stands for thwarting and frustrating effect the recalled products have brought to Chinese brands, implying disadvantages they will suffer in competition for business opportunities. Both roadblock and obstacle refer originally to a physical barrier set up across a road. In the discourse of Olympic Marketing, they creatively conceptualize the pressure from business competitors and difficulties in broadcasting the sports event. The last noun hurdle is a lexicalized metaphor, referring to a difficulty or problem. It points out that public acceptance is the problem Lenovo has to solve when it approaches the international market. The verb phrase clear the hurdle primarily describes the physical action to remove the impediment on the path in forward movement. In the discourse in question, they metaphorically construct the process of overcoming these difficulties in marketing. In summary, these metaphorical nouns dramatize economic problems in the preparation for Beijing Olympics and give light to difficulties domestic and foreign companies have to overcome.

Table 5.19 English metaphoric nouns for the DEFACILITATING FORCE scenario

Expression	Token	Metaphorical Use
burden	4	The government also sought donations to build structures such as the National Aquatics Centre. These measures helped to significantly reduce the financial **burden**. (BW, June 18, 2008)
curb	4	Businesses have been warned for months of Olympics-related **curbs** on traffic, construction and other activities. (BW, June 27, 2008)
bottleneck	3	Infrastructure **bottlenecks** and overbooking partially explain why flights are delayed or cancelled. (BW, February 29, 2008)
setback	2	Those widespread negative attitudes are a big **setback** for Chinese brands' global aspirations. (BW, October 8, 2007)
roadblock	2	Nike remains the No. 1 seller of footwear and athletic apparel in the world, but the acquisition of Reebok by Adidas-Salomon could throw up a considerable **roadblock** to the swoosh across Latin America and Asia. (NYT, January 28, 2006)
obstacle	2	The network already faces one **obstacle**: the five-hour time difference between London and the East Coast most likely will not allow for many marquee events in prime time. (NYT, August 17, 2008)
hurdle	1	To **clear the hurdle** of public acceptance, Lenovo decided to play down its Chinese heritage. (NYT, June 20, 2008)

In English discourse, the scenario of a difficult journey is also constructed by verbal expressions. Besides **curb**, there are **slow**, **halt** and **freeze**. The verb **slow** connotes the reduction of speed in movement. It stands for the restriction on Chinese architecture market. The other two metaphorical expressions **halt** and **freeze** take a further step by conveying complete pause and stop of some building projects, as the result of loud criticism on these megaprojects. This echoes the problems triggered by them that are highlighted in terms of **burden** metaphors. The only metaphoric adjective **rocky**, originally used for a risky way full of rocks, constructs hardship Olympic sponsors have experienced in the market. In a word, the DEFACILITATING FORCE scenario sheds light not only on difficulties individual companies and host cities have to overcome, but also on economic and technological problems produced by the Beijing Olympic Games.

Table 5.20   English metaphoric verbs and adjective for the DEFACILITATING FORCE scenario

Expression	Token	Metaphorical Use
slow	4	**SLOWING** DOMESTIC MARKET (BW, July 2, 2008)
halt	4	Over the summer, a number of high-profile projects by foreign firms were **halted**, scaled back or savaged in the press. (NYT, September 19, 2004)
curb (v.)	2	If Beijing's air remains unacceptably sullied in the days leading up the Games, officials said, they would take "stringent steps" to **curb** polluting industries. (NYT, December 29, 2007)
freeze	2	City officials laid out an ambitious series of measures on Monday that will **freeze** construction projects, slow down steel production and shut down quarries in and around this capital during the summer in an attempt to clear the air for the Olympics. (NYT, December 29, 2007)
rocky	1	G.E. had a **rocky** April, falling short of profit projections. (NYT, August 17, 2008)

In the face of difficulties and impediments in the journey, there are linguistic devices that illustrate movement away from the destination and the lack of initiative for movement towards the destination. Different from **move forward, move away from** (2 instances) indicates opposite direction from the destination, implying giving up some earlier plans for the journey. In the discourse of Olympic Economy, it refers to the fact that the Chinese government has changed its principle for the construction projects. The phrasal verb **wind down** (1 instance) depicts deceleration in the construction of one of these projects—the country's main state television network.

(67) Construction is **winding down** on the new headquarters of the country's main state television network, China Central Television, or CCTV.

(NYT, May 2, 2008)

Another phrasal verb **back away** (2 instances) represents the reality that many famous sponsors have decided to give up competing for the sponsorship because of few profits they could get. The verb **stick** (2 instances) describes metaphorically the fact that some companies are fixed in certain position of competition in the Chinese market. The dormant status implies the adversity foreign companies must go through in the Chinese market.

In Chinese media, the noun **zhàng ài** [障碍] (1 instance) referring to barriers is the only linguistic realization of the mapping between physical obstacle and abstract difficulties Chinese companies have to face. However, functioning as a subtitle, it is projected to any problems surfacing in the rest of the discourse, including Chinese companies' lack of experience in marketing, limitation of opportunities due to the exclusive rights enjoyed by high-profile sponsors and threat from multinationals in the same line. All these factors will impose great pressure on Chinese companies. These difficulties could account for the formant state of some domestic sponsors and partners of the Olympics, which is expressed metaphorically by the verb **tíng liú** [停留] (2 instances) denoting the remaining in a place as well as the idiom **guǒ zú bù qián** [裹足不前] (2 instances) describing the state of binding foot without any move. Both of them share the same basic sense of hesitating to move forward. They imply these companies' reservations, frustration and confusion in the following examples:

(68) 一个令国内企业**裹足不前**的难题是，找不到自己在奥运赞助中准确的定位。

[A problem that prevents domestic companies from moving forward is not able to find a precise position in the Olympic sponsorship.]

(PD, January 21, 2004)

(69) 目前一些国内奥运"伙伴"和"赞助商"的做法还是**停留**在表面上，这不得不让人焦虑。

[We can't help worrying about the fact that at present many domestic Olympic partners and sponsors could only do some facial work.]

(CEW, August 4, 2008)

Chinese media address the negative aspects of Olympic building projects, too. Two compound nouns **bāo fú** [包袱] (5 instances) referring originally to a bundle wrapped in a cloth-wrapper and **zhòng fù** [重负] (1 instance) denoting heavy burden usually arouse negative emotional responses, since they primarily refer to some burden, both physical and psychological, that make people under great pressure. In the discourse of building projects, they capture the record investment of Beijing Olympics, as in the extract (70), in which the interrogative question expresses worry about the trouble huge investment will bring to the successful holding of the 2008 Beijing Olympics. Other instances, represented by (71), are concerned with the management of these projects after the Olympic Games. The BURDEN metaphor here is mixed together with the WAR metaphor that is activated by the word **tiǎo zhàn** [挑战]. Nested in the WAR metaphor, the huge financial pressure faced by the local government

134

is brought to light. We could infer that much work and effort is needed for it to avoid the similar problem that used to trouble the other host cities in the history of Olympics.

(70) 北京奥运能否承受类似的经济**重负**？

[Could Beijing Olympics bear such economic burden?]

(CEW, August 28, 2004)

(71) 奥运会后能否不使市政府背上**包袱**，将是重大的**挑战**。

[That will be a huge challenge not to make the municipal government troubled by such a burden after the Olympic Games.]

(PD, February 10, 2006)

The sharp quantitative disparity of the DEFACILITATING FORCE scenario between these two media, with 31 English tokens against 11 Chinese one, implies that American media give more space to the negative side of Olympic Economy in metaphorical reprsentations. Adopting more varied metaphorical expressions for the scenario, American media address not only difficulties faced by sponsors and partners, but also restrictive measures taken by the Chinese government in the preparation for Beijing Olympics. This metaphorical construction of the role played by the Chinese government in the DEFACILITATING FORCE scenario is absent in Chinese media. Although the two media use the same BURDEN metaphor for the problems in Olympic construction projects, English media do not show concern about their operation after the Olympic Games.

In conclusion, both media highlight the development achieved by companies in the Olympic marketing and effective measures taken by the Chinese government for the operation of Olympic Economy through FORWARD MOVEMENT and FACILITATING FORCE scenarios. The inherent positive evaluation of these two scenarios is strengthened by double JOURNEY metaphors and its mixture with other positive schema.

However, differences still arise in the quantity and function of the same conceptual scenario. American media adopt more varied metaphorical expressions with much higher frequency for the DEFACILITATING FORCE scenario. One of its functions is to highlight restrictive measures taken by the Chinese government in the preparation for Beijing Olympics, which is totally absent in Chinese media. Another difference comes from different aspects of Olympic Economy the two media foreground by virtue of the FACILITATING FORCE scenario. Chinese media highlight positive effects of the Olympic Games on the economic development of the host country, while American media dramatize the efforts made by companies in the Olympic market.

In addition, two media use different scenarios for the same aspect of the target domain. For the aim companies want to achieve, American media construct it in the PATH scenario by the general term **goal**, whilst Chinese media refer to it in the FORWARD MOVEMENT scenario by virtue of directional prepositions in metaphoric phrasal verbs. In this connection, American media create a goal-oriented journey against the process-orientated one constructed by Chinese media, which is justified by its outnumbered variations of **pace** and **step** metaphors.

5.4 Representation of Olympic Economy as Sports and Games

5.4.1 Introduction

Both American and Chinese media conceptualize Olympic Economy as competitive sports and games. 170 and 173 SPORT and GAME metaphors are identified in Chinese and American media respectively. This means they produce 1.39 and 2.13 SPORT and GAME metaphors per 1,000 words. These two conceptual domains share the common feature that different participants compete to see which one is better in certain

136

aspects and gets some prize for the advantage. General terms, such as **jìng zhēng** [竞争] as a noun (45 instances) and its English counterpart **competition** (15 instances) conflate such source domains with the business competition in the following two extracts:

(72) 中外品牌的**竞争**方面东道主并没有绝对的优势。

[The host has no absolute advantage in the competition among brands from home and abroad.]

（PD, June 24, 2005）

(73) Foster & Partners, the British architectural firm, won the design **competition** less than five years ago.

(NYT, May 2, 2008)

However, apart from conventional metaphors, Chinese media establish close association between the business competition and the Olympic Games in a creative way through **shāng ào huì** [商奥会] (3 instances) meaning business Olympics, as in the title (74), **jīng jì ào yùn** [经济奥运] (2 instances) meaning economic Olympics, as in (75) and **ào yùn huì** [奥运会], as the Chinese equivalent of the word "Olympics" in the quotation mark (1 instance) in (76). These metaphors enable us to transfer easily the characteristics of this international sports event to Olympic Economoy, and figure out indirectly density, depth, and width of the competition in Olympic Economy the media want to imply.

(74) 更长、更久、更激烈的**商奥会**

[Another More Lasting, Even Longer, and Much Fiercer Olympics in the business world]

(CEW, September 1, 2008)

(75) 距离 2008 北京奥运还有将近两年的时间，但赛场外的 **"经济奥运"** 早已**硝烟弥漫** [7]。

[The 2008 Beijing Olympics is nearly two years away, but the "business Olympics" outside the arena has already been covered with smoke.]

（CEW, October 9, 2006）

(76) 另一场"**奥运会**"的成绩也即将揭晓，那就是赞助商和非赞助商、大企业和小公司、外国企业和本土公司之间的商业**较量**[8]。

[The result of another "Olympics" will be out. It is the business competition between sponsors vs. non-sponsors, big enterprises vs. small companies and foreign vs. local companies.]

（CEW, September 1, 2008）

Such metaphors generate a coherent network of entailments that provides the ground for certain inferences about business processes. Companies involved in Olympic Economy are described conventionally as **players** (15 instances), **rivals** (14 instances), **competitor** (10 instances) and **contenders** (2 instances) in the English data with 41 instances in all. Except for **players**, all of these expressions highlight the competitive feature of the event. The Chinese corpus has the corresponding conventional expressions including **duì shǒu** [对手] (15 instances), **jìng zhēng zhě** [竞争者] (1 instance) and **xuǎn shǒu** [选手] (1 instance), to perform the same function. However, it does not concern the collective efforts of different businesses in the same line or different employees from a same company, which is highlighted in the English corpus by the conventional metaphor **team** (25 instances) that refers basically to a group of people who play a particular sport or game against other similar people, as exemplified in the following extract:

(77) The National Swimming Center's international and multidisciplinary design **team** is composed of the Australian architecture firm PTW, engineers from the Sydney office of Arup, and a group from CCDI.

(BW, July 2, 2008)

The two media employ metaphorical expressions to describe the process of competition in Olympic Economy, including the verbal group **jìng xiāng zhēng duó** [竞相争夺] (2 instances) with the basic sense of contending, and the word **jìng zhēng** [竞争] (4 instances) modified by the adverb **pīn lì** [拼力] and the adjective **jī liè** [激烈], which mean sparing no efforts and being intense respectively. They can convey the intensity of business competition in the Olympic market. In the English corpus, we find such expressions as **compete** (11 instances), **square off** (4 instances) and **go out for** (1 instance) that create the same scenario. The conventional metaphor **compete** collates with **head-to-head** in two cases to depict the fierce competition among different companies.

These SPORT metaphors entail fair and open competition among domestic and foreign firms for the marketing opportunities under the guidance of certain rules, with winners and losers as the result. The winner will be awarded with the **prize** (4 instances), referring to more consumers and higher brand awareness that will bring more profits to companies in the discourse of Olympic Economy. The prize any players inspire most is the **gold medal** (5 instances) or its Chinese equivalent **jīn pái** [金牌] (5 instances). They stand for creatively the most efficient marketing program in the discourse of Olympic Economy. Their collocation with the verbal groups **go for, capture, win** in the English corpus and **zhēng duó** [争夺], **chōng jī** [冲击], **déle** [得了] in the Chinese corpus describe the companies' efforts to realize this inspiration and how it has come true. The Chinese nominal groups **duó jīn mì jué** [夺金秘诀] and **duó jīn diǎn** [夺金点], with the basic sense respectively related to the secret and the vital point to capture gold medals, metaphorically correspond to efficient measures that enable companies to get inspired results in the competition. The successful company is named as **winner** (5 instances) in the English corpus and **guan jūn** [冠军] (1 instance) in the Chinese corpus. The success in the market corresponds to the victory of players in the sports field, which is conveyed by the English metaphoric verb **win** (7 instances), the Chinese metaphors **shèng chū** [胜出] [to excel] (6 instances) and **lì cuò** [力挫] [to beat] (1 instance). There are other expressions that indicate the result in a sports event, such as **wèi liè dì èr míng** [位列第二名] (1 instance), and its corresponding English expression **come in second place** (1 instance).

5.4.2 The RACE Scenario

Companies competing in diverse marketing programs and construction projects in the Chinese market are constructed metaphorically as players in the match court engaging in a variety of sports items.

A RACE scenario is constructed by virtue of 27 Chinese and 37 English metaphors respectively. This scenario promotes the free market ideology, which highlights the idea that companies need mobility in order to be competitive (Boers, 1997).

In the RACE scenario, different types of races correspond to specific features of the Olympic marketing and diverse phases in a race are projected to different periods the marketing programs are supposed to go through. The verb **qǐ pǎo** [起跑] (1 instance), with the basic sense of starting a race, stands for the initiative of marketing programs. Another verb **kuài pǎo** [快跑] (2 instances), which primarily emphasizes the fast speed of a race, describes the fast development of the agent concerned. The leading position in a race expressed by the word **lǐng pǎo** [领跑] (2 instances) is mapped to Yili Milk Industry's advantage in the brand awareness among Chinese companies. The long-distance race of **cháng pǎo** [长跑] (1 instance) highlights continuous efforts made by China Bank in its marketing programs. The scenario in which different racers rush for the best track embedded in the structure **zhēng duó pǎo dào** [争夺跑道] (1 instance) constructs the competition of sports equipment producers for business opportunities in the sports exposition. Chinese media give special attention to the final spurt in a race signaled by the term **chōng cì** [冲刺] (7 instances) with the highest frequency. It stands for intense and strong efforts exerted by sponsors and partners in the final period of Beijing

140

Olympic Marketing Programs in order to achieve as best results as possible. The media also give more light to the race result through **chuàng jì lù** [创记录] or **dǎ pò jì lù** [打破记录] (7 instances in all) and **chā jù** [差距] (6 instances). The first two expressions describe successful companies in the Olympic industry who have achieved goals concerning sales of Olympics-related products, Olympic broadcasting or the huge investment in Olympic construction projects that all the companies in the same line have never arrived at before, just like excellent runners who will set or break a record on the track. The expression **chā jù** [差距] shows in a metaphorical way the disparity between competitive companies and other participants in Olympic Economy.

Similarly, American media also use metaphors derived from race. **Set a record** and **gap** (11 instances in all) perform the same function as their Chinese equivalents **chuàng jì lù** [创记录] and **chā jù** [差距] respectively. Used as both noun and verb, the general notion **race** (2 instances) constructs metaphorically competition between the most famous sportswear brands in the Chinese market, as expressed in (78).

(78) China is better known for making most of the world's sports shoes rather than wearing them, but the world's biggest athletic shoe brands are in a **race** here to change that.

(NYT, January 25, 2005)

The leading position (1 instance) expresses the same meaning as the Chinese word **lǐng pǎo** [领跑]. Like the two phrasal verbs **head the pack** (1 instance) and **lag behind** (5 instances), it describes the racer's position in a race. In the discourse under investigation, the three expressions imply respectively the advantageous and disadvantageous states of the companies in a variety of marketing programs. For example, in the following discourses, Nike is reported to take the lead in competition in Chinese sports shoes market, while InBev's situation is not promising in the Chinese market.

141

(79) Nike **heads the pack**, with 10% of the market.

(BW, March 14, 2005)

(80) Even though InBev is the largest brewer in the world, it has **lagged behind** in the world's largest beer market: China.

(BW, July 14, 2008)

Like the Chinese expression **chōng cì** [冲刺]，**do the victory lap** (1 instance) corresponds metaphorically to the fact that sponsors are ready to take measures in the final period of their Olympic marketing. As the English equivalent of **chōng cì** [冲刺], **sprint** is used only once in the title "a **marathon** rather than a 100m **sprint**" (BW, May 8, 2008) for the theme of technology in the Olympic Games. The **marathon** metaphor is repeated twice in a similar discourse, highlighting the necessity of continuous efforts if China wants to hold a High-Tech Olympics successfully.

The compound noun **finish line** (1 instance) in one title standing for the completion of building projects also triggers the RACE scenario with the entailment that taking part in the building projects is like competing in a race. Such entailment is extended by a set of verbal groups, including **catch up** (3 instances) besides **race** and **set a record**. They talk about reducing the gap between domestic and foreign building firms, the efforts to finish the construction of the new airport in a limited period of time, and the largest investment Beijing pours for Olympic projects respectively.

In the English corpus, we find world-famous sneaker makers are identified as horse riders in a horse race when they compete with each other in the Chinese market, as expressed in the following discourse:

(81) It is now a two-horse **race** between Nike and Adidas.

(NYT, January 28, 2006)

The HORSE RACING scenario is re-activated by such conventional metaphors as **neck-and-neck**, **jockey** and **free-rider** (3 instances in all) when journalists structure ad makers and sneaker makers as horse riders to engage in a horse race. The metaphoric verb **spur** figures significantly in

142

such a scenario with 6 instances. Originally, it depicts the action of a rider, who urges his horse by the spur fixed on the heel of his boot. In the discourse of Olympic Economy like (82), companies, described as horses are urged to take certain strategies. The leaders of these agencies that perform the role of horse riders in the HORSE RACING scenario are back grounded.

(82) Those concerns have **spurred** big foreign agencies to seek out local expertise.

(BW, June 25, 2005)

The HORSE RACING metaphor is particular to American media. This may be explained by the historical root and public popularity of this sport in Western cultures.

We can see that there is no obvious quantitative disparity in the RACE scenario between these two media. Except the particular use of HORSE RACE metaphors in American media, they both adopt concepts concerning the human race to construct various aspects of business competition, in which Chinese media express much concern for efforts in the last period, besides addressing different status of companies in competition as American media do. In addition, the RACE scenario in American media enjoys a wider scope (Kövecses, 2002: 108). Besides the Olympic marketing, it is alluded to in the representation of Olympic technology and building projects.

5.4.3 The BALL GAME Scenario

The media also use lexical terms in ball game sports, including table tennis in Chinese media and basketball or baseball in American media. The metaphorical expressions are listed in Table 5.21, with English terms followed by Chinese ones in the order according to their number of token.

We can see that American media are superior in both type and frequency of this conceptual scenario. The six types of linguistic expressions in it produce nearly three times as many BALL GAME metaphors as the two expressions in Chinese media.

Table 5.21   English and Chinese metaphors for the BALL GAME scenario

Expression	Token	Example of Metaphorical Use
cheerlead	4	Western Olympic Ads **Cheerlead** for China (NYT, July 20, 2008)
score	3	It also **scores** well on the environmentally friendly front, particularly crucial given the current call for greener building practices. (NYT, September 19, 2004)
break into big leagues	3	It's unclear how long it will take the Chinese to really **break into the global big leagues**. (BW, April 24, 2008)
face off against	2	It still has to prove it can **face off against** Nike and Adidas in Beijing and Shanghai—let alone the U.S., where Li-Ning in January opened a small design office in Nike's backyard, Portland, Ore. (BW, May 1, 2008)
beat out	1	The winning team **beat out** two other finalists—Foster & Partners and the United States firm of Kohn Pedersen Fox. (NYT, September 19, 2004)
cry foul	1	Even some leading Chinese architects and urban planners are **crying foul**. (NYT, May 2, 2008)
cā biān qiú [擦边球]	3	各种类型的**擦边球**，还有很多不可控的因素影响着赞助商们奥运营销的效果。 [All kinds of clip-shots as well as many uncontrollable factors will influence marketing results of the sponsors.] (CEW, August 11, 2008)
hǎn tíng [喊停]	2	近期国家体育场工程部分**喊停**，无疑是有关奥运的第二大新闻。 [Recently, the construction of some national sports venues has been called off. This is no doubt the second dramatic news about Olympics.] (CEW, August 23, 2004)

144

The verb **score**, often used together with the noun "point", and the phrasal verb **beat out** construct metaphorically the development achieved by some companies in the Olympic marketing and Olympic building projects. Another phrasal verb **face off against** depicts the action of the competing sides on the court at the beginning of a football or basketball game. In the discourse of Olympic Economy, it implies metaphorically the direct challenge faced by leading domestic sneaker makers when world-famous brands Adidas and Nike were entering Chinese market. The idiom **beak into big leagues** originally alludes to playing a professional sport at the highest level. In the discourse involved, it is concerned with the development of Chinese construction firms and acknowledgement they will receive in the international market. In addition, the verbal phrase **cry foul** conventionally describes the situation when referees give fouls to players who infringe rules. In the English corpus, it creatively refers to the loud voice of some leading Chinese architects and urban planners suggesting to stop some expensive and fashionable megaprojects. The same phenomenon is addressed in the Chinese corpus by the metaphorically used expression **hǎn tíng** [喊停] with the basic sense of calling off.

Moreover, American media use the BALL GAME metaphor to represent the aspect of sports events ignored by Chinese media. For example, the function of cheerleaders in a match, which is constructed by such expression as **cheerlead** in the English corpus. In a match, the cheerleader will organize the audience to cheer for the players to make the match more exciting. In the discourse of marketing, some foreign ad cooperates and sponsors are depicted as cheerleaders since they promote China's nationalism in their marketing programs by cheering for Chinese teams.

Cā biān qiú [擦边球] originally refers to a clip-shot in a table tennis match. A player takes risks by making the ball cut the corner that the contender is desperate to receive. Conventionally, it categorizes any behavior that is on the edge of violating the law and cuts every corner of the regulations. In the discourse concerned, it refers to the strategies adopted by non-official sponsors who spare no efforts to connect with the Olympics. Such a metaphorical representation sheds light on the risks taken and lucky results enjoyed by those sponsors, and thus conceal negative effects official sponsors will suffer. The latter is emphasized in the WAR metaphor in the English data, which will be discussed in the section 5.5.2.

In all, Chinese media have much less SPORT metaphors derived from ball games, but it has metaphors **miáo zhǔn** [瞄准] (4 instances) and **jiàn zài xián shàng** [箭在弦上] (3 instances) that are drawn originally from the sport of shooting. The former basically describes the action of taking aim at the target by gun or arrow. In the marketing discourse, it refers to the inspiration of book developers and business people from Taiwan to obtain business opportunities in Olympic Economy. The latter primarily refers to the moment when the arrow is ready on the string, and conventionally stands for the vital situation that forces people to take action. Correspondingly, in the marketing discourse, it's urgent for companies to adopt measures to offer satisfactory service in the Olympic Games, and try to solve such problems as recessive marketing programs and sustainment of the fast development after the Olympics.

5.4.4 The POKER and CHESS GAME Scenario

The above analyses show that history and public popularity of certain sports items could explain the different choices made by the two media in the use of the SPORT metaphor. However, the more obvious difference between Chinese and American media lies in their conceptualization of Olympic Economy as a game. While its corresponding term "card" or "poker" appear only twice in the English

146

corpus, the lexical term **pái** [牌] appears 23 times in the Chinese corpus, with varying collocations, such as **ào yùn pái** [奥运牌], **wén huà pái** [文化牌], **lǜ pái** [绿牌], **cí shàn pái** [慈善牌]. With the literal meaning of Olympic card, culture card, green card and charity card respectively, they represent in a fresh way diverse marketing strategies, including establishing close relation with the Olympics, promoting local culture, spreading the idea of environmental protection and taking part in charity shows. Apart from the nominal metaphors standing for strategies in the business competition, the verbal group **xǐ pái** [洗牌] [to shuffle] (2 instances) describing the mixing up of the cards for a new game corresponds to the huge change Olympic Economy has brought to some industries. For example, in (83), the participation and performance in the video broadcasting of the Olympics resulted in a new setup of the relevant industry.

(83) 视频牌照与奥运授权是视频网站的一个契机，同时也导致了视频网站行业的重新"**洗牌**"。

[Video licenses and authorization of Olympic Committee offer an opportunity to the video web, but at the same time lead to the new "shuffle" in this line.]

(CEW, August 11, 2008)

Apart from the poker game, there are Chinese metaphors derived from the chess game, such as **bó yì** [博弈] (1 instance) and **yī pán qí** [一盘棋] (2 instances) with the basic sense of playing chess and a game of chess respectively. They stand for metaphorically the general competition among companies in the marketing program. In a typical example (84), the scenario of playing chess is enriched by a new metaphorical expression **xīn zhāo** [新招] (1 instance) conveying a new move on the chess plate besides the repetition of the same metaphorical expression **yī pán qí** [一盘棋]. The identifying progress in this discourse alludes directly to the new marketing strategies adopted by companies.

147

(84) 把赞助奥运会比做**一盘棋**，众多赞助企业各显神通的**竞争**策略则成为**这盘棋**上不断走出的**新招**。

[If comparing the Olympics with a chess game, competitive strategies demonstrated continuously by every business will become the new moves on the board.]

(CEW, January 1, 2004)

Other metaphorical expressions, including **yí chū qí zhāo** [一出奇招] (1 instance) meaning an odd move and **yī zhāo miào qí** [一招妙棋] (1 instance) denoting a smart move perform the similar function, standing for novel and marvelous strategies adopted by marketing competitors. Our knowledge about the chess game tells us the decisive role played by one move for the final result. This enhances the vital position of important strategies in the total marketing program for a company. The scenario of playing chess is also extended by the lexicalized metaphor **jú miàn** [局面] (1 instance) standing primarily for changes on the chessboard. It is used in the discourse of Olympic Economy to describe the general situation in the business competition. The word **shōu gōng** [收官] (1 instance), depicting the end of a weiqi game is employed for the last period of the Olympic marketing programs. These rich game scenarios dramatize the central position of marketing strategies in Chinese media.

In sum, the GAME metaphor is much productive in Chinese media than in American media. It enables the media to foreground measures taken by companies in the business competition and address the influence of Olympic Economy on China's industry.

5.4.5 The GAMBLING Scenario

Comparatively, American media have few instantiations of the GAME metaphor. However, it conceptualizes the businesss competition in terms of gambling. The word **stakes** (5 instances) referring originally to

148

money risked in a gamble is mapped to abstract risk faced by sponsors and partners, since they have to pay a great amount of money for their exclusive rights, but are in the danger of not getting the promised returns. Moreover, ticketing system is described as a **lottery** (2 instances), in which people, who are lucky enough to get the ticket for the Olympics, are like the winners by random selection in a gambling.

The metaphorical construction of high risks faced by sponsors and partners is echoed in Chinese media by expressions taken from the same source domain of gambling, including **bó** [博] (3 instances) and **dǔ** [赌] (2 instances) with the same basic sense of gambling, **yā bǎo** [押宝] (2 instances) as the equivalent of the English verb "stake", and **yíng jiā** [赢家] (3 instances) referring to the winner in the gambling. The verb **bó** [博], used together with the quantifier **yī bǎ** [一把] means gambling only once, implying Chinese brands' plan to make participation in Olympic Economy as a turning point in their development. Another verb **dǔ** [赌] establishes the direct mapping between participating in Olympic Marketing with gambling. While the nominal group **háo dǔ** [豪赌], referring originally to the high-stake gambling highlights the high price that sponsors or partners have to pay, with the risk not obtaining proportional returns for their investment. The uncertainties of such investment are enhanced by the verb **yā bǎo** [押宝] in the discourse concerning ad corporates who bet on sports stars to promote their brands. The successful sponsors and partners called **yíng jiā** [赢家] in such a risky business activity are as lucky as winners in a gambling.

The analyses of the GAMBLING metaphor illustrate that both Chinese and American media highlight the risk, hazard, uncertainty and related costs and values of the Olympics. Despite of this common point, Chinese media alone shed light on opportunities faced by Chinese companies.

All in all both media shed light on fair and open competition in

Olympic Economy through converging it with sports events and games. In spite of this overarching similarity, they give priority to different scenarios for the same target concept in the business competition. This could be explained by the popularity of different sports and games in these two cultures. More linguistic realizations of the POKER and CHESS GAME scenario in Chinese media demonstrate its special attention to the importance of efficient strategies in the marketing and opportunities given to domestic companies. What's more, the problems of Olympic construction projects, which are highlighted by JOURNEY and LIVING ORGANISM metaphors, are stressed again, but from a different perspective. Instead of the financial pressure on the host city, negative response of domestic experts is highlighted this time in both media. As far as building projects are concerned, American media use more metaphors to dramatize the open and fair competition in the bid and construction between leading building firms. Among them, the disadvantages of Chinese firms have been emphasized.

5.5 Representation of Olympic Economy as a War

5.5.1 Introduction

Metaphors from the domain of conflict have been found to be prolific across a range of domains including argument and love, because it is the basic component of both animal and human interaction (Kövecses, 2002: 74-75; Lakoff & Johnson, 1980: 62; Liu & Yu, 2007). It includes a wide range of violent activities, from fist-fights to military attacks (Ritchie, 2003: 135) and emphasizes the confrontational, competitive, aggressive and potentially destructive effects of the target domain, more generally antagonistic nature of it. In the discourse concerned, we found 182 and 186 instances of the CONFLICT metaphor in Chinese and American media respectively. For example, the idiom **míng zhēng àn dòu** [明争暗斗] with the basic sense of striving openly and secretly dramatizes various forms of competition among the enterprises concerned in the Chinese discourse (85). The English idiom **gang up on** in (86) primarily describes the situation in which a group is formed to attack someone. This corresponds to the disadvantageous situation Nike was in when several rivals united to compete against it in the sportswear market.

(85) 这三家企业本是业内**明争暗斗**的角色。

[These three enterprises are the rivals in the same line striving openly and secretly.]

（PD, March 17, 2006）

(86) Nike was operating at 80 percent efficiency under Mr. Perez— an awkward position to be in when its biggest rivals are **ganging up on** it.

(NYT, January 28, 2006)

The great majority of metaphorical terms for CONFLICT metaphors, amounting to 92.9% and 89.2% respectively in both corpora indicate that they conceive of Olympic Economy as a war. Both of them use general notions, including **zhàn zhēng** [战争], **zhàn yì** [战役], **zhàn dòu** [战斗], and corresponding English words **war** or **battle**, **campaign**, **struggle** to refer to competition in sponsorship, licensing programs, broadcasting rights, and the intense construction of Olympic venues. In all, they reach 10 and 54 instances in Chinese and American media respectively. The sharp disparity in quantity lies in the most prevalent metaphorical expression **campaign** with the total token of 44. This could be explained by its entrenchment in the English vocabulary to link the business world and the war. As in the following examples, the above general terms in most cases dramatize the aggressive feature of intense competition in Olympic Economy.

(87) 一场没有硝烟的**战争** [9] 伴随着奥运的临近愈演愈烈。

[A war without fire becomes increasingly fierce with the arrival of the

Olympics.]

(88) Analysts and executives agree that the biggest **battle** will unfold in China.

(NYT, January 28, 2006)

Our knowledge of war tells us the main participants in a war are armed forces from two or more states or countries. They are supposed to fight for territory or resources at the cost of many people's life and a large amount of money. The war takes place on the battleground, involving both generals and soldiers. The generals are commanders, deciding on the strategies and arms; the soldiers will be positioned in different ranks due to their experiences in the battle. The war will go through different stages, leading to a decisive victory of one side.

Correspondingly, in Olympic Economy, two or more companies will compete for business opportunities in Chinese market and in certain lines with their human and financial resources. The crew and boss are like the soldiers and commander, with the latter having the power and intelligence to develop marketing strategies. Successful strategies will enable companies to obtain sponsorship, licensing, broadcasting rights and the bid for megaprojects that promise bigger market share, more economic profits and higher brand awareness. These various aspects of Olympic Economy as the target conceptual domain are structured by a number of metaphorical scenarios, including ARMED FORCES, BATTLE FIELD, STRATEGY, and BATTLE. The ARMED FORCES scenario is realized by 16 types of Chinese metaphors with 25 tokens and 5 types of English metaphors with 7 tokens. In such a scenario, companies are decribed as different types of armies or soldiers, such as the Chinese expressions **lǐng jūn rén wù** [领军人物] [the leading character] (2 instances), **háng wǔ** [行伍] [soldiers] (2 instances), **zhèng pái jūn** [正牌军] [a regular army] (1 instance) and **yóu jī duì** [游击队] [a guerrilla] (1 instance), and the English expressions **veteran** (3 instances) and **combatant** (1 instance). Companies in cooperation are represented by the equivalent Chinese and English expressions **lián méng** [联盟] (3 instances) and **alliance** (1 instance). In the BATTLE FIELD scenario, the host city and co-host cities are depicted as the battle ground, which is realized by 8 types of Chinese metaphorical expressions with 12 tokens and only one type of English metaphorical expression. For example, **qián xiàn** [前线] [front line] (3 instances), **bīng jiā bì zhēng zhī dì** [兵家必争之地] [spots of fighting] (1 instance) and **battle line** (1 instance) highlight the important position of these cities in the business competition. In the rest of this chapter, detailed analyses will be presented for another two scenarios, which figure more significantly due to much higher frequency of realizations.

5.5.2 The BATTLE Scenario

The most outstanding scenario constructed by WAR metaphors in Chinese and American media is that of a battle, accounting for 44.8% and 39.7% of the total WAR metaphors with 59 and 60 instances in the two media respectively (see Table 5.22 and Table 5.23). First of all, the Chinese noun **tiǎo zhàn** [挑战] and its English counterpart **challenge** denote the potential of a war, in which one country or state threatens or enrages the other that stimulates two sides to prepare for the coming war. Such situation is conventionally transferred to the discourse of Olympic Economy, framing the difficult tasks, huge threat and fierce competition it had produced. However, the highlighted origin, content and target of the challenges are quite different between these two media.

In Chinese media, international business rules and operations, the fresh experiences as sponsors or licensers, threat from international companies and competition among domestic companies in the same line impose great pressure on domestic businesses, as expressed in the following sentences.

(89) 举办奥运会基本上按商业原则和市场的规则来办，这将是内资面临的**挑战**。

[Holding Olympics basically follows business regulations and market rules. This will become a challenge to inner financed companies.]

(PD, October 29, 2006)

(90) 除了对自身品牌运作和市场营销能力的考验，赞助商面对的另一个**挑战**来自于竞争对手。

[Besides standing up to the tests of their brand' operation and marketing capacity, sponsors have to face challenges from their rivals.]

（CEW, August 11, 2008）

Table 5.22　Chinese WAR metaphors for the BATTLE scenario

Sub-conceputal Element	Express-ion	Pinyin	English Translation	Individual Token	Sub-token
INITIATION	挑战	tiǎo zhàn	challenge	10	17
	备战	bèi zhàn	ready for the war	3	
	迎战	yíng zhàn	to accept a challenge	2	
	立军令状	lì jūn lìng zhuàng	to write a pledge to receive military punishment because of the failing	1	
	实战演习	shí zhàn yǎn xí	drilling of actual combat	1	

154

continued:

Sub-conceputal Element	Expression	Pinyin	English Translation	Individual Token	Sub-token
ATTACK & DEFENCE	进军	jìn jūn	to advance	4	13
	突围	tū wéi	to break out of an encirclement	2	
	挺进	tǐng jìn	to advance forward	2	
	攻防	gōng fáng	attack and defence	1	
	防御	fáng yù	to defend	1	
	围攻	wéi gōng	siege	1	
	集中发力	jí zhōng fā lì	to exert collective force	1	
	扩张	kuò zhāng	to expand	1	
MANNER	抢滩	qiǎng tān	to forestall	4	13
	大战	dà zhàn	a large-scale battle	3	
	决战	jué zhàn	a decisive battle	2	
	争夺战	zhēng duó zhàn	the war to fight for something	1	
	拦击阻截	lán jī zǔ jié	to intercept and block	1	
	闪电战	shǎn diàn zhàn	a blitz	1	
	攻坚战	míng zhēng àn dòu	to strife openly and secretly	1	

continued:

Sub-conceputal Element	Expression	Pinyin	English Translation	Individual Token	Sub-token
	进驻	jìn zhù	to enter and occupy	3	
	一举拿下	yī jǔ ná xià	to take down at one stroke	2	
	登陆	dēng lù	to land	1	
	占据	zhàn jù	to occupy	1	
	占领	zhàn lǐng	to occupy	1	
	战胜	zhàn shèng	to conquer	1	
RESULT	重创	zhòng chuāng	heavy losses	1	11
	一炮打响	yī pào dǎ xiǎng	to win initial success	1	
	三国鼎立	sān guó dǐng lì	separation of powers among three kingdoms	1	
	划分势力范围	huà fēn shì lì fàn wéi	to divide areas for forces	1	
	重整格局	chóng zhěng gé jú	to reconstruct situation	1	

continued:

Sub-conceputal Element	Expression	Pinyin	English Translation	Individual Token	Sub-token
STATE	硝烟弥漫	xiāo yān mí màn	be full of smoke of gunfire	1	5
	如火如荼	rú huǒ rú tú	be like a raging fire	1	
	呐喊声	nà hǎn shēng	the sound of whooping	1	
	群雄争霸	qún xióng zhēng bà	a large number of heroes contend for hegemony	1	
	火药味	huǒ yào wèi	the smell of gunpowder	1	

In the face of these challenges, domestic companies are willing to engage in Olympic Economy, like armies are brave enough to "accept the war". They get ready for the impending difficulties through a variety of means including motivating and training their employers or getting familiar with international practices. This sub-scenario is instantiated in Chinese media through such linguistic devices as **bèi zhàn** [备战], **yíng zhàn** [迎战], **lì jūn lìng zhuàng** [立军令状] and **shí zhàn yǎn xí** [实战演习]. Thse expressions are often used together with such expressions as **jī huì** [机会] and **fā zhǎn** [发展], indicating opportunity and development are companions to difficulties for Chinese businesses. This implies the companies' performance in Olympic Economy is quite vital for their future development and constitutes one part of their total developing strategy.

Apart from difficulties individual companies would overcome in

Olympic Economy, Chinese media represent metaphorically the pressure that China's economy as a whole has to face. For example, the following discourse talks about the challenge to sustain the fast development of China's economy by taking advantage of Olympic infrastructure after the Beijing Olympic Games.

(91) 但是奥运会后如何因应这些基础硬件建设的发展**带动**产业、不影响奥运会后的公共事业投资等，都将是重大**挑战** [10]。

[This will be great challenges to facilitate industries by the development of infrastructure construction and not to affect investment into public projects after the Olympic Economy.]

(PD, February 10, 2006)

Table 5.23   English WAR metaphors for the BATTLE scenario

Sub-conceputal Element	Expression	Individual Token	Sub-token
INITIATION	challenge	21	22
	recruit	1	
ATTACK & DEFENCE	fight	9	13
	wage on	2	
	launch offensive	2	
MANNER	ambush	16	22
	blitz	3	
	catapult	1	
	foray	1	
	expand	1	
RESULT	withdraw	1	3
	give some ground to	1	
	conquer	1	

While in American media, the extracts concerning challenges refer to both domestic and foreign companies, with 8 tokens to the former and 10 to the latter. For Chinese companies, the media foreground their poor

158

brand value and the emergency to promote them, but never mention the threat coming from the foreign company directly. Look at one of such examples (92). The media seem to highlight the first step Chinese companies should take is to overcome their own drawbacks before they could stand up against the external threat.

(92) The long-term **challenge** for companies is to invest to develop goods of greater value that can sell for higher prices both at home and abroad.

(BW, October. 8, 2007)

As far as foreign companies are concerned, the challenges come from China's regional market and the communication with local governments, as expressed in (93) and (94), besides the threat from Chinese companies, which is highlighted in (95). It is not very hard to explain since Beijing, as the host city of the Olympics, has created a lot of business opportunities attracting many foreign companies. Their new arrival must lead to conflict with the local businesses.

(93) One **challenge** for global agencies is tailoring ads to the regional sensibilities of China's 1.3 billion citizens.

(BW, June 25, 2005)

(94) N.B.A.'s **challenge** has been to win government agencies' approval for arena construction.

(NYT, September 19, 2007)

(95) A looming **challenge** for all the market leaders is likely to be fast-developing Chinese upstarts.

(BW, March 14, 2005)

Based on the above analyses, we can conclude that Chinese media create a more complex scenario of initiating a war than the American counterpart, in which Chinese companies face the threat not only from domestic rivals, but also from multinationals. Confronted with a large number of competitive foreign enterprises, domestic companies are forced to make breakthrough in various aspects, just like soldiers in the battlefield who have been surrounded by powerful enemies and have to choose to "break out of an encirclement" for the hope of survival. A series of metaphoric verbs **jìn jūn** [进军], **tū wéi** [突围], **tǐng jìn** [挺进], **wéi gōng** [围攻], **jí zhōng fā lì** [集中发力] and **kuò zhāng** [扩张] establish the association between the maneuver of armies toward their intended destination and marching into new territory with the attempts of domestic companies to enter new lines and markets. The media also conceptualize companies' fight for profits and against competition in the market through linguistic expressions **gōng fáng** [攻防] and **fáng yù** [防御] as soldiers attack and defend in the war. As for the competition with domestic businesses, intertextual metaphors (Zinken, 2003) that are specifically culturally situated are chosen to frame this complex and abstract phenomenon. For example, **qún xióng zhēng bà** [群雄争霸] and **sān guó dǐng lì** [三国鼎立] in (93) remind us of a specific historical period when the Three Kingdoms—Wei, Shu and Wu—divided China from A.D. 222 to A.D. 228. Their division of political power is transferred to the head-to-head competition among the three leading producers in the beer market. They are so equal with each other that it is quite difficult for each of them to obtain decisive advantages over the other two. This sub-scenario associates the turbulent historical period with the competition among many companies, and thus enhances the intensified competition among different beer producers in the Chinese market and establishes the close relationship between the political event and the business activity. Another interesting point about this discourse is that it is a typical instance of mixed metaphors. The discussed WAR metaphors are embedded in the PERFORMANCE metaphors activated by the verbal expressions **shàng yǎn** [上演] and **chàng** [唱], and the nominal expressions **xì** [戏], **hǎo xì** [好戏] and **wǔ tái** [舞台]. The PERFORMANCE metaphor will be discussed in the section 6.4. Such juxtaposition highlights the exciting competition of Olympic Economy.

(96) 啤酒市场上正**上演**着**群雄争霸**的**好戏**……在奥运经济的**舞台**上，**三国鼎立**的**戏**恐怕更不好**唱**。

[In the beer market, a good play is just beginning. Many heroes contend for hegemony… On the stage of Olympic Economy, it is not easy to put on the play about the three kingdoms who contend for hegemony.]

(PD, March 12, 2006)

In contrast, American media highlight threat faced by internationals whose competition has shifted from the traditional market of the United States to the quite new one in China and will become much fiercer, which is implied by the neighboring adverb "increasingly" and the superlative "biggest" that modify the action of **wage** and the event of **battle** in (97). More than one term from the concept of war, including **war, fought, wage** and **battle** are used in the same discourse. This means the same scenario has been activated more than once. Such double metaphors enhance the aggressive nature of the competition between big internationals.

(97) The sneaker **wars**, once **fought** on the basketball courts and football fields of the United States, are increasingly being **waged** on the track fields of China. …Analysts and executives agree that the biggest **battle** will unfold in China, the world's most populous country.

(NYT, January 28, 2006)

In the construction of the BATTLE scenario, the noun **ambush** stands out with 18 tokens. It originally means an attack from a concealed position. When put together with "marketing" or "marketer" in the following discourses, a blended conceptual space is produced, in which some companies adopt recessive marketing strategies with the purpose to promote themselves in connection with the Olympic Games without paying the sponsorship fee and avoid breaking any laws. The high frequency (32%) of this metaphor indicates that American media show deep concern about this phenomenon, which is back grounded in Chinese media, since only once do the latter use the nominal phrase **yǐn xìng yíng xiāo shì chǎng** [隐性营销市场] [recessive marketing] in its discourse to refer to the same phenomenon and do not dramatize it with the WAR metaphor. In American media, the nominal metaphors with **ambush** act as the identified in the relational processes. For example, in (98), it is identified as a **flashpoint**, conceptualizing the unofficial sponsor's marketing in terms of dangerous things that could lead to explosion. The negative categorization implies recessive marketing programs will impose threat on the interests of official sponsors.

(98) **Ambush marketing** has long been a **flashpoint** at the Olympics.

(NYT, July 11, 2008)

In other cases, these nominal metaphors appear in material processes as goals at which metaphoric actions such as **clamp down** in (99) and **fight off** in (100) are directed. All these expressions convey the necessity to restrict this unofficial marketing, pointing to an ideologically vested negative evaluation of "the ambush marketers" as victims. These echo and to some extent, strengthen the negative attitude of the media towards this marketing strategy. In this connection, the official sponsors are justified to **fight back** and **launch its offensive** to protect themselves.

(99) The restrictions are meant to **clamp down** on so-called **ambush marketers**.

(100) They also try to **fight off ambush marketers** as best they can.

(NYT, June 1, 2008)

The representation of the recessive marketing in terms of **ambush** and **cā biān qiú** [擦边球] reveals different perspectives of American and Chinese media to look at the same business phenomenon. Chinese media think about it from the point view of non-official sponsors or suppliers who don't enjoy advantages in the Olympic market, whilst American media consider it from the perspective of official sponsors or suppliers, for whom such a marketing strategy will threaten their exclusive rights in the market. The different perspectives reflect their different views on the recessive marketing.

Except for difficulties official sponsors and partners have to overcome, the metaphoric verb **fight** dramatizes difficulties the host country has to deal with in such collocations as "**fight** piracy", "**fight** Olympic Traffic" and "**fight** against environmental degradation". These social and economic issues, including property rights, traffic problems and environmental pollution have raised a great deal of criticism across the world in the preparation for Beijing Olympics.

All the other terms in Table 5.23 with the semantic orientation to describe the process of a battle are employed by American media to represent various marketing activities carried out by famous multinational companies covering a variety of lines.

(101) Rival sportswear brands like Reebok and Nike have **recruited** sports stars like Yao Ming, the Shanghai-born center of the Houston Rockets, and Liu Xiang, China's gold-medalist hurdler, as icons of a confident sports-loving nation.

(NYT, January 25, 2005)

(102) There is, in fact, one famous example of a company that **catapulted** over its rival by tying itself to the Olympics.

(NYT, June 1, 2008)

(103) Major League Baseball and the National Football League are making strong pushes to do their own marketing **blitzes** in China.

(NYT, August 27, 2008)

(104) Auntie Anne's Pretzels plans to open three outlets in Beijing in the coming months, its first **foray** into China.

(NYT, March 30, 2008)

(105) Adidas and Nike, the world's two biggest sneaker brands, are **aggressively expanding** retail outlets in China and bringing over some of their biggest athletic stars, forceful or determined: an aggressive salesman.

(NYT, September 13, 2008)

The metaphoric verbs **recruit** and **catapult** originally mean enlisting people for military service and shooting forwards or upwards violently respectively in the concept of war. In the above examples, **recruit** is used to metaphorize the preparation of international companies to enter the Chinese market by inviting super sports stars in China to perform as their image prolocutors, while **catapult** connotes that the agent, the Vista, used to win decisive advantage over its rivals by engaging into Olympic marketing programs and created great losses to its competitors. The metaphoric nouns **blitz** and **foray** denote the violent and sustained attack by enemy aircraft and the initial attempt in military advance respectively in the battlefield. In the discourse of Olympic Economy, the former constructs how the sports organizations have carried out intense and large-scale promotion activities that produce overwhelming effect in the Chinese market and the latter indicates the hotel concerned has succeeded in opening its first branch in China. This way to conflate business activities with the manner of fight is realized by more varied Chinese metaphors, including **qiǎng tān** [抢滩], **dà zhàn** [大战], **jué zhàn** [决战], **zhēng duó zhàn** [争夺战], **lán jī zǔ jié** [拦击阻截], **shǎn diàn zhàn** [闪电战], **gōng jiān zhàn** [攻坚战]. Comparatively, the verb **expand** in (105) is more conventional, implying the sportswear producer of Adidas has increased its investment and intensified its activities in China and obtained more market share in this area. The collocation of the metaphoric adverb **aggressively** shows its forcedness and determinedness for such strategies.

Both Chinese and American media conflate the result of a battle with that of the business competition. However, there are 10 types of Chinese linguistic metaphors and only 3 types of English metaphors for this function. Apart from the sharp disparity in quantity, the progress of domestic companies in the Olympic marketing and their success in obtaining acknowledgement in the global market are depicted only in Chinese media through such metaphorical expressions as **yī jǔ ná xià** [一

举拿下], **dēng lù** [登陆], and **zhàn lǐng** [占领]. In addition, the Chinese expressions **rú huǒ rú tú** [如火如荼] and **xiāo yān mí màn** [硝烟弥漫] describe the Chinese market as a battle field, where domestic and foreign companies are involved in a bitter war. Such metaphorical representation is absent in American media.

In this connection, we can conclude that Chinese media construct a more comprehensive battle scenario. It covers not only competition among domestic brands, but also that between domestic and foreign companies instead of focusing on the latter alone as American media do. It dramatizes difficulties as well as opportunities that domestic companies face in Olympic Economy. More varied metaphors describing the fight and situation on the battle field imply jointly the intense competition in the Chinese market. American media shed more light on difficulties companies, especially multinationals have to overcome in Olympic Economy by virtue of the BATTLE scenario. The media also emphasize the frustration suffered by Chinese companies.

5.5.3 STRATEGY Metaphors

Besides the BATTLE scenario, STRATEGY metaphors are another important group representing Olympic Economy as a war in both Chinese and American media, with 43 Chinese and 18 English tokens respectively. They have equivalent expressions, such as **strategy** and **tactic** against **zhàn lüè** [战略], **cè lüè** [策略] and **zhàn shù** [战术]. Among them, **strategy** and **zhàn lüè** [战略] are significant, taking up 83.3% and 70.1% of English and Chinese STRATEGY metaphors. As conventional metaphors in English and Chinese languages, they perform the same function in the discourse of Olympic Economy to represent marketing measures taken by companies, as exemplified by the following discourses:

(106) 从企业自身的**战略**来讲，赞助奥运也是公司国际化品牌**战略**的关键举措。

[As far as companies' strategy is concerned, sponsoring the Olympics is a vital measure for their strategy of brand internationalization.]

(CEW, March 19, 2007)

(107) In China, the Western multinationals will pursue a much more **aggressive strategy**.

(BW, April 22, 2008)

The Chinese discourse (106) represents that participation in Olympic Economy is an important step in the internationalization, linking companies' performance in Olympic Economy with their holistic development. The English discourse (107) conflates the efforts of multinationals in the Chinese market with the strategies taken by armed forces on the battle field. Modified by another CONFLICT metaphor **aggressive** in its comparative degree, the media shed light on the intense marketing competition these foreign companies had never experienced.

When we examine the co-text of STRATEGY metaphors more closely, we find in American media some metaphors with Chinese cultural background, including **Mao Zedong strategy** and **paper-tiger strategy** in the following extracts:

(108) "Li-Ning is using the **Mao Zedong strategy**: build expertise in second- and third-tier cities," says Zou Marketing General Manager Terry Rhoads, an industry veteran who spent nine years with Nike China before founding Zou two years ago.

(BW, March 14, 2005)

(109) Some branding experts say the **paper-tiger strategy** is paying off.

(BW, May 1, 2008)

The WAR metaphor **Mao Zedong strategy** is quite outstanding due to its rich Chinese historical background in spite of its low frequency in the English corpus. As the first president of People's Republic of China, Mao used to propose a rich set of strategies that have been of importance in the Chinese revolution and construction.

The co-text of this metaphor "second- and third-tier cities" activates the source domain of the first civil war in China that broke out at the end of 1920s. **Mao Zedong strategy** refers to the military principle put forward by Mao Zedong at that time. It led the people in the fight to establish revolutionary bases in areas where the enemy's control was weak and encircle cities from rural areas. BW uses this military strategy creatively when it reports the marketing programs of Li-Ning, one local sportswear enterprise that is threatened by such powerful international enterprises as Nike and Adidas: open the expertise in middle- and small-sized cities instead of competing directly with the international giants in big cities like Beijing and Shanghai. Through the conceptual blending that is illustrated in Figure 5.1, we can infer that the company has chosen to strengthen its base in small cities ignored by its international rivals before it grows as strong as them. This highlights how Chinese local companies survive in the fierce competition, and simultaneously makes it clear that they are not competitive enough to accept the challenge launched by international rivals.

Such negative evaluation of Chinese companies is highlighted in another conceptualization of Li-Ning's marketing strategy, **paper-tiger strategy**. **Paper tiger** is the literal English translation of the Chinese phrase **zhǐ lǎo hǔ** [纸老虎], meaning something that seems as threatening as a tiger, but is really harmless. **Paper-tiger strategy** dramatizes the reality that Li-Ning tries to create the illusion of being a global enterprise despite its nearly-total reliance on its home market. The satirical tone of this metaphor enhances the media's negative attitude towards Chinese businesses and illuminates the unbalanced power between them and internationals in the competition.

Among 43 Chinese STRATEGY metaphors, 5 of them address Olympic construction projects. Without any exception, all these 5 instances are used in the context concerning the contribution of these construction projects to the development of the host city. Look at one typical example:

Source (Input space 1)	Generic Space	Target (Input space 2)
the Red Army led by Mao Zedong	a weak party	Li-Ning
the National Revolutionary Army	a strong party	big internationals
a war	a conflict	business competition
establish political and military base in countries and small cities where strong enemies have not occupied	specific strategy used by the weak party	build expertise in second- and third-tier cities
the survival and increasing strength of the Red Army	the perceived goal through such strategy	the goal the company wants to achieve in the marketing

Blending Space

Li-Ning has chosen to strengthen its power in small cities ignored by its international rivals before it grows as strong as them.

Figure 5. 1   Conceptual blending of the metaphor "Mao Zedong strategy"

(110) "两轴、两带、多中心"的**战略**规划，使人们的居住理念正在逐渐改变。

[The strategic planning of "two axes, two districts and diverse centers" is changing people's residential concept gradually.]

(PD, June 17, 2005)

The context tells us these metaphors emphasize that Olympic construction projects should be integrated into the macro planning of Beijing, and will bring profound changes to people's life. This function is absent in English STRATEGY metaphors.

In sum, the two media represent marketing measures of both domestic and foreign companies in Olympic Economy in terms of conventional

STRATEGY metaphors, in which American media depict the actions of leading Chinese companies through conceptual blends **Mao Zedong strategy** and **paper-tiger strategy**. The entailments point to the inferiority of Chinese companies in the business competition, which implies negative evaluation of the media on Chinese enterprises. Apart from marketing, Chinese STRATEGY metaphors enjoy a wider scope (Kövecses, 2002: 108) in the sense of being adopted in the representation of Olympic construction projects, in which their contribution to the development of Beijing is metaphorically dramatized.

The above analyses demonstrate that both Chinese and American media conflate Olympic Economy with a war, drawing readers' attention to the aggressive and potentially destructive effect of the competition in Olympic Economy and great efforts the companies involved have to make for survival and triumph. However, Chinese media seem to have given more preference to the aggressive aspect of the competition, considering its richer varieties of linguistic realizations. The primary difference lies in the diverse BATTLE scenarios created by English and Chinese metaphorical representations. English metaphors emphasize the conflict between great internationals in the Chinese market and give little attention to Chinese businesses except in the topic of the recessive marketing, to which they express critical attitudes through the linguistic metaphor of **ambush**. In contrast, Chinese metaphors put Chinese companies in the central position of the BATTLE scenario that break out not only among themselves but between them and internationals. Such differences may be to some extent explained by their geographical locations, but still they reflect American media's negative attitudes towards Chinese participants in Olympic Economy in terms of influence and economic faith. Such negative evaluation is strengthened by some English STRATEGY metaphors, which don't concern the contribution of Olympic Economy to China's development that is a focus of Chinese metaphors.

5.6 Summary

The analyses of the four most frequent metaphorical patterns illustrate the overarching similarities between these two media in the representation of Olympic Economy. Both of them talk about the mobility in the business world and the progess made by business subjects in terms of biological growth of living organism and the advance in a journey. They also underscore the fair and open competition in Olympic Economy through convergence of it with sports events and games. The common WAR metaphor gives light to the aggressive and potentially destructive effects of the business competition and great efforts needed for survival and triumph in the market.

In these shared metaphorical patterns, common conceptual scenarios are constructed to perform the same functions. Both media construct Olympic Economy by virtue of basic human experience—including identifying the active participation of companies in Olympic Economy with human rational behaviors, and conflating the power of this international sports business and the state of companies in it with social status and relation of human beings. The PATH scenario represents metaphorically the whole process of business activities in Olymic Economy. FORWARD MOVEMENT and FACILITATING FORCE scenarios are created in the two media to highlight the achievements in both Olympic markeing and construction projects and the effective measures taken by the Chinese government for the operation of Olympic Economy. The DEFACILITATING FORCE scenario is used for the difficulties that have to be overcome by individual companies and local governments. RACE and BALL GAME scenarios highlight intense business competition in Olympic Economy. Its depth and extent is enhanced by the BATTLE scenario in the two media. The vital role of

170

strategies in business success is dramatized by the POKER GAME scenario and STRATEGY metaphors in the concept of war. Additionally, both media address the risks faced by economic subjects through the GAMBLING scenario. These shared scenarios are even realized by equivalent expressions in these two media.

In spite of overarching similarities, differences arise when we look at the quantitative disparity and diverse functions of the same conceptual scenario. As far as the quantitative disparity is concerned, Chinese media seem to have given more priority to the aggressive aspect of Olympic Economy, considering the richer varieties of linguistic realizations of the BATTLE scenario. The two conceptual elements, HUMAN LIFE and PLANT LIFE constitute the large majority of LIVING ORGANISM metaphors in American media, but only HUMAN LIFE metaphors enjoy priority in Chinese media. This difference shows that American media prefer to emphasize both rational reasoning and psychological factors in Olympic Economy on the one hand, and natural development without human interference on the other hand. In the common HUMAN LIFE metaphors, more instances of Chinese expressions drawn from human social relationship in the construction of Olympic Economy shed more light on the attraction of this business event. Similarly, priority given to the STRENGTH scenario and the LIFE SPAN as well as HEALTH scenrios in American and Chinese media respectively highlight different aspects of companies they signifcantly dramatize: companies' power and influence in the former and their growth and image in the latter. Apart from these, the DEFACILITATING FORCE scenario with much more tokens in American media transfer its inherent negative evaluation to anything it represent, including restrictive measures taken by the Chinese government in the preparation for Beijing Olympics, which is totally absent in Chinese media. By virtue of specific sports items, Chinese media highlight the importance of efficient strategies in the marketing and opportunities given to domestic companies, which is not addressed in American media.

Differences are also produced by different functions the same metaphor or scenario performs between the two media. For example, the shared metaphor COMPANIES ARE ANIMALS highlights diverse aspects of Olympic Economy in them: the fierce competition in Olympic Economy and its positive influence on some industries emphasized by Chinese media and the negative attitudes of American media towards construction projects for Beijing Olympics. The FACILITATING FORCE scenarios in them also dramatize different aspects of Olympic Economy: positive effects of the Olympics on the economic development of the host country in Chinese media, while the great efforts made by companies in the Olympic market in American media. In addition, American media use the BATTLE scenario to emphasize the conflict between great internationals in Chinese market and give little attention to Chinese businesses except in the topic of the recessive marketing, to which they express critical attitudes through the **ambush** metaphor. In contrast, Chinese media put Chinese companies in the central position of the BATTLE scenario, in which the war breaks out not only among themselves but between them and internationals. Such differences may be to some extent explained by their geographical locations, but still they reflect American media's negative attitudes towards Chinese participants' influence and economic faith in the market.

For the same scenario, the lexical choice could underline different aspects of related entities and events in Olympic Economy. For instance, some metaphorical expressions derived from rational human behaviors in the representation of companies reveal the social responsibility Chinese media emphasize that companies should take up in Olympic Economy. This social aspect of companies is not addressed in American media. Moreover, the neighboring co-text of a metaphor could activate specific conceptual blending. For example, the modifiers of STRATEGY

172

metaphors in American media results in particular evaluative meaning.

Besides, the two media use different scenarios for the same aspect of the target domain. For the inspiration of companies, American media address it in the PATH scenario by the general term **goal**, whilst Chinese media refer to it in the FORWARD MOVEMENT scenario, in which directional prepositions in metaphoric phrasal verbs mark the destination explicitly. This leads to a goal-oriented journey created by American media against the process-oriented one in Chinese media. What's more, different metaphorical patterns, the SPORT and GAME metaphor and the WAR metahpor for recessive marketing programs reflect their different perspectives to talk about the same business phenomenon.

Generally, Chinese media shed more light on the positive side of Olympic Economy, especially opportunities given to companies and China's economy in spite of its representation of abnormal competition and failure of some companies in the competition for partnership by virtue of HUAMN BEHAVIOR metaphors. Comparatively, American media dramatize negative aspects of Olympic Economy, especially problems concerning technology, megaprojects and environmental pollution in the preparation for Beijing Olympics, which echoes wide debates inside China and doubts outside China. They even emphasize problems produced by the fast development of China's economy.

Notes:

[1] We sub categorize the verb **grow** in the mapping OLYMPIC ECONOMY IS A PLANT and the phrasal verb **grow up** in the mapping OLYMPIC ECONOMY IS A HUMAN LIFE in accordance with their basic senses in dictionary and current literature review. Accordingly, Chinese verb **chéng zhǎng** [成长] [to grow up] is categorized in the mapping OLYMPIC ECONOMY IS A HUMAN LIFE.

[2] We categorize the idiom **mó quán cā zhǎng** [摩拳擦掌] [to rub hands and clench fists in preparation for fight] (2 instances) as well as verbal phrase **zhì zào má fán** [制造麻烦] [to create difficulties] (1 instance) as instantiations of the CONFLICT metaphor. The former describes the situation when companies are spoiling for the coming competition, showing their eagerness and determination to participate; the latter depicts the competition between business rivals. Although they personify companies as agents in the preparation and competition of Olympic Economy, behaviors they depict belong to the concept of conflict.

[3] We categorize those metaphoric verbs conveying human physical upward move into the LIVING ORGANISM metaphor and categorize another group of verbs, such as **zǒu** [走] and **mài** [迈] conveying human physical forward movement into the JOURNEY metaphor. They construct the FORWARD MOVEMENT scenario, in which the agent is depicted as traveler who approach the destination in a journey.

[4]The metaphoric adjective **sizzling** defining extremely high temperature usually depicts economy with an unsustainable growth rate. The phrasal verb **pour into** activates the LIQUID metaphor, in which investment is described as liquid that flows into the country that is constructed as a container. They are classified into sub-metaphors of PHYSICAL ENVIRONMENTAL PHENOMENON metaphors that will

be discussed in detail in the section 6.2.

[5]The verb **propel** is classified as a metaphoric verb that construct the FACILITATING FORCE scenario in JOURNEY metaphors in this study.

[6] With the basic sense of referring to the terminal point of a journey or race, the metaphoric noun **goal** can be categorized as the JOURNEY or SPORT metaphor. In most cases, we regard it as a JOURNEY metaphor, but in the following discourse the neighboring SPORT metaphor **set a new record** helps us to classify it as a SPORT metaphor.

NBC's biggest remaining **goal** is to **set a new record** in what is called cumulative audience.

(NYT, August 17, 2008)

[7] In the discourse (75), the SPORT metaphor "经济奥运" is embedded in another metaphor SPORTS EVENT IS A WAR activated by the word **xiāo yān** [硝烟]. Such metaphor is prevalent in both American and Chinese culture (Xiao, 2006; Yang, 2004; Yuan, 2004).

[8] Discourse (76) is a typical example of double metaphor, in which the verb **jiào liàng** [较量] is another word derived from the domain of sport, meaning having the trial of strength.

[9] In this discourse, the Chinese noun **xiāo yān** [硝烟] is another WAR metaphor that has been included in Table 5.22. As the equivalent of "a war without fire", the structure "没有硝烟的战争" is the result of conceptual blending of two conceptual inputs of war and business competition.

[10] (91) is another typical example for mixed metaphors. The verb **dài dòng** [带动] activates the mechanical domain, showing the power of machines. In this discourse, it stresses the facilitating force of Olympic infrastructure construction for the development of industries.

Chapter 6   Analysis of Less Frequent

Common Metaphorical Patterns

Apart from these prominent metaphorical patterns, both media share other metaphorical patterns, such as MACHINE and PHYSICAL ENVIRONMENTAL PHENOMENON metaphors. They do not have as high frequency as predominant ones, but they demonstrate a sharp quantitative disparity between the two media (see Table 5.1). All these metaphors have much more realizations in Chinese media than American media.

6.1 Representation of Olympic Economy as a Machine

94 tokens of MACHINE metaphors are picked out in Chinese media. 96.8% of these metaphors talk about the operation and function of Olympic Economy in terms of machines' motion and power. They are realized in four conceptual scenarios in Chinese data that are listed in Table 6.1 in the order of their frequency of tokens.

It shows that the MECHANICAL POWER scenario is much more productive than the other three conceptual scenarios, taking up nearly 42.6% percent of all Chinese MACHINE metaphors. It is realized in the material processes constructed by the verbs **lā dòng** [拉动], **dài dòng** [带动] and **qū dòng** [驱动] with the same basic sense denoting the mechanical drive. In those processes constructed by these three metaphoric verbs, specific agents are described as running machines that could transform their mechanical power to their patients and put them in a dynamic state.

Table 6.1 Chinese MACHINE metaphors

Sub-conceptual Element	Express-ion	Pinyin	English Translation	Individual Token	Sub-token
MECHANICAL POWER	拉动	lā dòng	to drive	21	40
	带动	dài dòng	to spur on	18	
	驱动	qū dòng	to drive	1	
PROCESS	加速	jiā sù	to accelerate	8	22
	运作	yùn zuò	to operate	5	
	运行	yùn xíng	be in motion	4	
	试运行	shì yùn xín	test run	3	
	提速	tí sù	to accelerate	2	
IGNITION	启动	qǐ dòng	to switch on	16	16
MECHANICAL SOURCE	动力	dòng lì	motive power	9	13
	引擎	yǐn qíng	engine	2	
	助推器	zhù tuī qì	booster	1	
	发动机	fā dòng jī	engine	1	

The concrete examples demonstrate that the agents concerned are concepts associated with the Olympics. Besides 5 instances referring to this sports event directly, like the agent in (1), the others include direct investment in (2), and legacy of the Olympics, as expressed in (3).

(1) 奥运会**带动**最大的是我国发展相对滞后的现代服务业。

[The Olympics gives the greatest impetus to our comparatively lagging modern service industries.]

(PD, September 19, 2008)

(2) 因奥运会引起的投资和消费需求，将**拉动**北京国民生产总值增长速度平均每年提高约 1.7 个百分点，有望达到 11％左右。

[The investment and consumer demand spurred by the Olympic Games will accelerate the growth of Beijing's national gross product to reach as high as 11% with 1.7% up each year.]

(PD, February 18, 2003)

(3) 奥运会给我们留下宝贵的历史文化遗产，会**拉动**地区经济高速发展。

[The Olympics has left us precious historical and cultural relics, which will drive the fast development of local economy.]

(PD, February 10, 2006)

Altogether, they point to the profound influence of the Olympics and associated economic and social phenomena on various industries, local as well as national economy. The extent of its influence is strengthened by some co-text modifiers, such as the adverb **gāo sù** [高速] in (3) donnoting the sense of high speed.

MACHINE metaphors in the Chinese corpus also foreground the value of Olympic construction projects. For example, they are described in (4) as a machine that could spur the development of other industries, just like its operation could drive the running of other linked mechanical parts.

(4) 但是奥运会后如何因应这些基础硬件建设的发展**带动**产业、不使市政府背上**包袱**、不影响奥运会后的公共事业投资等，都将是重大**挑战**。

178

[However, it will be a huge challenge after the Olympics if we make the infrastructure development spur other industries without imposing any burden on municipal government and preventing investment in public services.]

(CEW, February 10, 2006)

Here, the MACHINE metaphor signified by **dài dòng** [带动] is used together with the BURDEN metaphor and the WAR metaphor activated respectively by **bāo fú** [包袱] and **tiǎo zhàn** [挑战]. Such juxtaposition shows that to make infrastructure of Beijing Olympics facilitate the development of other industries is a big concern of China. Its success will reduce the burden of the government.

A set of metaphoric verbs converge the dynamic state of a machine with the operation of Olympic Economy and the development of China's economy under its influence. For example, the verb **yùn zuò** [运作] constructs metaphorically how companies participate in marketing programs like operating on a machine in (5). The trial operation of a machine, expressed in the expression **shì yùn xín** [试运行] stands for the licensing program before the official starting of Beijing Olympic Marketing Programs after the 2004 Athens Olympic Games in (6). China's fast-developing economy is also represented by virtue of a couple of synonym **jiā sù** [加速] and **tí sù** [提速] as a fast-running machine, which speeds up in (7) as well as in (8) and whose smooth operation is the very concern of the media, as is expressed in the title (9) through the verb **yùn xíng** [运行].

(5) 作为一家毫无"奥运经验"的中国公司，**运作**如此大的营销**战略**毕竟"还是第一次"。

[As a Chinese company without any "Olympic experience", it is the real "first time" for the company to operate such a big marketing strategy.]

(CEW, August 11, 2008)

(6) 特许商品计划**试运行**一年，实现销售 6 亿多元。

179

[After one-year trial run of the licensed product plan, sales reached more than 60 millions yuan.]

(PD, November 4, 2005)

(7) 通过举办奥运会，将使北京的建设大大**加速**。

[Thanks to the hosting of the Olympics, the construction of Beijng will be greatly accelerated.]

（PD, December 16, 2005）

(8) 奥运带给中国的间接影响包括城市基础设施的改善和现代化进程**提速**。

[The indirect influences of the Olympics on China include the improvement of urban infrastructure and the acceleration of modernization.]

(CEW, September 7, 2008)

(9) 如何保持奥运后期的平稳**运行**

[How to Sustain Smooth Operation in the Later Period of the Olympics]

(PD, February 10, 2006)

In the scenario of starting a machine mainly signaled by **qǐ dòng** [启动], a rational agent will operate on a machine. Correspondingly, in the following examples, a variety of marketing programs, including the market development, licensing programs, sponsorship, suppliership and other promotions related to the Olympics, are organized by the government, IOC, COC and companies.

(10) 中国奥委会在北京发布了新商用徽记，并**启动**了 2009-2012 年市场开发。

[Chinese Olympic Committee (COC) issued the new trade emblem in Beijing and started the market development from 2009 to 2012.]

(PD, May 9, 2008)

(11) 奥组委将陆续**启动**适合中小企业参与的供应商计划和特许计划。

180

[Olympic Committee will start successively suppliership and licensing programs that are suitable to middle-and-small-sized enterprises.]

(PD, May 20, 2005)

The beginning of a construction project is also constructed like operating on a machine by the same metaphor **qǐ dòng** [启动] in the following two extracts:

（12）先**启动**什么，后**启动**什么，牵涉到，是整个城市为奥运服务，还是奥运促进城市发展的根本问题。

[What is started first and what is started next have something to do with the fundamental issue whether the whole city services the Olympics or the Olympics facilitate the development of the city.]

（PD, August 28, 2004）

（13）中国科学技术馆新馆则成为了最先**启动**的奥运工程代建项目。

[The new building of Chinese Science and Technology Museum became the first Olympic construction project to start.]

(PD, September 23, 2005)

In terms of these inanimate metaphors, such objects as various marketing programs and construction projects in these processes are described as powerful machines that are operated and controlled by agents according to the overall plans and mechanisms.

The facilitating power of the Olympics and related economic phenomena is more explicitly constructed in the MECHANICAL SOURCE scenario, in which there is direct identity of the Olympics as well as concomitant economic activities with inseparable parts of a machine that ignite and control its formal operation. Such identity is foregrounded in the identifying process, which defines the participant (Halliday, 2000[1994]: 119-122) and has been acknowledged as "the most straightforward model for presenting a comment or judgment" (Hodge & Kress, 1988: 113).

In the typical examples (14) and (15), the verbs **shì** [是] and **chéng**

wéi [成为] link the identified **ào yùn huì** [奥运会] and **ào yùn jīng jì** [奥运经济] with the identifiers that are referred to by metaphorical expressions **yǐn qíng** [引擎] and **zhù tuī qì** [助推器] with the basic sense of an engine and a booster. In this way, the Olympics and Olympic Economy are defined with the precise nature of being a mechanical source. The scenario of propelling mechanical source is also mapped to companies and local governments' underlying initiative for their active participation in various marketing programs.

(14) 在中国政治文化中心北京举办的奥运会和在中国经济中心上海举办的世博会，将成为 21 世纪初促进我国改革开放和经济社会发展的 "**双引擎**"。

[The Olympics held in Beijing, the political and economic center of China and Expo 2010 held in Shanghai, another economic center, will become "the double engines" to facilitate China's open-up and reform and accelerate its economic and social development in the 21st century.]

(PD, June 24, 2005)

(15) 商用徽记和新一轮的企业合作计划无疑是这个宏伟蓝图的**助推器**。

[The commercial emblem and the new round of enterprise partnership are undoubtedly the boosters of this grand blueprint.]

(PD, June 24, 2005)

In some cases, the MECHANICAL SOURCE scenario is activated more than once. In the discourse (16), it is constructed by the expressions **dòng lì** [动力] and **fā dòng jī** [发动机] with the same semantic orientation in the frame of mechanical world. Another discourse (17) illustrates that the dominant scenarios produced by MACHINE metaphors are not separated. The scenario of MECHANICAL SOURCE activated by **dòng lì** [动力] and the MECHANICAL POWER scenario activated by **lā dòng** [拉动] join together to represent the positive effect of exhibitions about Beijing Olympics on the local economy. The positive power of business activities related to the Olympics is stressed when the MECHANICAL SOURCE scenario is created together with the FACILITAING FORCE scenario constructed by the JOURNEY metaphor that is signified by the verb **cù jìn** [促进] in the representation of Olympic Economy in (16). In the same discourse, the verb **tí shēng** [提升] [to elevate] activates the conventional schematic image of GOOD IS UP, which highlights the positive evaluation of Olympic Economy.

(16) 奥运经济是一个**动力强大的发动机**，在**促进**地方经济快速发展的同时，也大大**提升**了相关上市公司的业绩增长预期。

[Olympic Economy is a powerful engine. It has accelerated the development of the local economy and at the same time promoted growth prospects of the listed companies concerned.]

(PD, April 8, 2005)

(17) 综观近期在北京以奥运为主题的会展，对**拉动**经济增长的巨大**动力**已经显现。

[In the overview of Olympics-themed exhibitions held in Beijing recently, there is already a manifestation of the strong impetus to stimulate economic growth.]

(PD, June 24, 2005)

In a word, the application of MACHINE metaphors enables Chinese media to shed light on the vitality of Olympic Economy and its positive influence on China's development and companies' growth.

There are only 26 tokens of MACHINE metaphors in the English discourse and are almost equally distributed in four conceptual scenarios that are listed in Table 6.2.

MECHANICAL POWER and MECHANICAL SOURCE scenarios are also constructed in American media. These two scenarios are realized by English equivalents of Chinese metaphorical expressions, such as **engine** for **yǐn qíng** [引擎] and **fā dòng jī** [发动机], **booster** for **zhù tuī qì** [助推器], **drive** for **lā dòng** [拉动] in the following examples:

Table 6.2   English MACHINE metaphors

Sub-conceptual Element	Expression	Individual Token	Sub-token
MECHANICAL POWER	drive	7	7
REPAIR	gear	5	7
	overhaul	1	
	retool	1	
MALFUNCTION & STOPPAGE	pull the plug	3	5
	glitch	1	
	backfire	1	
MECHANICAL SOURCE	engine	2	5
	machine	2	
	booster	1	
IGNITION	jump-start	2	2

(18) A Big, Dirty Growth **Engine**

(BW, August 22, 2005)

(19) The Olympics is a revenue **booster**.

(BW, August 7, 2007)

(20) Li-Ning now is counting on next year's 2008 Beijing Olympics to **drive** its branding efforts.

(BW, October 8, 2007)

With low frequency, they perform similar functions, highlighting the dynamic state of the Chinese market in (18), emphasizing huge benefits produced by Beijing Olympics in (19), and underlining in (20) the contribution of Beijing Olympics to brand development.

The obvious difference between the two media lies in two particular conceptual scenarios that have constructed in the English corpus: REPAIR as well as MULFUNCTION and STOPPAGE. The metaphoric verb **gear**

184

in the representation of Olympic Economy describes the host country, companies and the market as machines that are fixed or set again for Beijing Olympics, as exemplified by the following extract:

(21) With China **gearing** up to host the Olympics in August, these should be especially heady days for the tourism business.

(BW, April 3, 2008)

In the domain of mechanics, both **retool** and **overhaul** concern the action of close examination and the accompanying repair. In the discourse of Olympic Economy, **retool** conceptualizes the reality that sponsors and partners carry out certain marketing strategies and produce related products in order to adapt to the Olympic market and **overhaul** constructs the process in which companies try to improve their reputation and image. So the REPAIR scenario implies that all the relevant entities, ranging from the host country to individual companies need adapt to the new situation in Olympic Economy.

The metaphoric noun **glitch** originally refers to a sudden instance of malfunctioning or irregularity in an electronic system. In the discourse of Olympic Economy, it represents the problems construction projects have to deal with. The verb **backfire** represents the reality that some inefficient marketing tactics have brought disaster to its operators. The verbal phrase **pull the plug** frames the fact that some sponsors including Kodak and Lenovo in (22) decide to give up continuing their cooperation with IOC, which implies difficulties and frustrations sponsors will go through in Olympic Economy.

(22) High-profile Beijing Olympics sponsors Kodak and Lenovo are **pulling the plug** on future Games.

(BW, July 31, 2008)

We can see that nearly half of MECHANICAL metaphors used in American media allude to the adjustment of machines, stopping of machine's operation and abnormal working of an engine.

In conclusion, besides the sharp statistic disparity, the two media foreground different aspects of the source domain through different significant scenarios created by MACHINE metaphors. Firstly, American media highlight the adjustment, repair and even stopping of a machine, which are absent in Chinese media. Secondly, Chinese media underline the positive power of a machine's working, while the American counterpart mentions the result of its abnormal operation. Taking the target domain of Olympic Economy into consideration, these two differences indicate that two media attach importance to different phenomena in Olympic Economy: its dynamic operation and positive effects on China's economy in Chinese media and its problems and complication in American media.

6.2 Representation of Olympic Economy as a Physical Environmental Phenomenon

The distinguished gap in statistics also appears in metaphors of physical environmental phenomena, with 69 instances in Chinese media against 35 in American media. Such metaphor is composed by WEATHER metaphors, metaphors for natural physical or chemical phenomena and metaphors for natural geographical feature.

The WEATHER metaphor is mainly realized linguistically in Chinese by the character **rè** [热] meaning the high temperature. As a metaphoric adjective, it is sometimes used independently as in the following discourse, describing that Olympics-related products are well received in the market.

(23) 随着雅典奥运会的进行，奥运图书销售逐渐**热**了起来。

[With the arrival of the Athens Olympic Games, Olympic books have gradually become a craze in the market.]

(PD, August 20, 2004)

Table 6.3 Chinese PHYSICAL ENVIRONMENTAL PHENOMENA metaphors

Sub-conceptual Scenario	Expression	Pinyin	English Translation	Individual Token	Sub-token
WEATHER scenario	热	rè	hot	23	37
	过热	guò rè	overheated	7	
	升温	shēng wēn	heat up	5	
	冷	lěng	cold	2	
NATURAL PHYSICAL & CHEMICAL PHENOMENA scenario	泡沫	pào mò	bubble	11	19
	催化	cuī huà	catalyze	5	
	飓风	jù fēng	hurricane	1	
	爆发	bào fā	burst of explosive	1	
	喷发	pēn fā	eruption	1	
NATURAL GEOGRAPHICAL FEATURE scenario	高潮	gāo cháo	high waves	8	16
	热潮	rè chao	upsurge	7	
	冲击	chōng jī	lash	1	

However, in 17 out of 23 instances, the character **rè** [热] is used as a morpheme in various compound expressions, including nominal groups **ào yùn rè** [奥运热] meaning Olympic craze，**dì chǎn rè** [地产热] standing for an estate wave，**lǚ yóu rè** [旅游热] denoting tourism wave and **shōu cáng rè** [收藏热] referring to collection wave. It also appears in the verbal group **rè xiāo** [热销] depicting Olympic products that go like hot cakes, and the adjective group **huǒ rè** [火热] with the basic sense of being burning hot. They all represent generally business vitality in the Chinese market, especially the fast development of specific industries spurred by Olympic Economy, such as real estate, tourism and collection. The business jargon **guò rè** [过热] shares the common basic sense of defining extremely high temperature with the English equivalents

overheated and **sizzling**. They usually correspond to economy with an unsustainable growth rate and imply the media's worry about China's economy. However, their negative evaluation is overshadowed by brisk business constructed by all the other WEATHER metaphors realized by **rè** [热]. Its antonym **lěng** [冷] represents depression of some industries in the preparation for Beijing Olympics, but appears with only 2 instances.

In addition, the expression **shēng wēn** [升温] primarily conveying the change in temperature is employed in the representation of China's economy to construct the quick expansion of business activities and the powerful influence of Olympic Economy on both national and local economy. For example, the discourse (24) dramatizes the influence of Olympic Economy on the tourism industry:

(24) 奥运旅游悄然**升温**。

[Olympic Tourism has gradually heated up.]

(PD, May 12, 2006)

Table 6.4 English PHYSICAL ENVIRONMENTAL PHENOMENA metaphors

Sub-conceptual Scenario	Expression	Individual Token	Sub-token
WEATHER scenario	hot	2	6
	sunny	1	
	clouded	1	
	overheated	1	
	sizzling	1	
NATURAL PHYSICAL & CHEMICAL PHENOMENA scenario	bubble	7	9
	catalyst	2	
NATURAL GEOGRAPHICAL FEATURE scenario	surge	8	18
	wave	5	
	sea	2	
	high-water mark	1	
	landscape	1	
	waters	1	

Besides **overheated** and **sizzling**, American media use the adjectives **hot, sunny** and **clouded** (3 instances in all) that primarily describe weather conditions to conceptualize respectively the intense competition in the market, favorite or distressed situations for companies.

Apart from **guò rè** [过热], **lěng** [冷] and **overheated** that convey negative evaluation of the fast-developing economy in China by invoking unpleasant feelings associated with very extreme temperatures, another couple of equivalent metaphorical expressions **bubble** and **pào mò** [泡沫] with equal 6 instances in both corpora is another kind of conventional metaphorical construction of highly developing economy. Drawn from the sub-domain of chemical phenomenon, they usually depict the false appearance of vitality in business. The other Chinese expressions primarily depicting natural physical and chemical phenomena include **cuī huà** [催化], **jù fēng** [飓风], **bào fā** [爆发] and **pēn fā** [喷发]. They basically allude to powerful and sudden change in physical or chemical environment. Through these linguistic metaphors, an overnight successful company is described as an explosive or volcano, licensing programs are talked about in terms of hurricanes and exhibitions are constructed as vital forces to spur the local development. They point together to the effects of Olympics-related business activities on China's economy and imply great changes it has experienced. For example, in (25), the Olympics-themed exhibition is described as a catalyst that will bring change to China's economy and Chinese society. Its English equivalent **catalyst** performs the same function.

(25) 会展会对一个城市或地区的国民经济和社会进步产生难以估量的影响和**催化**作用。

[Exhibitions will have an inestimable influence and cause tremendous changes to the national economy and social development of a city or district.]

(PD, June 24, 2005)

The NATURAL GEOGRAPHICAL FEATRUE scenario is realized mainly by the Chinese nominal groups **gāo cháo** [高潮] and **rè cháo** [热潮]. They are lexical metaphors, denoting the climax in Olympic Marketing Programs, such as the development and sales of Olympics-related products in (26) and active participation of local governments in the bid for the Olympic mascot in (27).

(26) 面对无限商机，奥运图书的开发也推向了一个小**高潮**。

[Faced with endless business opportunity, the development of Olympic books has come to a small climax.]

(PD, August 20, 2004)

(27) 这是奥运会开办 109 年来第一次由地方政府推动的 "申吉**热潮**"。

[This is the first "upsurge in the bid for the Olympic mascot" facilitated by the local government in the 109-year history of the Olympic Games.]

(PD, November 11, 2005)

In English discourse, the term **surge** is significant with 8 tokens. Used as both verb and noun, it indicates the conceptual identity in the development of economy and sudden, powerful forward movement of huge waves, as is expressed in the discourse "Beijing's economy **surged** in recent years". Another metaphoric noun **wave** performs the same function, dramatizing the fast development of construction and the tourism industries due to the coming Olympics. Their basic sense implies a sudden outburst of the forward movement, which is hard to predict. Simultaneously, the movement of huge waves is a dangerous force that is difficult to control. All these work together to emphasize the unpredictable and complicated nature of China's economy. **High-water mark, sea** or **waters,** and **landscape** with much less tokens stand for the high prices for sponsorship, a brisk advertisement market before the Olympics, and the general situation in the Olympic market respectively.

190

The above analyses reveal that Chinese media are different from its American counterpart in that in spite of the negative evaluation of the fast developing economy in China, which is expressed by some jargons in economics, it still sheds more light on China's flourishing economy as the product of Olympic Economy and underscores positive factors contributing to it through more varied linguistic metaphors with higher tokens. The unpredictability and complicated situation of China's economy highlighted by English NATURAL GEOGRAPHICAL FEATURE metaphors form a sharp contrast with its mechanism dramatized by Chinese MACHINE metaphors that were discussed in the last section.

6.3 Representation of Olympic Economy as a Building

Metaphors from the source domain of building typically carry a strong positive evaluation and are adopted to express aspiration to desired business goals. Both Chinese and American media use metaphors that converge efforts made by companies over an extended period of time for abstract desired outcome with the staged process of activities in the building, which are activated by the verb **build** and the phrasal verb **build up** in English (10 instances in all) and the corresponding Chinese verbs **jiàn shè** [建设] (9 instances) and **shù lì** [树立] (5 instances). In most cases (90%), they are used conventionally in the discourse about brand development, as expressed in (28)-(30). They also construct the process of establishing close relationship with local governments and consumers in the discourses (31) and (32).

(28) 赞助商的身份，用好了能使企业在品牌**建设**的**道路**上**一步登天**。

[Successful sponsorship could help sponsors reach the sky in a single bound on the road of building up their brands.]

(PD, March 17, 2006)

191

(29) 雷士时刻抓住**树立**中国本土品牌不放松。

[Lei Shi never for a moment relaxes and misses no opportunity to build up its Chinese domestic brand.]

(CEW, August 11, 2008)

(30) Lenovo does have a pretty massive task in front of us, to **build** its brand globally.

(NYT, June 20, 2008)

(31) 奥运带来了**建设**客户关系的机会。

[The Olympic Games offer opportunities to build up consumer relations.]

（CEW, October 9, 2006）

(32) Sponsors may **stay the course** and try to **build** on their relationship with Chinese consumers.

(BW, May 28, 2008)

Like the JOURNEY metaphors, these metaphors highlight the need for patience, effort and not to expect instant outcome. In some discourses, like (28) and (32). BUILDING and JOURNEY metaphors are mixed, in which the JOURNEY metaphor is realized by **dào lù** [道路] and **stay the course** respectively. The entailed pre-determined goal of business activities and the aspiration to desired business goals of these two metaphors make them compatible in enhancing companies' efforts in Olympic Economy.

Chinese media produce more than twice as many BUILDING metaphors as American media, with 50 instances against 29 instances. Besides depicting efforts in the marketing through an archetypal creative activity, Chinese media use metaphors referring to various parts of a building, including **mén kǎn** [门槛] (20 instances) and **rù kǒu** [入口] (2 instances) with the basic sense of threshold and entrance respectively. In the discourse of Olympic Economy, these metaphors construct sponsorship, licensing and supplying programs as a building and describe the basic requirement to enter the building as its entrance, as expressed in one typical example (33), in which **mén kǎn** refers to the minimal price for sponsorship.

(33) 北京奥运会赞助商的**门槛**要上亿元，成为奥运供应商也要数千万元。

[The threshold of sponsorship for the Beijing Olympic Games requires billion dollars, and an Olympic supplier also needs tens of millions.]

(PD, September 28, 2008)

In line with the metaphor OLYMPIC ECONOMY IS A BUILDING, companies who are denied to participate in Olympic Economoy are described as people that are kept out of this building, as expressed in the following English extract.

(34) Even some marketers that have been **shut out of** the Beijing Games have found ways to profit from them.

(BW, March 14, 2005)

Companies who want to enter this building must go through the entrance, which means they are required to pay an amount of fee; otherwise, they will be shut out of the building. If a building is a worthwhile goal, entering this building by paying some price is like achieving this goal by making some sacrifice. These metaphors emphasize the effort and sacrifice needed for Olympic Economy.

Besides various Olympic marketing programs, Chinese market is also described as a building. This is invoked by a group of Chinese phrasal verbs, including **jìn rù** [进入] (3 instances), **dǎ kāi** [打开] (2 instances), **qiāo kāi** [敲开] (2 instances) and **jǐ jìn lái** [挤进来] (1 instance) with the basic sense of entering, opening up, knocking up and pushing in respectively and the English expressions **enter** (3 instances), **head into** (1 instance), **break into** (1 instance), **get into** (1 instance), **shut out** (1 instance) as well as the English verb phrases **open the door** and **pull up**

the drawbridge with 1 instance respectively. The extracts (35) and (36) are two typical examples, in which companies' success in the Chinese market is depicted as a successful entry into a building.

(35) 去年以来，国际知名酒店管理集团的顶级品牌相继**进入**中国。

[Since last year, top brands of famous international hotel group have entered China in succession.]

(PD, November 24, 2004)

(36) Aramark **entered** China in 2004 and provides food and housekeeping services to such clients as Lenovo and the U.S. Embassy in Beijing.

(BW, April 22, 2008)

6.4 Representation of Olympic Economy as a Performance

The PERFORMANCE metaphor is much more productive in Chinese media, with the total 53 instances that are realized by 14 types of expressions concerning various components of the conceptual domain of performance, including the stage where performances take place, the relevant people and their show, different stages of performances and their effects.

They have created comprehensive scenarios of a performance, in which the element of stage is quite significantly signified by the metaphor **wǔ tái** [舞台], which outnumbers greatly the other expressions. It stands for a huge market produced by the Olympic Games, as expressed in the discourse (37), implying opportunities for companies that are personalized as performers who are competing for applause and acknowledgement. Our knowledge about the stage gives rise to a set of entailments, especially the limelight shed on the stage. It corresponds to close and intense attention the Chinese market has obtained due to the holding of the Olympics in its capital city of Beijing.

(37) 奥运会为众多商家提供一个面向世界充分展示自我的大舞台。

[The Olympic Games provide a huge stage for a great number of companies to show off themselves at the best before the whole world.]

(PD, October 29, 2001)

Table 6. 5 Chinese PERFORMANCE metaphors

Sub-conceptual Element	Express-ion	Pinyin	English Trans-lation	Meta-phorical Meaning	Individual Token	Sub-token
STAGE	舞台	wǔ tái	stage	market	23	23
PERFORMING (14)	亮相	liàng xiàng	to strike a pose on the stage	initial participation in OE	5	14
	走上前台	zǒu shàng qián tái	to come to proscenium	increasing importance of tourism industry	4	
	表演	biǎo yǎn	to perform	to participate in OE	2	
	登场	dēng chǎng	to come on stage	to begin competing with business rivals	2	
	对歌	duì gē	to sing in antiphonal style	to compete with rivals	1	

195

continued:

Sub-conceptual Element	Expression	Pinyin	English Translation	Metaphorical Meaning	Individual Token	Sub-token
PLAY (9)	大戏	dà xì	a full-scale drama	full-scale competition in OE	2	9
	好戏	hǎo xì	an exciting drama	fierce competition in OE	2	
	开场	kāi chǎng	the beginning of a performance	the beginning of Olympic market development	2	
	序幕	xù mù	prolude	the beginning of Olympic sponsorship	2	
	舞步	wǔ bù	dance steps	concrete marketing programs	1	
ROLE (5)	角色	jué sè	a role in a play	status of a company in competition	3	5
	主角	zhǔ jué	hero		2	
EFFECT (2)	紧锣密鼓	jǐn luó mì gǔ	wildly beating gongs and drums	intense production of Olympic commodities	1	2
	叫座	jiào zuò	a great draw	successful marketing program	1	

The metaphoric noun **stage**, used in the nominal group "the world stage" in English discourse has the same metaphorical meaning as its Chinese equivalent term **wǔ tái [舞台]**, referring to the huge Olympic market. However, in the discourse (38), it is used as a verb. With the primary sense of performing a play, it conflates China's holding the Olympic Games with putting on a drama on the stage. The other expressions elaborate on this scenario, in which the public attention is compared to the **limelight** on the stage, the promotion of products in marketing programs is like a special kind of performance depicted by the word **trumpet**, and concrete measures to hold up the Beijing's proclaim for a Green Olympics is talked about in terms of the script for a drama that is conveyed by the noun **playbook**. These jointly point to the specific way Western media think of Beijing Olympics.

(38) The Chinese will spend $3 billion to $4 billion to **stage** the Summer Games in Beijing.

(NYT, June 1, 2008)

Table 6.6   English PERFORMANCE metaphors

Sub-conceptual Element	Expression	Metaphorical Meaning	Individual Token	Sub-token
STAGE	stage (n.)	market produced by Olympics	6	9
	limelight	great attention given to successful companies in Olympic Economy	3	
PERFORMING	stage (v.)	to hold the Beijing Olympic Games	4	8
	trumpet	to carry out intense market promotion	4	
SCRIPT	playbook	projects for Olympic market development	3	3

Apart from this, PERFORMANCE metaphors are mixed together with dominant WAR, SPORT and GAME metaphors in Chinese media, such as the expression **sān guó dǐng lì de hǎo xì** [三国鼎立的好戏] [a great play about the division of power among three kingdoms] in the example (96) in the section 5.5.2. The compound noun **hǎo xì** [好戏] refers basically to the biggest part of a story full of contradiction. Used together with the BATTLE scenario constructed by the historical metaphor **sān guó dǐng lì** [三国鼎立], which describes a turbulent phase in Chinese history, it enhances the intensity of business competition in the Olympic Marketing.

(39) 奥运竞标**胜出**只是雷士的第一次**亮相**。

[The successful bid for the Olympics was only Leishi's first pose on the stage.]

(CEW, August 11, 2008)

The discourse (39) is characterized by a mixture of PERFORMANCE with SPORT and GAME metaphors that are activated by the compound noun **liàng xiàng** [亮相] and the verb **shèng chū** [胜出] respectively. **Liàng xiàng** [亮相] is used to represent the successful bid for an Olympic project by the Chinese company of Leishi. With the basic sense of a pose on the stage, it indicates important influence of this success on the company's image in the public. Modified by "the first time", it implies subsequent efforts of the company. The discourse is one of typical instances to conflate Chinese companies' business activity in the marketing with players' performance on the stage. It is not hard to explain when we think of China's eagerness to demonstrate its power and prosperity after its 30 years' openness and reforms in this international event.

6.5 Representation of Olympic Economy as Natural Resources

Both Chinese and American media represent Olympic Economy as a place that is rich in natural resources, but still there are sharp differences in quantity, type and form. In Chinese media, there are nominal metaphors that link directly this business phenomenon with natural resources. The expressions **jīn shān** [金山] (1 instance) and **jù bǎo pén** [聚宝盆] (3 instances) primarily referring to golden mountains and treasure basins respectively are employed to identify Olympic Economy in the title (40) and the extract (41), in which Olympic Economy is described as rich natural resources that could bring great fortunes to any one who could take advantage of them.

(40) 如何挖掘奥运**金山**

[How to Dig the Golden Mountain of the Olympic Games]

(PD, January 21, 2004)

(41) 奥运这个招牌，用好了是个**聚宝盆**。

[If you make a good use of the Olympic Games, it will become a treasure basin.]

(PD, April 21, 2006)

However, most of NATURAL RESOURCES metaphors are realized by verbs in Chinese media, including **kāi fā** [开发] (30 instances), **wā jué** [挖掘] (5 instances) and **kāi jué** [开掘] (1 instance) with the basic sense of exploring, unearthing and digging natural recourses. Compared with the last two, **kāi fā** is a lexical metaphor used in the expression **shì chǎng kāi fā** [市场开发] in most cases, referring to the market development. In the other cases, this metaphor, used as both noun and verb, dramatize the development of Olympic products and the utilization of Olympic infrastructure after the Olympic Games. For example, it addresses the development of Olympic books in (42) and concerns how to make good

199

use of Olympic venues after the Olympic Games in (43). In both cases, the metaphor **kāi fā** conveys the process Olympic products and Olympic venues are exploited as natural resources that could benefit the producers and users.

(42) 图书市场上对奥运图书的**开发**已经掀起了小的高潮。

[The book market has set up a fairly upsurge in the development of Olympic books.]

(PD, April 20, 2004)

(43) 用奥运体育场馆是社会的不是孤立的、是开放的不是封闭的、是大众的不是专业的理念，深度**开发**游览功能、展示功能、教育功能。

[Holding the concept that the Olympic arena is social, open and common instead of being isolated, enclosed and professional, we will have in-depth exploitations of their functions for sightseeing, exhibition and education.]

(PD, July 24, 2005)

In contrast, the NATURAL RESOURCES metaphor is realized in American media by only one type of metaphor **tap**. Without any exception, its 8 instances talk about the development of the Chinese market during the period of the Olympic Games by both domestic and foreign companies, as expressed in (44).

（44）The analyst urged infocomm vendors to look outside Beijing and Shanghai to **tap** into the second- and third-tier cities across the Chinese mainland.

(BW, June 21, 2007)

Analyses show that the NATRUAL RESOURSES metaphors are more productive in Chinese media than in the American counterpart, with 40 tokens against 8. In addition, there are more types of metaphorical expressions in Chinese media, which talk about not only the huge Chinese market, but also rich economic resources the Olympics grant to China.

200

6.6 Summary

The sharp disparity in quantity demonstrates that Chinese media show favor to these above discussed metaphorical patterns. The prevalence of the PERFORMANCE metaphor can be explained by the social background of the Beijing Olympic Games. The preference for the other patterns implies Chinese media's positive attitudes towards Olympic Economy and the bright image the media intend to build. Metaphors from the source domain of BUILDING carry a strong positive connotation because they express aspiration towards desired social goals (Charteris-Black 2004: 70-73). Benefits human beings get from natural resources are transferred to subjects and events related to Olympic Economy in NATURAL RESOURCE metaphors. The positive images established by them in Chinese media are enhanced by comparative analyses of different scenarios structured by MACHINE and NATURAL ENVIRONMENTAL PHENOMENA metaphors between these two media.

Chapter 7 Analysis of Particular Metaphorical Patterns

7.1 Particular Metaphorical Patterns in Chinese Discourse

Table 7.1 shows that four metaphorical patterns are particular to Chinese media. They are drawn from conceptual domains of food, examination, art and fortune. Next, we will examine the linguistic realizations and functions of each pattern in detail.

Table 7. 1 Particular metaphorical representations in Chinese discourse

Source Domain	Express-ion	Pinyin	English Translation	Individual Token	Total Token
FOOD	蛋糕	dàn gāo	cake	20	36
	馅饼	xiàn bǐng	pie	6	
	大餐	dà cān	a big meal	3	
	热炒	rè chǎo	to stir craze for	3	
	甜头	tián tou	pleasant flavor	2	
	分食	fēn shí	to share and eat	1	
	饕餮	tāo tiè	to eat voraciously	1	

continued:

Source Domain	Expression	Pinyin	English Translation	Individual Token	Total Token
EXAMINA-TION	难题	nán tí	a difficult question	6	12
	答卷	dá juàn	examination paper	2	
	题目	tí mù	examination questions	1	
	榜眼	bǎng yǎn	the second place at palace examinations	1	
	加分	jiā fēn	to score some points	1	
	减分	jiǎn fēn	to take some points away	1	
ART	塑造	sù zào	to mold	8	12
	传奇	chuán qí	a legend	3	
	经典	jīng diǎn	a classic	1	
FORTUNE	含金量	hán jīn liàng	gold content	3	9
	资本	zī běn	capital	2	
	财富	cái fù	fortune	2	
	金	jīn	gold	2	

7.1.1 FOOD Metaphors

Eating occupies a quite important place in Chinese culture (Liu, 2002: 64-71). Chinese obsession with food has turned cooking and dining into an artistic feat, which makes eating enjoy special social functions. As a result, FOOD metaphors have found ways into the business world, including Olympic Economy, in which marketing programs are described as delicious food or drink and pleasant taste by virtue of a set of metaphorical expressions that are listed in Table 7.1. As metaphoric nouns and verbs, they appear in the following examples:

(1) 仅北京市政府就投资 2800 亿元的奥运**蛋糕**，企业将如何**分食**？

[The Beijing municipal government alone has invested on the Olympic cake that is worth as much as 280 billion yuan. How do enterprises share this big cake?]

(PD, January 21, 2004)

(2) 既然有"奥运**蛋糕**"，当然也会有"奥运**馅饼**"了。

[Since there is the "Olympic cake", there must have the "Olympic pie".]

(PD, December 16, 2005)

(3) 受益于北京奥运，VISA 已经再次尝到了"**甜头**"。

[Because of the Beijing Olympic Games, VISA has benefited again.]

(CEW, August 11, 2008)

(4) 媒体在**热炒**"奥运钢铁**大餐**"。

[The press is stirring the craze for the Olympic steel industry.]

(PD, April 26, 2004)

(5) 奥运这一旅游业的**大餐**，北京该如何**饕餮**？

[How should Beijing enjoy voraciously the Olympic Games as a big meal of tourism?]

(PD, June 24, 2005)

Dàn gāo [蛋糕] is much more pervasive than the other FOOD metaphors. It refers to huge business opportunities and possible benefits official marketing programs and investment projects in Olympic Economy can bring to the market. **Xiàn bǐng** [馅饼], as a food that is more popular in the masses, stands for benefits any companies other than official sponsors, partners and suppliers could obtain due to the brisk Olympic market. Companies that get economic returns, like VISA in (3) are compared to people who have enjoyed sweet taste of these delicious foods. FOOD metaphors are also used to talk about the bright prospect of some industries, such as the steel industry in (4) and the tourism industry in (5). The metaphor **dà cān** [大餐] describes the brisk business in these two industries as an opulent meal. It is compatible with another FOOD metaphor **rè chǎo** [热炒], which conveys the action of making food. Companies who inspire to benefit from Olympic Economy are depicted as hungry people who are eager to take in something, which is activated by metaphoric verbs **fēn shí** [分食] and **tāo tiè** [饕餮].

In a word, FOOD metaphors highlight a huge market and economic returns produced by the Olympic Games and express the media's concern about the way to exploit such a market.

7.1.2 EXAMINATION Metaphors

The EXAMINATION metaphor is identified only in Chinese media. It is realized by four metaphoric nouns and two metaphoric verbs with 12 instances that are also presented in Table 7.1.

In the following extracts about Olympic Economy, these metaphorical expressions conflate thorny problems that examinees have to solve with difficulties troubling the host city and local governments in Olympic Economy, such as difficulties of the operation in various industries in (6) as well as the management of Olympic venues after the Olympic Games in (7). Chinese companies that participate in Olympic marketing programs are described as examinees solving problems on the examination paper. They are eager to hand in one satisfactory paper, which will win the praise of the examiners, who are supposed to be the international world. Any companies that are successful in their marketing are described as the examinees who win the second place at palace examinations in (10).

(6) 与奥运有关的体育、旅游、文化产业出现运营困难等一系列**难题**值得关注。

[A series of tough problems are worth our attention, including difficulties of the operation in sports, tourism and culture industries that are related to the Olympic Games.]

(PD, December 17, 2007)

(7) 赛后的利用既要注重经济效益，也要注重社会效益。这是需要我们集思广益，精心策划来破解好的一个**题目**。

[The operation after the Olympic Games should concern both economic returns and social benefits. This is a subject that needs collaborating wisdoms and elaborate plans to deal with.]

(PD, April 22，2004)

(8) 如今，已经是该交出**答卷**的时候了，张辉也到了最为繁忙的时候。

[Now, it is time to hand in the examination paper. It is also the busiest time for Zhang Hui as manager of a famous domestic company.]

(CEW, September 1, 2008)

(9) 很多奥运赞助商都是上市公司，要等着他们的年报和相关调查出来之后再来评价他们买下这块金字招牌到底是**加分**还是**减分**。

[Many Olympic sponsors are listed companies, so we can not tell whether they score points or not after getting the hallmark of sponsorship until the annals and results of other relevant research come out.]

(CEW, August 11, 2008)

(10) 奥运营销已带来 150 亿元品牌价值，"国家电网"以 1116.42 亿元的品牌价值首次登上**榜眼**。

[The Olympic marketing has brought 15-billion brand values and enables State Power Grid Company to enter the Brand Rand with the new brand value of 111.642 billion.]

(CEW, August 11, 2008)

We can conclude that EXAMINATION metaphors address challenges both governments and companies have to face in Olympic Economy and show the media's concern for the final results of the relevant business competition.

This inclination towards EXAMINATION metaphors could be explained to some extent by the long history of China's examination system, which is indicated by the metaphor **bǎng yǎn** [榜眼] and the vital role of examination in China's contemporary social life. Besides that, Chinese are eager to show their achievement after the 30-year reform and opening-up when the Olympic Games would be held for the first time in a developing country and every other country fixes its eyes on its economic development.

7.1.3 ART Metaphors

The expressions **chuán qí** [传奇] and **jīng diǎn** [经典], originally meaning saga and classic, stand for the experience of successful sponsors and partners in the history of the Olympics. For example, in the title (11) for the discourse about Lenovo's Olympic story, the unusual experiences of this multinational in the Olympic Games are dramatized as a legend, implying adventure and unexpected success. In (12), as a successful sponsor in Olympic history, Samsung is described as a legend and a classic, which implies their successful experience has become a model for other sponsors.

(11) 营销奥运书写品牌**传奇**

[The Olympic Marketing Creates Brand Legend]

(PD, August 24, 2008)

(12) 三星由此成为了奥运营销史上的"**传奇**"和"**经典**"

[Hence Samsung has grown to become a "legend" and "classic" in the history of the Olympic Marketing.]

(CEW, August 11, 2008)

Compared with these two creative metaphors, the more conventional metaphor **sù zào** [塑造] has more instantiations, which are realized in both nominal and verbal metaphoric expressions, such as **pǐn pái sù zào** [品牌塑造] [the development of a brand] and **sù zào pǐn pái** [塑造品牌] [to develop a brand]. With the basic sense of referring to the process of creating a piece of art work, it is used to represent participants' efforts to develop their brands in the Olympic Marketing，as constructed in the following extract:

(13) 联想成为全球奥运 TOP，为联想**塑造**全球品牌奠定了坚实的基础。

[Being Olympic TOP has laid a solid foundation for Lenovo's development of global brand.]

(PD, August 24, 2008)

In this way, the media elevate the business activity to the spiritual world of human beings by conflating marketing programs with art works.

7.1.4 FORTUNE Metaphors

Chinese media adopt FORTUNE metaphors to represent not only marketing programs, but also construction projects. The expressions **hán jīn liàng** [含金量] and **zī běn** [资本] construct unanimously the value of sponsorship in the following two titles:

(14) 奥运赞助商 "**含金量**" 知多少

[How Many Are "Gold Content" in Olympic Sponsorship]

(15) 引以为傲的 "奥运**资本**"

[A Sense of Pride with "Olympic Capital"]

(CEW, August 11, 2008)

The title (14) expresses the concern about actual benefits official sponsors could obtain in Olympic Marketing Programs. The other title (15) is about the phenomenon that sponsorship has become the resource for sponsors to reap even more economic returns and social benefits. Another metaphor **jīn** [金] sharing the same basic meaning as the English word

208

"gold" refers to the benefits of the Olympic market, as expressed in the following extract:

(16) 很多北京居民计划当个"奥运房东"，在奥运这个"黄金商机"中掘一桶**金**。

[Many Beijing residents plan to become "Olympic landlords" and unearth the first barrel of gold in such "gold business opportunity" as the Olympic Games.]

(CEW, November 5, 2007)

Construction projects are also talked about in the Chinese corpus by virtue of FORTUNE metaphors that are instantiated in the noun **cái fù** [财富]. For example, a large number of Olympic arenas are identified with precious wealth in (17), implying commercial and social functions of these building projects in a long term.

(17) 数量众多、规模巨大的奥运场馆是奥运会留给北京的宝贵**财富**。

[The numerous and enormous Olympic arenas are valuable wealth the Olympic Games grant to Beijing.]

(PD, September 19, 2008)

In a word, FORTUNE metaphors foreground economic and social benefits Olympic Economy bring not only to Beijing as the host city, but also to any enterprises and individuals who are engaged in related business competition.

7.2 Particular Metaphorical Patterns in English Discourse

There are only two metaphorical patterns particular to the American media concened. Their linguisitic realizations and the number of tokens are presented in Table 7.2.

Table 7. 2 Particular metaphorical representations in English discourse

Source Domain	Expression	Individual Token	Total Token
TEXTILE	pillow	7	22
	cushion	5	
	sheet	3	
	patch	2	
	knit	2	
	fabricate	2	
	weave	1	
CONNECTION	link	9	17
	tie (v.)	3	
	tie-up	2	
	tie (n.)	1	
	linkage	1	
	tie-in	1	

7.2.1 TEXTILE Metaphors

More than 20 instances of TEXTILE metaphors are identified in the English corpus. They are all adopted to represent Olympic construction projects. They provide the lexical means to refer to certain building elements. For example, **pillow** and its synonym **cushion**, with the basic sense of a comfortable bag filled with soft material, stand for the material that functions as the buffer in the structure of a building. And **sheet**, originally referring to a large rectangular piece of inner bed cover, is used to describe the broad and thin surface of a material.

American media also use lexical terms to refer to the process related to the structure and arrangement of a building, including **patch**, **knit**, **weave** and **fabricate**. Look at one typical example (18), in which the skillful process of putting together different parts to produce a piece of fabric is mapped to the architectural method to deal with the special material of ETFE, in which companies are personalized through the verb **partner** to become the agent of this process.

(18) The international companies, headquartered in Germany, **partnered** with a Chinese curtain-wall manufacturer to engineer, **fabricate**, and install the ETFE cushions.

(BW, July 2, 2008)

We can see TEXTILE metaphors focus on the combinary skills and are mainly concerned with assessing the architects' skill. By using such metaphors, American media highlight the intellectual and artistic process of making a building.

7.2.2 CONNECTION Metaphors

American media adopt the basic linkage schema in its representation of Olympic Economy. That is realized by the verbs **link** and **tie** with the similar basic sense conveying the connection between different objects and their corresponding nouns **linkage** and **tie** with another two words **tie-in** and **tie-up**. The verbal metaphoric expressions highlight the efforts of companies to establish relations with the Olympic Games, as in (19) and (20):

(19) According to the rules of the International Olympic Committee, the company is not authorized to **link** itself explicitly to the Olympics.

(NYT, June 1, 2008)

(20) Official sponsors or not, companies are rushing to **tie** their products to the Summer Olympics.

(BW, March 13, 2008)

The nominal metaphoric expressions in the following extracts describe abstract marketing phenomena, including the brand development and promotion activities as concrete substances, which have the connection with other concrete substances that in turn represent the Olympic Games and profitable industries.

211

(21) But Beijing may leave fans especially confused because so many Chinese brands want to establish themselves with Olympic **tie-ins**, official or otherwise.

(BW, March 13, 2008)

(22) Dozens of other companies have less extensive **tie-ups**, ranging from the "official wine supplier" (Great Wall) to Guangzhou Liby Enterprise Group, which is an official provider of detergent for sheets, shorts, and other laundry.

(BW, March 13, 2008)

(23) Global brands, in particular, see the Olympics and World Cup soccer as the two most important international sporting events; brand **linkage** to these events can boost brand awareness, preference and sales over competitors who cannot afford the global sponsorship prices set by the International Olympic Committee.

(BW, April 22, 2008)

7.3 Summary

We can see that Chinese media adopt more types of distinctive metaphorical patterns than the American counterpart, which results in quantitative superiority, with 69 against 39 tokens.

As far as the source domains of these metaphorical patterns are concerned, we can conclude that Chinese media prefer to describe Olympic Economy as physical objects that usually bring physical satisfaction, spiritual pleasure and concrete fortunes to people. The choice of these source domains is likely to arouse positive evaluation, which will be transferred to the target domain of Olympic Economy. This forms a sharp contrast with the neutral metaphorical patterns adopted by American media.

As far as various aspects of the target domain are concerned, we can figure out different business phenomena these two media emphasize. Besides common interest in the market opportunity and huge business returns, American media give more space to building projects in its representation.

Although particular metaphors in both media take up only a small fraction of their total metaphorical expressions (6.12% and 4.58% in Chinese and English corpora respectively), we can not ignore their important functions in the representation of Olympic Economy. Some of them enhance functions performed by the other scenarios. For example, the positive effect of Olympic Economy on China's economy underscored by the FACILITATING FORCE scenario in the JOURNEY metaphor, MECHANICAL POWER as well as MECHANICAL SOURCE scenarios in the MACHINE metaphor is stressed again by FORTUNE metaphors. Additionally, some particular metaphors talk about aspects of the target domain that are not discussed in the other patterns, such as the TEXTILE metaphors for the artistic process of building Olympic arenas. Most importantly, they demonstrate directly the difference in metaphorical representations between the two media.

Chapter 8   Discussion

This chapter will offer explanations for the collective results of the preceding four chapters from cognitive, social and cultural perspectives. First we will look at the common dominant conceptual projections with the aim to reveal the overarching similarities between these two media in looking at entities and events concerning Olympic Economy. These similarities demonstrate to some extent the change in China's economic ideology under the influence of Western values or the integration of different ideologies in this international sports economy.

8.1 Shared Mental Model of Olympic Economy

In both Chiese and Americna media, the conceptual domains of LIVING ORGANISM, JOURNEY, WAR, SPORT and GAME are often referred to in the metaphorical representations of business activities, participants and influenced social entities in Olympic Economy. Through such diversification (Goatly, 1997: 148-167), these significant metaphors jointly produce a shared understanding of Olympic Economy, as illustrated in Figure 8.1. LIVING ORGANISM and JOURNEY metaphors realize the mental model of development, in which the progress and development in the business world is talked about in terms of natural biological growth and spacial movement, emphasizing jointly the mobility in Olympic Economy. The WAR as well as SPORT and GAME metaphors reflect the mental model of competition of these two media, which look at Olympic Economy as an intense and open competition between different opposites.

Such a competitive model promotes the value of efforts and strategies.

Alfred Marshall in the 1890s argued that "economics should gradually become more biological in tone" (in Henderson, 1982: 149). The use of metaphor at lexical level in my data brings biological notion into the conceptualization of organizations and associated patterns of behaviors in Olympic Economy. The most popular pattern in both media is personification, which allows us to make sense of inanimate and possibly alien entities in terms of human motivation, characteristics, and activities. However, the results of data analyses show that personification is not a single unified general process in the representation of Olympic Economy. Different aspects of human beings are picked out to perform diverse functions (Lakoff & Turner, 1989: 33). In the scenario of intelligent agent, companies are described as rational people to take part in competition and cooperation. The sentimental aspects of human beings are drawn to reveal the attitudes of business communities towards Olympic Economy, which are the underlying motives of their concrete strategies. Another extension of conceptualizing Olympic Economy as a living organism activates the metaphors relating to physical growth and strength of human beings in the representation of development in marketing programs and construction projects, the competitive power of companies and the advance of China's economy. The human relations in the conceptualization of people as social beings are frequently resorted to in an attempt to describe the business community's devotion to the Olympics and the social status of companies. We can see that this underlying cognitive model of the organic world produces a number of anthropomorphic metaphors that serve as the cover for the vital relations of long-run process and motion. As Henderson (1994: 48) points out, "personification is a device often resorted to in order to talk about abstract forces or processes or to make us feel more at home in a hostile world". Such an animate metaphor also transforms the discussed entities and events into something concrete that could act or be acted upon.

This makes it possible to highlight the initiatives of entities on the one hand and the constraints imposed on them on the other hand, which are the core of free market ideology and socialist ideas respectively.

Another significant conceptualization reflecting the developmental model of Olympic Economy is the metaphor OLYMPIC ECONOMY IS A JOURNEY. The JOURNEY metaphor is a conventional way to represent any purposeful events (Charteris-Black, 2004; Lakoff, 1993). Conceptualizing Olympic Economy as a journey is compatible with great expectations and inspirations of business communities both at home and abroad. The Chinese party inspires to further their integration with the international system by taking advantage of Beijing Olympics and at the same time demonstrate to the world its rising power thanks to the thirty-year reform and opening up. While the foreign party, represented by the United States is eager to expand their market share in the frisk market of China. In this way, both media adopt the JOURNEY metaphor to talk about Olympic Economy to highlight what business communities intend to achieve in this international sport event and efforts they have made for that. There is the assumption that the entities concerned (domestic and foreign enterprises, China's economy) in the constructed journey have predetermined objectives to reach. Normally, we positively evaluate any measures and phenomena that could help achieve these objectives, because they are socially valued ones; as Hunston and Thompson (2000: 14) notes: "Something that is good helps to achieve a goal". In this way, JOURNEY metaphors in the representation of Olympic Economy have a strong positive orientation to highlight, which refers to the progress and achievement in this sports economy, even when negative aspects of the journey are addressed by the metaphor to highlight the need for patience since it will take time and effort to reach a destination (Charteris-Black, 2004: 94-95).

Besides, both Chinese and American media favor SPORT and GAME

216

metaphors to talk about Olympic Economy, in which companies, organizations, business activities, China's economy are conceived as animate entities engaging in a sports event or game, which has a clear result with the winner and loser. Such metaphors highlight strategic thinking, the team work, preparedness, and the glory of winning as well as the shame of defeat. These unique features of sport highlight American psyche and the American way of life, which value the equality of opportunity, hard work, competition, and prosperity (Liu, 2002: 14). To some extent, sport and business are conflated in American society. As a result, it is not hard to explain the popularity of the SPORT metaphor in American media, ranking only after the LIVING ORGANISM metaphor. It reinforces the economic ideology that proclaims free and open competition for success. In addition to the blurred boundary between sport and business, sport is closely tied to politics, since sport has been frequently used to promote the sense of national pride (Coakley, 1994). The Olympics had helped boost a strong sense of national pride among Chinese. A study by Ogilvy Group shows that 75% of Chinese say the Olympics make them proud of their country. And an even greater 87% see the Olympics as an opportunity to help Chinese brands become more international. After going through several serious crises earlier in 2008 and celebrating Chinese manned mission to the space and the succeeding successful spacewalk, a new wave of enthusiasm was driven by the chance to share exciting and inspiring Olympic moments with all people of the world and to write a new page in the history of the Olympics in the year that marks the 59th anniversary of the birth of PRC and the 30th anniversary of its reform program. The leader of China, President Hu Jintao used to elevate the contribution to and support for Beijing Olympics as the spirit of patriotism in his speech to celebrate the 110th anniversary of the birth of Beijing University. It is an urgent and positive response from the Chinese government in the face of many problems, including unrest in two Chinese minority areas—Tibet and Xinjiang, overseas attempts to disrupt, or even sabotage the Olympic torch relay, and foreign criticism on China's ability to deal with pollution and protection of intellectual property. This reflects China's determination to further improve her image on the world stage and strengthen its integration with the international world. The frequent reference to the sports world that embodies the national identity reflects as well as reinforces this underlying credo in the discourse of Olympic Economy. From this, we can see that while metaphors are often culture-specific, they are not culture-exclusive (Carroll, 1963) by the sense that the SPORT metaphor that is widely used in American society is adopted by the Chinese community in certain situation with a strong link between sport and politics. The popularity of SPORT metaphors may be also accounted for by the increasing attention given to the sports industry by the Chinese government under the spur of the Olympic Games. However, this assumption needs further justification by looking into more empirical evidence.

The competitive model of Olympic Economy in these two media is also realized by WAR metaphors. Essentially as an elaborate struggle with greater numbers and heavier weapons, the WAR metaphor is more appropriate than any other forms of conflict to represent the intense and prevalent competition in almost every field of business triggered by the Olympic Games that attracted so many domestic and foreign companies and organizations within a 7-year time span. It highlights the isomorphic relationships between the domain of business and war, in which there are shared scenarios for a ritualized sequence of activities: Initially there is a threat leading to the identification of an enemy; then there is a call to action in which allies are summoned; finally, a military struggle against an enemy leads to the victory, or surrender, or some form of punishment. The use of the WAR metaphor in both Chinese and American media successfully dramatizes the opposition between different companies and emphasizes the aggressiveness and seriousness of competition in Olympic Economy. Simultaneously, it creates an atmosphere of solidarity within a group and stimulates the members to stand together against a common enemy, such as foreign competitors faced by Chinese business community. The WAR metaphor is also used in relation to particularly serious and intractable problems that companies, organizations and governments came across in Olympic Economy and thus justifies the initiatives and strategies that were developed in order to solve these problems. These metaphors generally underscore the free market system by depicting a tough and relentless world of Olympic Economy, advocating the attitude of fittest survival: only the strongest could survive in Olympic Economy, leaving little room for joint problem solving and harmonious cooperation.

The developmental and competitive models of Olympic Economy are compatible with each other. They emphasize together the mobility of business events and entities in the conflict against others and the accompanying progress they can make. Such compatibility is best illustrated by the mixture of different metaphors deriving from these two models respectively. Take the following two extracts for instance. The two Chinese characters **lù** [路] and **zhàn** [战] in (1) activate the PATH scenario and the BATTLE scenario in JOURNEY and WAR metaphors respectively. They concern how Lenovo's performance in the marketing competition related to Beijing Olympics will contribute to the promotion of its brand. The Olympic marketing is described as a point in its long process of brand development. The English discourse (2) shows the compatibility of WAR and LIVING ORGANISM metaphors, in which Chinese fast-developing brands are personalized as powerful military forces that take the leading position in a battle. This highlights the value of strength in the business competition.

(1) 在联想的全球品牌推广之路上，怎样看待此次"奥运之战"的意义和作用？

[How do we look at the function and meaning of this "Olympic War" for Lenovo's global promotion of its brand?]

(CEW, October 9, 2006)

(2) Dozens of other companies are in the vanguard of China's growing number of powerful brands.

(BW, August 2, 2006)

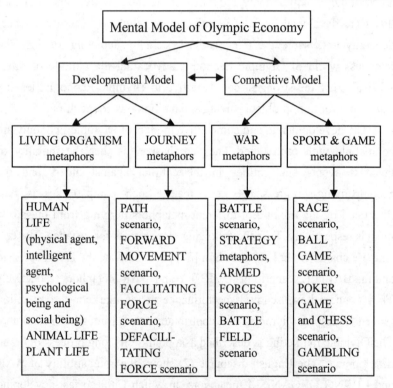

Figure 8.1 Shared mental model of Olympic Economy

All in all, the analysis of these four shared dominant metaphorical constructions demonstrates the common mental model of the two media in the understanding of Olympic Economy as an international sports business. It is conceived as a competitive event, in which companies like sentimental

220

and rational beings are fighting for limited resources following some open and fair regulations. The competition is accompanied with dynamic process in the business world and growth of the entities concerned. For success, the entities need strength, strategies and patience to overcome difficulties. To dramatize this understanding, they refer to intra-phenomena of the human being, mainly the physical, mental and emotional states of individuals and the inter-phenomena of human beings, mainly their social experiences, including war, sport and journey. The underlying motives reveal the dominance of free market ideology and the influence of political background on the metaphorical representation of Olympic Economy.

8.2 Differences in the Mental Model of Olympic Economy

In spite of the above similarities, there are still disparities in thinking of Olympic Economy between these two media, which are expressed through different or even particular metaphorical patterns or blends, different conceptual scenarios due to lexical choices within the same conceptual domain, and different grammatical co-texts for the linguistic metaphors. These give rise to differences in their developmental models, different BATTLE scenarios in their competitive model, diverse ways to look at companies as participants, business activities and related China's economy in both competitive and developmental models.

8.2.1 Differences in the Developmental Model between These Two Media

Both Chinese and American media highlight the development achieved by Olympic Economy as well as its positive effect on China's economy in the FORWARD MOVEMENT and FACILITATING FORCE scenarios constructed by a large number of metaphorical expressions conveying mobility and advance towards the destination in a journey.

Compared with Chinese one-sided emphasis on positive aspects of the journey, American media construct fairly comprehensive scenarios, with comparatively richer expressions for barriers on the path, and hindering forces accompanying the forward movement towards the destination. Such mixed scenarios stimulate both negative and positive evaluative meanings and emotive responses. In contrast, Chinese media represent Olympic Economy in terms of a much smoother journey that is realized by metaphors conveying forward mobility and facilitating forces. This highlights the fast development of China's sports industry due to the holding of the Olympics and implies positive effect of this sports event on China's economy. This is in line with the intended achievement of the Chinese government.

Goal-oriented and process-oriented journeys are constructed by American and Chinese media respectively. They use different metaphors to stand for the inspiration of companies. The English metaphor **goal** directly conflates their inspiration with the destination of a journey, while Chinese metaphors refer to it by the directional prepositions in the metaphoric phrasal verbs that construct the FORWARD MOVEMENT scenario. The process-orientated journey is further highlighted by outnumbered variations of metaphors standing for the forward movement in Chinese media. Such different orientations derive from diverse concerns of business communities addressed by these two media. American media focus on what companies could achieve in Olympic Economy, but Chinese media attach importance to how the achievement in Olympic Economy contributes to companies' future development.

In addition, the large majority of LIVING ORGANISM metaphors are divided in the English corpus mainly by two conceptual scenarios, HUMAN LIFE and PLANT LIFE. This is different from Chinese LIVING ORGANISM metaphors that are mainly realized by the HUMAN LIFE metaphor. This suggests that American media emphasize not only rational reasoning and psychological factors for the development of Olympic Economy, but also natural development without human interference. The latter aspect is not highlighted in Chinese media. This difference is also reflected by the choice of different kind of metaphoric verbs in the two media when they construct business events in terms of human actions.

8.2.2 Differences in the Competitive Model between These Two Media

The integration of free-market ideology into China's economic circle is best revealed by the frequent use of WAR metaphors in Chinese media, which even enjoy higher frequency of the WAR metaphor than the American counterpart. The intensity of aggressive and relentless scenarios dramatizes the challenges domestic companies have never faced before: They encounter threat from companies at home and abroad. On the one hand, they try to keep and at the same time expand their domestic market share. The historical metaphors alluding to the fighting for political dominance among several kingdoms imply the fierce competition among domestic companies who seem to engage in a war for survival. On the other hand, as inexperienced participants in Olympic Economy, they compete with experienced internationals, as soldiers defend their home territory against powerful foreign invaders and try to break through their encirclement to enter new markets, obtaining acknowledgment around the world. Comparatively, American media only focus on internationals, who are involved in a battle that is launched in a different market from those before. The fighting could be even more intense because of greater opportunities provided by the fast developing market in China. In this connection, two different BATTLE scenarios are constructed through metaphorical representations. In Chinese representations, multinationals depicted as foreign armed forces are competing to enter China and meet with challenges from domestic companies as the local forces who are attempting to break through obstruction to get into the foreign land besides defending their existing territory against any enemies. In English representations, multinationals enter the Chinese market as foreign armies are advancing into Chinese territory, fighting with each other and against local enemies. Correspondingly, two competitive models are produced, as illustrated in the following two figures, in which the rectangle in the middle stands for the Chinese market and circles for individual companies. The circles inside the rectangle represent domestic companies and those outside are internationals. The arrows show the direction of companies' development and the size of circles indicates their scale.

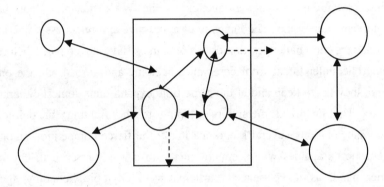

Figure 8. 2   The competitive model created in Chinese media

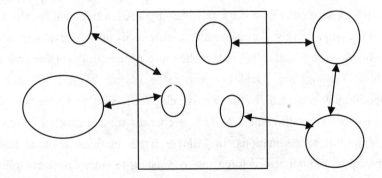

Figure 8.3   The competitive model created in American media

We can conclude that Chinese media create a more complicated model of competition, in which it not only concerns the entry of foreign companies into the Chinese brisk market that has become more attractive due to the hosting of Beijing Olympics, but also gives attention to the development of local companies beyond the boundary of the Chinese market, which is indicated by the dotted arrow in Figure 8.2. Such a model highlights both challenges and opportunities faced by local business communities.

8.2.3 Different Views on Companies as Participants in Olympic Economy

In the basic model of competition and development, the two media dramatize the features, activities and functions of companies as participants through a variety of metaphors. Based on the detailed analyses of lexical choices, the use of common and particular metaphorical patterns in the previous chapters, we can infer their differences on these aspects.

Firstly, American media stress the power of successful companies through such conceptual scenarios as the domination of intelligent people, big size and healthy state of human bodies and animals conveying conventionally positive meanings. At the same time, the media shed light on the interior status of Chinese companies in the competition in terms of their lagging position in the RACE scenario and by conflating them with Chinese Red Army in the 1920s who avoided direct conflict with the strong enemies in big cities by virtue of such intertextual metaphor as Mao Zedong strategy. This draws our attention to disadvantages of Chinese companies in the competition and at the same time stresses the value of free market ideology insisting that individual companies should be strong enough to compete with their rivals in the market.

Secondly, both Chinese and American media highlight the progress companies have achieved in Olympic Economy and any changes that have happened to them through the LIVING ORGANISM and JOURNEY metaphors. Apart from current progress, Chinese media take a more comprehensive perspective by considering the future development of companies, which is expressed by the metaphors of physical movement towards a destination with marked orientation. This demonstrates the difference between "what can we get in the Olympics?" and "what can we get after the Olympics?" The collective concern of these two issues in Chinese media may be explained by her role as the host country, which makes it regard the Olympics as an opportunity to further its local development and may be influenced by it for a long time. This makes Chinese media naturally look beyond the current event and link it with companies' future development.

Thirdly, we can witness the influence of free-market ideology in the emphasis of companies' mobililty by virtue of the RACE and FORWARD MOVEMENT scenarios in the two media. However, the active role of companies in Olympic Economy is enhanced more explicitly in American media in its convergence of companies' development with the self-propelling forward movement of a rational agent in the FACILITATING FORCE scenario. Although Chinese media depict companies as machines that have driving forces, our knowledge about machines tells us that they need external forces to make them run formally. In a word, American media give more priority to the initiative of economic subjects in Olympic Economy.

Fourthly, the social function of companies emphasized by MACHINE metaphors in Chinese media is also highlighted in its construction of companies as rational agents who have to take up social responsibilities. The underlying socialist values remind us of the vital role played by the central government in China's mixed economic systems. The positive role played by local and central governments in Olympic Economy is foregrounded through more than one scenario in Chinese metaphorical representations. HEALTH metaphors are adopted in the construction of measures against megaproject problems. The FORWARD MOVEMENT as well as FACILITATING FORCE scenarios structure the contribution made by the government to the progresss of Olympic Economy. All these convey positive evaluation of the government's function in Olympic Economy. Differently, the social role of companies is not the concern of American media. The government's role in the preparation for Beijing Olympics is constructed in American media by both FACILITATING and DEFACILITATING FORCE scenarios in JOURNEY metaphors. This implies a mixture of positive and negative evaluation of the government's functions in Olympic Economy.

Fifthly, both Chinese and American media concern cooperation between different companies apart from fierce competition. Chinese media attach importance to the interrelationship between companies by the concept of family in the representation of Olympic Economy as a social being. Besides the FAMILY metaphor, the SPORT metaphor is used by American media, highlighting the cooperation between different companies by constructing them as players who are engaged in team games. Such a difference may be explained to some extent by the profound influence of family and sports cultures in the societies these two media address. Still it could reveal their different ways of considering the cooperation in Olympic Economy. Chinese media prefer to consider it from the point of view of social network. Differently, American media consider competitive background apart from the social network companies belong to.

In a word, besides cultural factors and geographical locations, different thinking of companies between the two media and their diverse views on companies' roles in Olympic Economy demonstrate their disparate economic ideologies: American media adhere to the competitive model, emphasizing the power and initiative of individual companies for the success; while Chinese media put companies in the social network, highlighting their social as well as economic functions. They reveal the influence of free-market ideology and socialist values respectively.

8.2.4 Different Views on Events in Olympic Economy

Both media give attention to some phenomena that have triggered bitter arguments in the public, including problems of megaprojects in the preparation for Beijing Olympics, concrete business activities and their influence on local economy. Analyses on both linguistic and conceptual levels of metaphorical representations of these phenomena reflect different views between these two media.

As far as the megaprojects are concerned, both media underscore their financial problems bothering the host country and their negative influence on the development of local economy with regards to BURDEN metaphors. SPORT metaphors are employed to represent the result of wide debates over these problems, such as **cry foul** in American media and **hǎn ting** [喊停] in Chinese media, besides such JOURNEY metaphors as **halt** and **freeze**. Apart from these similarities, different metaphorical patterns are identified in these two media. As for the huge financial investment that sparked disputes, Chinese media talk about it as illness that plagues a patient besides the BURDEN metaphor. According to the logic of the HEALTH metaphor, the patient is not to be blamed for being affected by illness. Accordingly, the government is portrayed as an innocent victim suffering from ill health and its active and positive roles in the response are highlighted in the positive HEALTH metaphor **shòu shēn** [瘦身]. The negative side of megaprojects is further soft-pedaled by frequent representations of their positive social and economic functions, which are realized in the scenario of social human being and other metaphorical patterns, including STRATEGY metaphors highlighting their contribution to the development of Beijing, MACHINE metaphors depicting them as machines with powerful driving forces, NATURAL RESOURCES and

228

FORTUNE metaphors that shed light on their long-term benefits. Differently, American media express marked criticism by referring to animate metaphors with inherent negative evaluative meanings and arouse negative emotions among readers by the depiction of buildings' shape in terms of unfriendly movement of animals. As far as financial problems of those megaprojects are concerned, more than one metaphorical pattern (ANIMAL and JOURNEY metaphors) are adopted for the prominence of negative sides of these constructions. The binary opposition of positive and negative evaluation between Chinese and American media is further illustrated by MACHINE and PHYSICAL ENVIRONMENTAL PHENOMENA metaphors employed by them respectively in the representation of Olympic construction projects, in the sense that the MACHINE metaphor conflates mechanical mechanisms with the well-planned operation of these projects, while the the PHYSICAL ENVIRONMENTAL PHENOMENA metaphor foregrounds the instable and uncontrollable factors in the projects.

The opposite evaluation proceeds in their representations of specific business activities in Olympic Economy. They take different perspectives in their metaphorical construction of recessive marketing strategies by non-official sponsors, partners and suppliers, most of which are local companies. American media, on behalf of foreign companies, discuss about it in the BATTLE scenario realized by the conceptual blends of ambush marketing, in which a fight against the recessive marketing is justified to defend the right of official suppliers, partners and sponsors. Chinese media, however, express much concern over the development of local companies. It depicts the recessive marketing strategies taken by some domestic companies as effective strategies in the table tennis match whose success to a large extent depends on luck as well as skill. In this connection, the dubious attitudes of Chinese media form a sharp contrast with the critical view of American media. In addition, particular metaphorical patterns, including FOOD, ART and FORTUNE metaphors further foreground positive evaluation of business activities and their products in Chinese media.

Apart from specific business activities, their disparate views are also revealed in their metaphorical representations of China's economy. Both of them depict its fast development, but in different metaphorical patterns. Chinese media choose the JOURNEY metaphor and American media use the LIVING ORGANISM metaphor. The former describes the business process as a physical forward movement towards a pre-determined destination, implying necessary preparations for different stages, possible difficulties faced in the process and time plus patience needed to arrive at the destination; the latter converges the business progress with natural growth of an organism, implying the natural cycle of development China's economy will experience. In this connection, the two media talk about economic development in China during the Olympic Games from different perspectives. American media look at it as a normal stage of the growth cycle experienced by an economic entity, while Chinese media stress rational factors in the developing process of economy, implying the external forces outside of a business entity. This, to some extent is the conflict between different economic ideologies that either propose or oppose the interference of other social entities in the operation of business activities, such as the dispute about the government's role in economy.

As for contributing factors to China's economic development, both media shed light on the influence of Beijing Olympics on China's economy. Chinese media conceptualize the positive role played by Beijing Olympics through the FACILITATING FORCE scenario in JOURNEY metaphors, MECHANICAL SOURCE as well as POWER scenarios in MACHINE metaphors. In the MACHINE metaphor, the facilitating power of the Olympics is especially emphasized in the identified process that categorizes the Olympics directly as a running machine with powerful

230

driving forces. The same function in American media is mainly performed by the GROWTH scenario as patient in PLANT LIFE metaphors, in which the Olympics as an agent stimulates the growth of China's economy. But the positive voice is accompanied by negative one embedded in some verbal expressions that complete the construction of the same scenario. The same function is also performed by the material processes that contain expressions activating machine image, but with much less instances, compared with Chinese media. Moreover, the FACILITATING FORCE scenario for China's economy is totally absent in American media. These differences demonstrate that the benefits of Olympic Economy on China's development are demonstrated more strikingly by Chinese media. This is strengthened by its mixture of JOURNEY and MACHINE metaphors in the construction of China's economy. The inferred positive evaluation based on these metaphors to some extent justifies the country's efforts for the bid and preparations for the Olympics.

The negative voice expressed in the GROWTH scenario as patient in American media is echoed in more than one case. The image of sudden forward movement of waves in the NATURAL GEOGRAPHICAL FEATURE scenario, and unpleasant feelings aroused by WEATHER metaphors point together to the negative sides of fast-developing economy in China. They highlight the instability and unpredictability of China's economy, which is hard to control and predict, implying high risks besides opportunities for any related economic entities.

8.3 Summary

Because of the international nature of the topic in question and the influence of free market ideology, both media share a developmental and competitive mental model of Olympic Economy that is instantiated in JOURNEY, LIVING ORGANISM, WAR, SPORT and GAME metaphors.

These metaphors draw our attention to the fierce and open competition between different participants in Olympic Economy, and hard work as well as effective strategies that are needed for success. Simultaneously, such a mental model highlights intended goals, achieved progress and difficulties that have to be overcome in the whole process.

In spite of these similarities, the different roles played by these two countries in Beijing Olympics make them consider this competition from different perspectives, which leads to two different competitive models. The more complicated model created by Chinese media structures two battles engaging the local companies, implying the juxtaposition of challenges and opportunities for them. Besides, different views on China's economy, the political and economic significance of Beijing Olympics for China lead to differences in the developmental model. In addition, different economic ideologies, plus cultural elements drive them to consider participants in the model differently. The dominance of free market ideology drive American media to emphasize the power and initiative of individual companies in the market; while Chinese media, influenced by socialist ideas highlight the social functions of companies. Moreover, American media indicate negative evaluation of the competitiveness of Chinese companies, megaprojects and Beijing's transformation in the preparation for the Olympics and problems caused by the fast development of China's economy. Differently, Chinese media construct optimistic images in linking the economic event with political and social background in China. It also associates the current situation with companies' development in the future in an attempt to tone down the current problems.

Chapter 9   Conclusion

9.1 Major Findings of the Present Study

In the core of this dissertation, an integrated theoretical framework is adopted to study the cognitive patterns and linguistic realizations in the discourse of Olympic Economy through description, interpretation and explanation of metaphorical representations in both Chinese and American popular business discourse. The detailed and systematic analyses help us reach the following conclusions.

Firstly, the great number of metaphorical expressions identified in the corpora can be reduced to a fairly limited number of conceptual metaphors. They are employed for the construction of participants, process, consequences and major problems in Olympic Economy. The most frequent metaphorical patterns are shared by these two media. They are drawn from concepts concerning intra-phenomena of human beings, mainly the physical, mental and emotional states of individuals and the inter-phenomena of human beings, mainly their social experiences, including war, sport, game and journey. These support the basic idea of cognitive linguistics that the complex and abstract social phenomena are often discussed in terms of familiar objects and experiences, and thus demonstrate the experiential motivation of metaphor use.

Secondly, the shared salient metaphors also reflect the common mental model of Olympic Economy in these two media. Both of them regard Olympic Economy as a fierce and open competition between different companies in accordance with certain rules and practices. The success requires patience, strategies, hard work of the participants as well as overcoming the difficulties in the whole process. The shared mental model is largely decided by the nature of Olympic Economy as an international sports business with mature mechanisms. In addition, the similarity shows some effect of China's integration with the international market in its process of modernization, which is marked by the frequent presence of those metaphors adhering to free-market ideology.

Thirdly, the similarities of these two media do not hide their different thinking of entities and actions in Olympic Economy and thus demonstrate their different understanding of Olympic Economy: American media regard it as another business competition between powerful multinationals in a rising market and concern both positive and negative sides in these processes. It highlights the doubt on the competitiveness of local companies and expresses negative evaluations of China's fast development. Chinese media consider it as an opportunity to improve the image and raise awareness of local companies in the world and link this event closely with their development. What's more, positive evaluation is dominant in Chinese media by its soft-pedaling the problems.

Fourthly, differences between the two media are mainly revealed in diverse scenarios activated by lexical choices within the same conceptual domain, one media's favor for different metaphorical patterns and even particular cross-domain projections for the same topic. In addition, different functions of the same metaphorical pattern contribute to different views and opinions of these two media. These reflect the vital role lexical and grammatical analyses play in the revelation of metaphor functions and thus justify the detailed linguistic analysis in the study of metaphors' functions in discourse. The significance of the linguistic level is remarkable in diverse scenarios created within the same conceptual domain. Such scenarios activated by specific lexical choice could imply diversity in mentality that is easy to be ignored if we only confine the study to the macro cross-domain projections.

Fifthly, apart from diversification and multivalency (Goatly, 1997: 255) in the use of metaphor, there are many instances of double metaphors and mixed metaphors in the discourse about Olympic Economy. The same metaphorical pattern is activated more than once by the same or different expressions derived from the same conceptual domain in double metaphors. This consolidates the metaphorical representation concerned and thus highlights the specific way in the understanding of entities and events in Olympic Economy. In mixed metaphors, two concepts from different domains are drawn to dramatize the same entity and event. Concrete examples show that these different metaphors are compatible with each other that result in a more comprehensive representation of the target domain.

Sixthly, besides common metaphors, some metaphors are particular to either Chinese or English media. The analyses show that they mainly perform two functions: to complement frequent metaphorical patterns in the construction of Olympic Economy, such as TEXTILE metaphors in the structure of building projects; to enhance views and tones that have been implied in other metaphorical patterns. For instance, FOOD metaphors in Chinese echo the positive evaluation about Olympic Economy that is implied in JOURNEY and MACHINE metaphors. To some extent, we can see that particular metaphors give more explicit demonstration of evaluative meanings in spite of their low frequency.

Seventhly, both media use conventional and novel metaphors in the representation of Olympic Economy. Undoubtedly, conventional metaphors as a traditional way in a community to represent entities and events reflect its underlying values and opinions. Comparatively, novel metaphors could more easily draw readers' attention, in spite of their low frequency. The present study demonstrates their equal importance in the representation of economic ideologies in Chinese and American societies and their attitudes towards Olympic Economy related to Beijing Olympics.

Last but not least, the present study also demonstrates that analyses at the lexical and grammatical levels alone cannot fully explain the function of some metaphors, or the media's preference to one metaphorical representation than another, or different uses of the same metaphor between the two media. We need to look into historical, cultural, as well as political factors and economic ideologies lying behind the depicted business activities. Only through historical factors could we understand the implied meaning of a metaphor and the embedded evaluation in it. The case in point is the intertextual metaphor with a historical origin. Without corresponding cultural background knowledge, we could not infer the emotional effect of a metaphor or explain the popularity of specific metaphors in one media. Both media also use intertextual metaphors deeply rooted in the foreign culture. For example, the English metaphor **Mao Zedong strategy** draws from Chinese history and the Chinese metaphor **nián yú** [鲇鱼] is the literal translation of **catfish** that reflects enterprise culture of western countries. The political factors, including political issues accompanying the preparations for the Olympics and the political aims the host city and country want to achieve help us to explain the salience of the positive tone in Chinese media and its obscurity in the representation of problems. The metaphorical representations even reveal different economic ideologies of the two communities that decide their diverse ways of constructing the same entity and event: the dominance of free-market ideology in American society and the mixture of free-market and socialist ideas in Chinese society. These various contextual factors contribute to their mentalities that produce similar and different metaphorical representations of Olympic Economy in these two media, which in turn reinforce their ideologies and influence the opinions of readers and their perception of business activities related to Beijing

236

Olympics.

9.2 Implications of This Study

Although the study suffers from a few weak points due to its tentative nature, it still has a few important implications. Major findings contribute theoretically and methodologically to the discourse study of metaphors and media studies.

Theoretically, an integrated framework has been established in order to reveal the relation between societal structure and discourse of Olympic Economy related to the 2008 Beijing Olympics. In such a framework, metaphor as both conceptual and linguistic phenomena works as the interface not only between the cognitive structure underlying discourse and ideological structure dominating it, but also between discourse and its metaphoric realizations in text. Incorporation of the analytical tools and ideas from cognitive linguistics into the paradigm of CDA enables this study to carry out social, cognitive and linguistic analyses of metaphor use in popular business discourse. The findings support some basic ideas about metaphor, including its experiential motivation, conceptual and ideological nature and simultaneously demonstrate its function in the relevation of covert meanings in language use. Most importantly, this framework enriches social-cognitive research under the paradigm of CDA and thus responds to the doubt of the so-called over-interpretation of CDA.

Methodologically, the study of metaphor as ideologically tainted language in this research further blurs the boundary between conventional and novel metaphors. Not only conventional metaphors, but also novel metaphors and conceptual blending could reveal the users' specific perspective to think of entities and events. Even one-shot metaphors with quite low frequency could perform the similar function. These also reflect that the total dependence on the frequency of metaphorical patterns could not give a comprehensive interpretation and explanation of the function and special meaning of metaphor use. The manual search used in the identification of metaphors enables us to notice the co-text of each metaphor and interaction of different kinds of metaphorical patterns.

The comparative method adopted in the research clearly foregrounds underlying ideologies that nurture the diversity of metaphor use across different languages. It makes observations about one society outside the First World that draws world-wide attention due to Beijing Olympics. This responds to the criticism that CDA confines only to particular kinds of societies, which represent the core of the world system (Blommaert, 2005: 35) and thus advocates the idea that disparity across societies should be taken into account in the study of discourse in the contemporary world.

In application, these conclusions based on conceptual, linguistic and social analyses of metaphorical representations could contribute to the current literature of media studies in the critical approach by incorporating cognitive linguistics into empirical studies. As a fairly cognitively robust CDA, the dissertation enhances the belief that media discourse, including popular business discourse, is not always the complete and neutral representation of the reality, including the world of economy. The media is an effective channel to manipulate the public's understanding of important events, such as Beijing Olympics and related business activities. Metaphors play an essential role in such a process and could provide useful insights into it.

9.3 Limitations and Suggestions for Further Studies

This study is the first comparative research of metaphorical representations of Olympic Economy. Although it presents some meaningful findings, there are still limitations since it is only a tentative study, and more research is needed to confirm and complement the present

238

study.

Due to the limitation of time and energy, the self-established corpora are only based on the data chosen from two newspapers and two magazines within a fixed time span. In spite of discussion with one expert for ambigious cases and reference to authentic dictionaries based on a large corpus of modern Chinese and English in an attempt to reduce subjective identification of metaphorical expressions, we can not deny the possibility of missing some metaphors. Additionally, our way of categorizing some metaphors on the basis of the primary sense of metaphorical expressions defined by dictionaries, the current literature on metaphor study and the context of metaphor use may give rise to different opinions among researchers.

For further studies this research should be replicated with a larger size of data with the purpose of confirming the generalization of the results. The time range could be expanded to trace the response in the media longer after Beijing Olympics. Other kinds of data could also be considered, such as discourse from the tabloid instead of exclusive reference to the authentic magazines and newspapers. Apart from larger corpora, empirical studies of reactions could be adopted to enrich investigative methods in the study of metaphorical representations of Olympic Economy as a socio-cultural and psycholinguistic phenomenon.

References

Ahrens, K. (2010). *Politics, Gender and Conceptual Metaphors.* Basingstoke: Palgrave Macmillan.

Akin, A. A. (1994). The rhetorical construction of radical Africanism at the United Nations: Metaphoric cluster as strategy. *Discourse & Society,* 5 (1), 7-31.

Attia, M. (2007). A critical cognitive study: The Egyptian written media. In C. Hart & D. Lukes (Eds.), *Cognitive Linguistics in Critical Discourse Analysis* (pp. 81-106). Newcastle: Cambridge Scholars Publishing.

Bell, A. (1995). Language and the media. *Annual Review of Applied Linguistics,* 15 (1), 23-41.

Bichieri, C. (1988). Should a scientist abstain from metaphor? In A. Kramer, D. McCloskey & R. Solow (Eds.), *The Consequences of Economic Rhetoric* (pp. 100-116). New York: Cambridge University Press.

Billig, M. & Macmillan, K. (2005). Metaphor, idiom and ideology: The search for No Smoking Guns across time. *Discourse & Society,* 16 (4), 459-80.

Blommaert, J. (2005). *Discourse: A Critical Introduction.* Cambridge: Cambridge University Press.

Boers, F. (1997). "No Pain, No Gain" in a Free Market Rhetoric: A test for cognitive semantics? *Metaphor and Symbol,* 12 (4), 231-241.

Boers, F. (1999). When a bodily source domain becomes prominent: The joy of counting metaphors in the socio-economic domain. In R. W.

Gibbs & G. Steen (Eds.), *Metaphor in Cognitive Linguistics* (pp. 47-56). Amsterdam: John Benjamins.

Boers, F. (2000). Enhancing metaphor awareness in specialized reading. *English for Specific Purposes*, 19 (1), 137-147.

Boers, F. (2001). Remembering figurative idioms by hypothesizing about their origins. *Prospect*, 16 (3), 35-43.

Boers, F. (2003). Applied linguistics perspectives on cross-cultural variation in conceptual metaphor. *Metaphor and Symbol*, 18: 231-238.

Boers, F. & Demecheleer, M. (1997). A few metaphorical models in (western) economic discourse. In W. Liebert, G. Redeker & L. Waugh (Eds.), *Discourse and Perspective in Cognitive Linguistics* (pp. 115-130). Amsterdam: John Benjamins Publishing Co.

Boers, F., Demecheleer, M. & Eyckmans, J. (2004). Cross-cultural variation as a variable in comprehending and remembering figurative idioms. *European Journal of English Studies*, 8 (3), 375-388.

Boozer, R. W., Wyld, D. C. & Grant, J. (1992). Using metaphor to create more effective sales messages. *Journal of Business & Industrial Marketing*, 7 (1), 19-27.

Bratož, S. (2004). A comparative study of metaphor in English and Slovene popular economic discourse. *Managing Global Transitions*, 2 (2), 179-196.

Caldas-Coulthard, C. R. & van Leeuwen, T. (2003). Critical Social Semiotics: Introduction. *Social Semiotics*, 13 (1), 3-4.

Caers, E. (2006). When ministers were digging in for a fight: metaphors of liberal common sense during the Winter Of Discontent, 1978-1979. *Belgian Journal of English Language and Literatures*, 4 (1), 5-20.

Cameron, L. (2001). Operationalising "metaphor" for applied linguistic research. In L. Cameron & G. Low (Eds.), *Researching and*

241

Applying Metaphor (pp. 3-28). Shanghai: Shanghai Foreign Language Education Press.

Cameron, L. (2007) Patterns of metaphor use in reconciliation talk. *Discourse and Society*, 18 (2), 197-222.

Cameron, L. & Deignan, A. (2003). Combining large and small corpora to investigate tuning devices around metaphor in spoken discourse. *Metaphor and Symbol*, 18 (1), 149–160.

Carroll, J. B. (1963). Linguistic relativity, contrastive linguistics, and language learning. *International Review of Applied Linguistics in Language Teaching* 1(1), 1-20.

Charteris-Black, J. (2000). Metaphor and vocabulary teaching in ESP economics. *English for Specific Purposes Journal,* 19 (2), 145-165.

Charteris-Black, J. (2003). Speaking with forked tongue: A comparative study of metaphor and metonymy in English and Malay phraseology. *Special edition of Metaphor and Symbol,* 18 (4), 289-310.

Charteris-Black, J. (2004). *Corpus Approaches to Critical Metaphor Analysis*. New York: Palgrave.

Charteris-Black, J. (2005). *Politicians and Rhetoric. The Persuasive Power of Metaphor*. Basingstoke: Palgrave-Macmillan.

Charteris-Black, J. & Ennis, T. (2001). A Comparative study of metaphor in Spanish and English financial reporting. *English for Specific Purposes: An International Journal*, 20 (3), 249-266.

Charteris-Black, J. & Musolff, A. (2003). Battered "hero" or "innocent victim"? A comparative study of metaphors for euro trading in British and German financial reporting. *English for Specific Purposes*, 22 (2), 153-176.

Cheng, M. (2006). Constructing a new political spectacle: Tactics of Chen Shui-bian's 2000 and 2004 "inaugural speeches". *Discourse & Society*, 17 (5), 583-608.

Chilton, P. (2004). *Analyzing Political Discourse: Theory and Practice.*

242

London and New York: Routledge.

Chilton, P. (2005a). Manipulation, memes and metaphors: The case of Mein Kampf. In L. de Saussure & P. Schulz (Eds.), *Manipulation and Ideologies in the Twentieth Century* (pp. 5-45). Amsterdam & Philadelphia: John Benjamins.

Chilton, P. (2005b). Missing links in mainstream CDA: Modules, blends and the critical instinct. In R. Wodak & P. Chilton (Eds.), *A New Agenda in (Critical) Discourse Analysis: Theory, Methodology and Interdisciplinarity* (pp. 19-51). Amsterdam: John Benjamins.

Chilton, P. & Lakoff, G. (1995). Foreign policy by metaphor. In C. Schäffner & A. Wenden (Eds.), *Language and Peace* (pp. 37-60). Aldershot, Ashgate.

Chilton, P. & Schäffner, C. (2002). *Politics as Text and Talk: Analytical Approaches to Political Discourse.* Amsterdam: John Benjamins.

Coakley, J. (1994). *Sports in Society: Issues and Controversies* (Fifth Edition). St. Louis: Mosby.

Cornelissen, J. P., Kafouros, M. & Lock, A. R. (2005). Metaphorical images of organization: How organizational researchers develop and select organizational metaphors. *Human Relations,* 58 (12), 1545-1578.

Cortazzi, M. & Jin, L. (1999). Bridges to Learning, metaphors of teaching, learning and language. In L. Cameron & G. Low (eds.) *Researching and Applying Metaphor* (pp.149-176). Cambridge: Cambridge University Press.

Deignan, A. (2000). Persuasive uses of metaphor in discourse about business and the economy. In C. Heffer & H. Sauntson (Eds.), *Words in Context: A Tribute to John Sinclair on His Retirement.* Birmingham, England: ELR Discourse.

Deignan, A. (2001). Corpus-based research into metaphor. In L. Cameron & G. Low (Eds.), *Researching and Applying Metaphor* (pp.

177-199). Shanghai: Shanghai Foreign Language Education Press.

Deignan, A. (2003). Metaphorical expressions and culture: An indirect link. *Metaphor and Symbol*, 18 (4), 255-271.

Deignan, A. (2005). *Metaphor and Corpus Linguistics*. Amsterdam/Philadelphia: John Benjamins Publishing Company.

Deignan, A. (2006). Readership and purpose in the choice of economics metaphors. *Metaphor and Symbol*, 21 (2), 87-110.

Deignan, A. & Potter, L. (2004). A corpus study of metaphors and metonyms in English and Italian. *Journal of Pragmatics*, 36 (7), 1231-1252.

Dirven, R., Frank, P. & Hans-Georg, W. (2005). Cognitive linguistics, ideology and Critical Discourse Analysis. In D. Geeraerts & H. Cuckyens (Eds.), *Handbook of Cognitive Linguistics* (in press). Oxford: Oxford University Press.

Dirven, R., Frank, R. M. & Pütz, M. (2003). Introduction: categories, cognitive models and ideologies. In R., Dirven, R. M., Frank & M., Pütz (Eds.), *Cognitive Models in Language and Thought: Ideology, Metaphors and Meanings* (pp. 1-24). Berlin: Mouton De Gruyter.

Dudley-Evans, A. & Henderson, W. (1990). The language of economics: the analysis of economics discourse. *ELT Documents*, No.134, Modern Publications in Association with the British Council, London.

Emanatian, M. (1995). Metaphor and the expression of emotion: The value of cross-cultural perspectives. *Metaphor and Symbolic Activity*, 10, 163-182.

Eubanks, P. (2000). *A War of Words in the Discourse of Trade: The Rhetorical Constitution of Metaphor*. Carbonale and Edwardsville: Southern Illinois University Press.

Fairclough, N. (1989). *Language and Power*. London: Longman.

Fairclough, N. (1992). *Discourse and Social Change*. Cambridge: Polity

Press.

Fairclough, N. (1993). Critical Discourse Analysis and the marketization of public discourse: the universities. *Discourse & Society*, 4 (2), 133-168.

Fairclough, N. (1995). *Critical Discourse Analysis: The Critical Study of Language*. London: Longman.

Fairclough, N. (2003). *Analysing Discoure: Textual Analysis for Social Research*. USA and Canada: Routledge.

Fauconnier, G. (1998). *Mental Spaces: Aspects of Meaning Construction in Natural Language*. New York: Cambridge University Press.

Fauconnier, G. & Turner, M. (1998). Conceptual integration network. *Cognitive Science*, (2), 133-187.

Fauconnier, G. & Turner, M. (2002). *The Way We Think: Conceptual Blending and the Mind's Hidden Complexities*. New York: Basic Books.

Foucault, M. (ed. Colin Gordon). (1980). *Power/Knowledge: Selected Interviews and Other Writings*. New York: Pantheon Books.

Fowler, R. (1991). *Language in the News: Discourse & Ideology in the Press*. London: Routledge.

Fowler, R. Hodge, B., Kress, G., & Trew, T. (1979). *Language and Control*. New York: Routledge & Kagan Paul.

Gibbs, Raymond W. (1994). *The Poetics of Mind: Figurative Thought, Language and Understanding*. Cambridge: Cambridge University Press.

Gibbs, Raymond W. (1999). Embodied metaphors in perceptual symbols. *Behavioral and Brain Sciences*, 22 (4), 617-618.

Gibbs, Raymond W., Bogdanovich, Josephine M., Sykes, Jeffrey R. & Barr, Dale J. (1997). Metaphor in idiom comprehension. *Journal of Memory and Language*, 37(1), 141-154.

Gibbs, R. W. (2001). Researching metaphor. In L. Cameron & G. Low

(Eds.), *Researching and Applying Metaphor* (pp. 29-47). Shanghai: Shanghai Foreign Language Education Press.

Gibbs, R. W., Lima, P. L. C., & Francozo, E. (2004). Metaphor is grounded in embodied experience. *Journal of Pragmatics*, 36, 1189-1210.

Goatly, A. (1997). *The Language of Metaphors.* London and New York: Routledge.

Goatly, A. (2007). *Washing the Brain: Metaphor and Hidden Ideology.* Amsterdam: John Benjamins.

Grady, J. (1997a). THEORIES ARE BUILDINGS revisited. *Cognitive Linguistics,* 8 (2), 267-290.

Grady, J. (1997b). Foundations of Meaning: Primary Metaphors and Primary Scenes. Doctoral Paper. University of California, Berkeley.

Gwyn, Richard. (1999). "Captain of my own ship": Metaphor and the discourse of chronic illness. In L. J. Cameron and G. D. Low (Eds.), *Researching and Applying Metaphor* (pp. 203-220) Cambridge: Cambridge University Press.

Halliday, M. A. K. (2000[1994]). *An Introduction to Functional Grammar.* Beijing: Foreign Language Teaching and Research Press.

Hart, C. & Lukes, D. (2007). *Cognitive Lingusitics in Critical Discourse Analysis: Application and Theory.* Newcastle: Cambridge Scholars Publishing.

Hawkes, T. (1972). *Metaphor.* London: Methuen.

Hawkins, B. (2001). Ideology, metaphor and iconographic reference. In R. Dirven, R. Frank & C. Ilie (Eds.), *Language and Ideology. Volume II: Descriptive Cognitive Approaches* (pp. 27-50). Amsterdam & Philadelphia: John Benjamins.

Henderson, W. (1982). Metaphor in economics. *Economics*, 18(4), 147-153.

Henderson, W. (1986). Metaphor in economics. In M. Coulthard (Ed.), *Talking About Text* (Discourse Monographs, No. 13. English

Language Research) (pp. 109-127). Birmingham: University of Birmingham.

Henderson, W. (1994). Metaphor and economics. In R. E. Backhouse (Ed.), *New Directions in Economic Methodology* (pp. 343-367). London and New York: Routledge.

Hodge, R. & Kress, G. (1988). *Social Semiotics.* Oxford: Polity.

Hodge, R. & Kress, G. (1993). *Language as Ideology* (2nd Edition). London: Routledge

Hunston, S. & Thompson, G. (2000). *Evaluation in Text: Authorial Stance and the Construction of Discourse.* Oxford: Oxford University Press.

Johnson, M. (1987). *The Body in the Mind: The Bodily Basis of Meaning, Imagination, and Reason.* Chicago: University of Chicago Press.

Kail, P. J. E. (2001). Projection and necessity in Hume. *European Journal of Philosophy*, 9 (1), 24-54.

Koller, V. (2003). Metaphor Clusters in Business Media Discourse: A Social Cognition Approach. Doctoral Paper. Vienna University.

Koller, V. (2004). *Metaphor and Gender in Business Media Discourse: a Critical Cognitive Study.* New York: Palgrave Macmillan.

Koller, V. (2006). Of critical importance: Using electronic text corpora to study metaphor in business media discourse. In A. Stefanowitsch & S. Th. Gries (Eds.), *Corpus-Based Approaches to Metaphor and Metonymy* (pp. 237-265). Berlin, New York: Mouton de Gruyter.

Kövecses, Z. (1986). *Metaphors of Anger, Pride, and Love: A Lexical Approach to the Study of Concepts.* Amsterdam: Benjamins.

Kövecses, Z. (1991). Happiness: A definitional effort. *Metaphor and Symbolic Activity*, 6 (1), 29-46.

Kövecses, Z. (1995a). American friendship and the scope of metaphor. *Cognitive Linguistics*, 6 (2), 315-346.

Kövecses, Z. (1995b). Anger: Its language, conceptualization, and physiology in the light of cross-cultural evidence. In J. R. Taylor &

247

R. Maclaury (Eds.), *Language and the Cognitive Construal of the World* (pp. 181-196). Berlin: Mouton de Gruyter.

Kövecses, Z. (2000). *Metaphor and Emotion: Language, Culture and Body in Human Emotion.* Cambridge: Cambridge University Press.

Kövecses, Z. (2002). *Metaphor: A Practical Introduction.* New York: Oxford University Press.

Kövecses, Z. (2003). The scope of metaphor. In B. Antonio (Ed.), *Metaphor and Metonymy at the Crossroads: A Cognitive Perspective* (pp. 79-92). Berlin, New-York: Mouton de Gruyter.

Kövecses, Z. (2004). Introduction: cultural variation in metaphor. *European Journal of English Studies,* 8 (3), 263-274.

Kövecses, Z. (2005). *Metaphor in Culture: Universality and Variation.* Cambridge: Cambridge University Press.

Kövecses, Z. & Szabo, P. (1996). Idioms: A view from cognitive linguistics. *Applied Linguistics,* 17 (3), 326-355.

Kress, G. (1990). Critical Discourse Analysis. *Annual Review of Applied Linguistics,* 2 (11), 84-99.

Kress, G. (1996). Representational resources and the production of subjectivity. In C. Caldas-Doulthard & M. Coulthard (Eds.), *Texts and Practics: Readings in Critical Discourse Analysis* (pp. 15-31). London and New York: Routledge.

Kress, G. & Hodge, R. (1979). *Social Semiotics.* Ithaca, NY: Cornell University Press.

Kress, G. & T. van Leeuwen. (1996). *Reading Images: The Grammar of Visual Design.* London: Routledge.

Kress, G. & T. van Leeuwen. (2001). *Multimodal Discourse: The Modes and Media of Contemporary Communication.* Arnold: London.

Lakoff, G. (1987). *Women, Fire and Dangerous Things: What Categories Reveal about the Mind.* Cambridge: Cambridge University Press.

Lakoff, G. (1991). Metaphor and War: the metaphor system used to justify war in the Gulf. http://www.uoregon.edu/~uophil/metaphor/lakoff-l. htm.

Lakoff, G. (1993). The contemporary theory of metaphor. In A. Ortony (Ed.) *Metaphor and Thought* (pp. 302-351). Cambridge: Cambridge University Press.

Lakoff, G. (1996). *Moral Politics: What Conservatives Know That Liberals Don't.* Chicago: Chicago University Press.

Lakoff, G. (2002). *Moral Politics: How Liberals and Conservatives Think.* Chicago: The University of Chicago Press.

Lakoff, G. (2004). *Don't Think of an Elephant: Know Your Values and Frame Your Debate.* White River Junction, VT: Chelsea Green.

Lakoff, G. & Johnson, M. (1980). *Metaphors We Live By.* Chicago: University of Chicago Press.

Lakoff, G. & Johnson, M. (1999). *Philosophy in the Flesh: The Embodied Mind and Its Challenge to Western Thought.* New York: Basic Books.

Lakoff, G. & Kövesces, Z. (1987). The cognitive model of anger inherent in American English. In D. Holland & N. Quinn (Eds.), *Cultural Models in Language and Thought* (pp. 195-221). Cambridge: Cambridge University Press.

Lakoff, G. & Turner, M. (1989). *More Than Cool Reason.* Chicago: University of Chicago Press.

Lazar, G. (1996). Using figurative language to expand students' vocabulary. *ELT Journal*, 50 (1), 43-51.

Levitt, H., Korman, Y., & Angus L. (2000). A metaphor analysis in treatments of depression: Metaphor as a marker of change. *Counseling Psychology Quarterly,* 13, 23-36.

Liu, Dilin. (2002). *Metaphor, Culture, and Worldview: the Case of American English and the Chinese Language.* Lanham, New York, Oxford: University Press of America, Inc.

Louis Wei-Lun, L. & Kathleen, A. (2008). Ideological influence on BUILDING metaphors in Taiwanese presidential speeches. *Discourse & Society*, 19 (3), 383-408.

Maalej, Z. (2004). Figurative language in anger expressions in Tunisian Arabic: An extended view of embodiment. *Metaphor and Symbol*, 19 (1), 51-75.

Maalej, Z. (2007). Doing Critical Discourse Analysis with the contemporary theory of metaphor: Towards a discourse model of metaphor. In C. Hart & D. Lukes (Eds.), *Cognitive linguistics in Critical Discourse Analysis* (pp.132-158). Newcastle: Cambridge Scholars Publishing.

MacArthur, F. (2005). The competent horseman in a horseless world: Observations on a conventional metaphor in Spanish and English. *Metaphor and Symbol*, 20 (1), 71-94.

Mason, M. (1990). Dancing on air: Analysis of a passage from an economics textbook, In A. Dudley & W. Henderson (Eds.), *The Language of Economics: The Analysis of Economic Discourse* (ELT Documents 134) (pp.17-28). London: Modern English Publications.

McCloskey, Donald N. (1985). *The Rhetoric of Economics*. Madison: University of Wisconsin Press.

Mey, J. L. (1994). *Pragmatics: An Introduction*. Oxford: Blackwell.

Musolff, A. (2003) Ideological functions of metaphors: The conceptual metaphors of health and illness in public discourse. In R. Dirven, R. M. Frank & M. Pütz (Eds.), *Cognitive Models in Language and Thought: Ideology, Metaphors and Meanings* (pp. 327-352). Berlin: Mouton De Gruyter.

Musolff, A. (2004). *Metaphor and Political Discourse: Analogical Reasoning in Debates about Europe*. Basingstoke: Palgrave Macmillan.

Musolff, A. (2006). Metaphor scenarios in public discourse. *Metaphor and*

Symbol, 21(1), 23-38.

Musolff, A. (2007). Which role do metaphors play in racial prejudice? The function of anti-Mein Kampf. *Patterns of Prejudice,* 41 (1), 21-44.

O'Halloran, K. (2003). *Critical Discourse Analysis and Language Cognition.* Edinburgh: Edinburgh University Press.

O'Halloran, K. (2007). Casualness vs commitment: The use in Critical Discourse Analysis of Lakoff and Johnson's approach to metaphor. In C. Hart & D. Lukes (Eds.), *Cognitive Linguistics in Critical Discourse Analysis* (pp.159-179). Newcastle: Cambridge Scholars Publishing.

Olson, H. A. (1998). Mapping beyond Dewey's boundaries: Constructing classificatory space for marginalized knowledge domains. *Library Trends*, 47 (2), 233-254.

Ortony, A. (1996). Metaphor, language, and thought. In A. Ortony (Ed.), *Metaphor and Thought* (Second Edition) (pp. 1-16). Cambridge: Cambridge University Press.

Oswick, C. & Montgomery, J. (1999). Images of an organization: the use of metaphor in a multinational company. *Journal of Organizational Change Management*, 12 (5), 501-523.

Öztel, H. & Hinz, O. (2001). Changing organizations with metaphors. *The Learning Organization: An International Journal*, 8 (2), 153-168.

Pancake, Ann S. (1993). Taken by storm: The exploitation of metaphor in the Persian Gulf War. *Metaphor and Symbolic Activity*, 8 (2), 281-295.

Peters, W. & Wilks, Y. (2003). Data-driven detection of figurative language use in electronic language resources. *Metaphor and Symbol*, 18 (2), 161-173.

Phillips, B. (1998). Energy and performance: The power of metaphor. *Career Development International*, 3 (1), 18-22.

Pielenz, M. (1999). *Argumentation und Metapher.* Tubingen: Gunter Narr

Quinn, N. (1991). The cultural basis of metaphor. In J. W. Fernandez (Ed.), *Beyond Metaphor: The Theory of Tropes in Anthropology* (pp.57-93). Stanford, CA.

Rash, F. (2005). Mein Kampf. Metaphorik. de 9: 74-111.

Reder, M. W. (1999). *Economics: The Culture of a Controversial Science.* Chicago and London: The University of Chicago Press.

Ritchie, D. (2003). "ARGUMENT IS WAR"—Or is it a game of chess? Multiple meanings in the analysis of implicit metaphors. *Metaphor and Symbol,* 18 (2), 125-146.

Rohrer, T. (1995). The metaphorical logic of (political) rape: The new world order. *Metaphor and Symbolic Activity,* 10 (1), 115-137.

Sanday, P. R. (1994). Trapped in a metaphor. *Criminal Justice Ethics,* 13 (2), 32-38.

Santa Ana, Otto. (1999). Like an animal I was treated: Anti-immigrant metaphor in US public discourse. *Discourse & Society,* 10 (1), 191-224.

Santa Ana, Otto. (2002). *Brown Tide Rising: Metaphors of Latinos in Contemporary American Public Discourse.* Austin: University of Texas Press.

Santa Ana, Otto. (2003). Three mandates for anti-minority policy expressed in U.S. public discourse metaphors. In R., Dirven, R. M., Frank & M., Pütz (Eds.), *Cognitive Models in Language and Thought: Ideology, Metaphors and Meanings* (pp. 199-228). Berlin: Mouton De Gruyter.

Semino, E. (2002). A sturdy baby or a derailing train? Metaphorical representations of the euro in British and Italian newspapers. *Text,* 22 (1), 107-139.

Semino, E. (2006). A corpus-based study of metaphors for speech activity in British Enlgish. In A. Stefanowitsch & S. Th. Gries (Eds.), *Corpus-Based Approaches to Metaphor and Metonymy* (pp. 36-62).

Berlin, New York: Mouton de Gruyter.

Semino, E. (2008). *Metaphor in Discourse.* Cambridge: Cambridge University Press.

Semino, E. & Masci, M. (1996). Politics is football: Metaphor in the discourse of Silvio Berlusconi in Italy. *Discourse & Society,* 7 (1), 243-269.

Smith, A. (1776). *An Inquiry into the Nature and Causes of the Wealth of Nations.* London: Methuen & Co., Ltd.

Smith, T. (2005). Metaphors for navigating negotiations. *Negotiation Journal,* 21(4), 343-364.

Steen, G. (1994). *Understanding Metaphor in Literature.* New York: Longman.

Steen, Gerard, J. (2007). *Finding Metaphor in Grammar and Usage: A Methodological Analysis of Theory and Research.* Amsterdam/ Philadelphia: John Benjamins Publishing Company.

Stefanowitsch, A. & Stefan Th. Gries (eds). (2006). *Corpus-based Approaches to Metaphor and Metonymy.* Berlin: Mouton de Gruyter.

Sweetser, E. (2002). *From Etymology to Pragmatics: Metaphorical and Cultural Aspects of Semantic Structure.* Beijing: Peking University Press.

Taylor, J. & Mbense, T. (1998). Red dogs and rotten mealies: How Zulus talk about anger. In A. Athanasiadou & E.Tabakowska (Eds.), *Speaking of Emotions: Conceptualization and Expression* (pp.191-226). Berlin: Mouton de Gruyter.

Turner, M. (1991). *Reading Minds: The Study of English in the Age of Cognitive Science.* Princeton: Princeton University Press.

Vaghi, F. & Venuti, M. (2004). Metaphor and the Euro. In A. Partington, J. Morley & L. Haarman (Eds.), *Corpora and Discourse* (pp. 369-382). Bern: Peter Lang AG.

Van der Valk, I. (2003). Right-wing parliamentary discourse on immigration in France. *Discourse & Society,* 14 (2), 309-348.

van Dijk, T. A. (1977). *Text and Context: Explorations in the Pragmatics of Discourse.* London: Longman.

van Dijk, T. A. (1984). *Prejudice in Discourse: An Analysis of Ethnic Prejudice in Cognition and Conversation.* Amsterdam: John Benjamins.

van Dijk, T. A. (1987). *News Analysis: Case Studies of International and National News in the Press.* Hillsdale, NJ: Lawrence Erlbaum Associates.

van Dijk, T. A. (1988). *News as Discourse.* Hillsdale, NJ: Erlbaum.

van Dijk, T. A. (1991). *Race and the Press: Critical Studies in Racism and Migration.* New York: Routledge.

van Dijk, T. A. (1993). Principles of Critical Discourse Analysis. *Discourse & Society,* 4 (2), 249-283.

van Dijk, T. A. (1995). Discourse semantics and ideology. *Discourse & Society,* 6 (2), 243-289.

van Dijk, T. A. (1997). The study of discourse. In T. A. van Dijk (Ed.), *Discourse as Structure and Process* (pp. 1-34). London and California: Sage Publications, Ltd.

van Dijk, T. A. (2001a). Mutltidisciplinary CDA: A plea for diversity. In: R. Wodak & M. Meyer (Eds.), *Methods of Critical Discourse Analysis* (pp. 95-120). London: Sage.

van Dijk, T. A. (2001b). Knowledge and News. http://www.discourse. org/teun.htlm

van Dijk, T. A. (2001c). Political Ideology. http://www.hum.uva.nl/teun/dis-pol-ideo.htm

van Dijk, T. A. (2001d). Discourse, ideology and context. http://www.uva.nl/teun/Discourse-Ideology-Context.htm

van Dijk, T. A. (2002). Political discourse and political cognition. In P.

254

Chilton & C. Schäffner (Eds.), *Politics as Text and Talk: Analytic Approaches to Political Discourse* (pp. 203-237). Amsterdam: John Benjamins.

van Dijk, T. A. (2006a). Introduction: Discourse, interaction and cognition. *Discourse Studies*, 8 (1), 5-7.

van Dijk, T. A. (2006b). Discourse, context and cognition. *Discourse Studies*, 8 (1), 159-177.

Voss, J. F., Kennet, J., Wiley, J. & Schooler, T. Y. (1992). Experts at debate: The use of metaphor in the US senate debate on the Gulf crisis. *Metaphor and Symbolic Activity*, 7 (1), 197-214.

Wee, L. (2001). Divorce before marriage in the Singapore-Malaysia relationship: The Invariance Principle at work. *Discourse & Society*, 12 (3), 535-549.

White, M. (1997). The use of metaphor in reporting financial market transactions. *Cuadernos de Filologı̀a Inglesa*, 6 (2), 233-245.

White, M. (2003). Metaphor and economics: the case of growth. *English for Specific Purposes*, 22 (2), 131-151.

White, M. & Herrera, H. (2003). Metaphor and ideology in the press coverage of telecom corporate consolidations. In R. Dirven, R. M. Frank & M. Pütz (Eds.), *Cognitive Models in Language and Thought: Ideology, Metaphors and Meanings* (pp. 277-326). Berlin: Mouton De Gruyter.

Wodak, R. (1996). *Disorders of Discourse*. London: Longman.

Wodak, R. (1997). Das Ausland and anti-semitic discourse: The discursive construction of the "other". In S. H. Riggins (Ed.), *The Language and Politics of Exclusion* (pp. 65-88). London: Sage.

Wodak, R. (1999). Critical Discourse Analysis at the end of the 20th century. *Research on Language and Social Interaction*, 32 (2), 185-193.

Wodak, R. (2001). What is CDA about—a summary of its history, important concepts and its development. In R., Wodak & M., Meyer (Eds.), *Methods of Critical Discourse Analysis* (pp.1-13). London: Sage.

Wodak, R. (2006). Mediation between discourse and society: Assessing cognitive approaches in CDA. *Discourse Studies*, 8 (1), 179-190.

Wodak, R. & Meyer, M. (2001). *Methods of Critical Discourse Analysis*. London: Sage.

Wolf, H. G. & Polzenhagen, F. (2003). Conceptual metaphor as ideological stylistic means: An exemplary analysis. In R. Dirven, R. M. Frank & M. Pütz (Eds.), *Cognitive Models in Language and Thought: Ideology, Metaphors and Meanings* (pp. 247-276). Berlin: Mouton De Gruyter.

Yang, G. (2002). Love and its conceptual metaphors in Mandarin: Aspectual classification. Unpublished manuscript, Department of Linguisitics, University of California at Berkeley.

Yu, N. (1995). Metaphorical expression of anger and happiness in English and Chinese. *Metaphor and Symbolic Activity*, 10, 59-92.

Yu, N. (1998). *The Contemporary Theory of Metaphor: A Perspecitve from Chinese*. Amsterdam: John Benjamins.

Yu, N. (2004). The eye of sight and mind. *Journal of Pragmatics,* 36 (3), 663-686.

Zinken, J. (2003). Ideological imagination: Intertextual and correlational metaphors in political discourse. *Discourse & Society,* 14 (4), 507-523.

Zinken, J., Hellsten, I. & Nerlish, B. (in press). What is "Cultural" about conceptual metaphors? *International Journal of Communication*.

陈家旭，（2003），英汉语基本颜色的隐喻认知对比，《西南民族大学学报》，（12），283-286.

陈家旭，（2007a），《英汉隐喻认知对比研究》，上海：上海学林出版社.

陈家旭，（2007b），英汉语"喜悦"情感隐喻认知对比分析，《外语与外语教学》，（7），36-37.

冯晓虎，（2004），《隐喻——思维的基础篇章的框架》，北京：对外经济贸易大学出版社.

洪艳青，张辉，（2002），认知语言学与意识形态研究，《外语与外语教学》，（2），5-9.

黄华，（2002），试比较概念隐喻理论和概念整合理论，《四川外语学院学报》，（1），93-96.

孔德明，（2002），从认知看经济语篇中的概念隐喻，《外语与外语教学》，（2），13-16.

李耸，冯奇，（2006），"风"和"wind"隐喻映射的文化透视对比，《南昌大学学报》，（4），157-160.

廖美珍，（1992），英语比喻的语篇衔接作用，《现代外语》，（2）：32-35.

廖美珍，（2007），隐喻语篇组织功能研究——标题与正文之间的组织关系，《外语教学与研究》，（3），177-183.

林书武，（1998），"愤怒"的概念隐喻，《外语与外语教学》，（2），8-13.

刘余红，余晓红，（2007），现代汉语中的军事隐喻研究，《语言教学与研究》，（3），12-20.

卢卫中，路云，（2006），语篇衔接与连贯的认知机制，《外语教学》，（1），13-18.

罗晨杰，（2006），概念隐喻理论与概念整合理论的联系与区别，《西昌学院学报》，（3），48-51.

任绍曾，（2006a），概念隐喻与语篇连贯，《外语教学与研究》，（1），91-100.

任绍曾，（2006），概念隐喻及其语篇体现——对体现概念隐喻的语篇的多维分析，《外语与外语教学》，（10），17-21.

束定芳，（2004），隐喻研究中的若干问题与研究方向，束定芳，《语言的认知研究——认知语言学论文精选》（pp. 428-441），上海：上海外语教育出版社.

辛斌，（2007），批评语篇分析的社会和认知转向，《外语研究》，

（6），19-25.

许伟利，周可容，（2006），从"水"的隐喻看中西文化的差异，《云南民族大学学报》，（4），77-81.

魏纪东，（2005），从博喻看篇章隐喻的逻辑和信息建构，《中国外语》，（4）.

魏纪东，（2006a），论篇章隐喻中博喻的结构类型和组篇特征，《国外外语教学》，（1），1-9.

魏纪东，（2006b），从博喻的元功能看其对建构英语篇章隐喻的作用，《四川外语学院学报》，（1），71-76.

魏纪东，（2006c），论博喻的非元功能对建构英语篇章隐喻的作用，《外国语》，（1），45-51.

魏在江，（2006），隐喻的语篇功能——兼论语篇分析与认知语言学的界面研究，《外语教学》，（5），10-15.

文旭，罗洛，（2004），隐喻 语境 文化——兼论情感隐喻"人比黄花瘦"，《外语与外语教学》，（1），11-14.

文旭，吴淑琼，（2007），英汉"脸、面"词汇的隐喻认知特点，《西南大学学报》，（6），140-144.

肖鸿波，（2006），体育新闻中的语言暴力，《新闻知识》，（3），17-19.

辛斌，（2007），批评语篇分析的社会和认知取向，《外语研究》，（6），19-24.

许家金，（2007），兰卡斯特汉语语料库简介，《中国英语教育》，（3）.

杨春生，（2004），英汉语中与"吃"有关的隐喻比较，《外语与外语教学》，（12），46-48.

杨菲菲，（2005），体育新闻语言军事化的认知基础，《修辞研究》，（6），67-69.

袁影，（2004），论战争隐喻的普遍性及文化渊源，《外语研究》，（4），36-39.

张辉，（2000），汉英情感概念形成和表达的对比研究，《外国语》，（5），27-32.

张辉，江龙，（2008），试论认知语言学与批评话语分析的融合，《外语学刊》，（5），12-19.

张建理，丁展平，（2003），时间隐喻在英汉词汇中的对比研究，《外语与外语教学》，（9），3.

张玮，张德禄，（2007），隐喻性特征与语篇连贯研究，《外语学刊》，（1），99-103.

张玮，张德禄，（2008）隐喻构型与语篇组织模式，《外语教学》，（1），7-11.

周榕，（2000），时间隐喻表征的跨文化研究，《现代外语》，（1），58-66.